American Foreign Policy
Since Détente

Contributors

Michael L. Baron, Columbia University

Robert J. Bresler, Pennsylvania State University—Capitol Campus

Leon Gordenker, Princeton University

Robert C. Gray, Franklin and Marshall College

Miles Kahler, Yale University

Carl Leiden, University of Texas at Austin

Stanley J. Michalak, Jr., Franklin and Marshall College

Karl M. Schmitt, University of Texas at Austin

Jerome Slater, State University of New York at Buffalo

American Foreign Policy Since Détente

ROBERT C. GRAY
STANLEY J. MICHALAK, JR.
Franklin and Marshall College

HARPER & ROW, PUBLISHERS, New York
Cambridge, Philadelphia, San Francisco,
London, Mexico City, São Paulo, Sydney

1817

Sponsoring Editor: Jean Hurtado
Project Coordinator: Editing, Design & Production, Inc.
Printer and Binder: R. R. Donnelley & Sons Company

American Foreign Policy Since Détente

Library of Congress Cataloging in Publication Data

Main entry under title:

American foreign policy since détente.

   Contents: Introduction—The United States and
the Soviet Union / Robert C. Gray—The United States
and arms control / Robert J. Bresler—The United
States and China / Michael L. Baron—[etc.]
   1. United States—Foreign relations—1945–
—Addresses, essay, lectures.   2. Détente—Addresses,
essays, lectures.   I. Gray, Robert C.   II. Michalak,
Stanley J.
E840.A63   1984   327.73   83-12667
ISBN 0-06-044424-X

For our parents
Mildred S. Gray and Robert A. Gray
and
Rose M. Michalak and Stanley J. Michalak

Contents

Preface

The following nine essays, written especially for this volume, describe and assess key issues in U.S. foreign policy in the 1970s and 1980s and are appropriate for courses in international politics, American foreign policy, and foreign policy analysis. The chapters have been carefully designed to provide the student with an outline of U.S. policy since the inception of détente—from the Nixon administration through the first two years of the Reagan administration. In addition, each chapter discusses enduring problems that future American decision makers will face. Thus, this volume should help bridge the gap between a standard chronological history of American foreign policy since World War II, on the one hand, and the annual year-end issue of *Foreign Affairs*, on the other.

In Chapter 1, Robert C. Gray discusses the evolution of United States-Soviet relations from détente to the surge of cold war rhetoric under Reagan and Andropov. In Chapter 2, Robert J. Bresler focuses on the most crucial Soviet-American dialogue, arms control. Michael L. Baron, in Chapter 3, traces the gradual and uneven process of normalizing relations with the People's Republic of China. Jerome Slater, in Chapter 4, deals with the Arab-Israeli component of the Middle East crisis. In Chapter 5, Carl Leiden assesses the challenges facing the United States in the Persian Gulf. Karl Schmitt examines U.S. policy toward Latin America in Chapter 6. In Chapter 7, Leon Gordenker addresses the problems of sub-Saharan Africa. Stanley J. Michalak, Jr., in Chapter 8, outlines a variety of North-South issues that have surfaced at the United Nations. And in Chapter 9, Miles Kahler explains the importance of U.S. economic relations in an increasingly interdependent world.

We would like to express our gratitude to Franklin and Marshall College for a grant, which assisted us in editing this book. Rose Musser typed various drafts and provided cheerful assistance above and beyond the call of duty. Jean Hurtado was an exceptionally helpful editor. We thank her and the entire staff of Harper & Row.

Robert C. Gray and Stanley J. Michalak, Jr.

Introduction

The American foreign policy agenda changed more significantly in the last decade than at any time since the 1940s. Thus, to evaluate options for the future, it is imperative to understand developments of recent years. By the beginning of the 1970s, the challenges of the first quarter-century of the cold war seemed to have been met. Western Europe, for example, had recovered economically from the destruction of World War II. The Soviet Union had been contained in Europe. The People's Republic of China had not advanced beyond her territorial boundaries of 1951. And, with the notable exception of Indochina, decolonization in Asia and Africa had been achieved with surprisingly little violence. In sum, the United States had achieved a high degree of success in attaining its major postwar objectives.

Success, however, led to the emergence of new problems. With the apparent success of containment, East-West relations improved in the early 1970s as the United States disengaged from Vietnam and simultaneously pursued détente with the Soviet Union and normalization of relations with the People's Republic of China. Consequently, a new challenge was posed for American policy—balancing the delicate triangular relationship between Washington, Moscow, and Peking.

A strong Europe and Japan meant greater economic competition for the United States in the international arena and an influx of western European and Japanese products in the American domestic market. The dollar-shortage problem of the late 1940s became a dollar-surplus problem in the 1970s.

The decolonization of the Third World had unintended consequences for the United States, for the emergence of new nations presented a host of complex issues for American decision makers. Most of the Third World countries found that decolonization did not mean political stability, viable economies, or decent living standards. Dictatorships—some benign, but many brutal—quickly became the mode of government in many of the developing countries. Corruption, mismanagement, and high birth rates led to poverty, hunger, and malnutrition of staggering proportions. But rather than looking within their own societies for the causes of their economic problems, Third World leaders blamed the postwar liberal international economic system instead and called for a New International Economic Order (NIEO).

While most of the demands made by the Third World were not new, Western elites began to take them more seriously after the Arab oil boycott and OPEC price increases of 1973. Economically, Third World countries attempted to charge higher prices for their raw materials. Politically, they used their numerical majority in the United Nations to emphasize issues (such as Palestinian autonomy and apartheid in South Africa) that the United States found awkward. And in terms of legal issues, the Third World demanded the writing of new international codes on the nationalization and expropriation of foreign property and the conduct of multinational corporations.

Some analysts in the 1970s argued that East-West détente, economic tension among the Western nations, and the North-South conflict had created a new agenda for American foreign policy. In the early 1980s, however, the primary challenge facing the United States increasingly came to resemble that of the late 1940s. To be sure, North-South issues and economic tensions in the West persisted, but détente seemed to be giving way to a renewed adversarial relationship between the United States and the Soviet Union.

From Angola and the Horn of Africa to Indochina, Soviet-backed forces were exploiting instability in the Third World. With the confusion that followed the fall of the Shah of Iran and the Soviet invasion of Afghanistan, an increasing number of observers believed that the Soviets would use their positions in Africa and Afghanistan to reap benefits from internal turmoil in the Middle East. In addition to Third World adventurism, the Soviet buildup of nuclear and conventional arms throughout the 1970s also alarmed many observers. The expansion of Soviet nuclear forces ended America's position of strategic superiority. The Soviets had superiority at the theater nuclear level in Europe. And the Soviet conventional buildup improved its military position in Europe and its capacity to deploy forces in Third World areas previously beyond its reach.

American reactions to these Soviet efforts were mixed in the Carter administration. Little was done to confront Soviet-backed forces in the Third World. And although the United States did respond to the Soviet arms buildup with American and NATO arms modernization programs, a SALT-II treaty was also completed and signed by Presidents Brezhnev and Carter in June 1979. The future of this treaty and the entire SALT process became unclear in 1980, however, for the Soviet invasion of Afghanistan caused President Carter to request a suspension in Senate consideration of the treaty. During 1980, a mood favoring higher defense expenditures and greater efforts to offset Soviet power emerged in the United States. Thus, as the new decade began, the potential for Soviet-American discord was high.

These were the circumstances facing the Reagan administration when it took office in 1981. An effort was made to restore the East-West conflict to center-stage. Emphasis was placed on a substantial buildup of American military forces, and strategic arms control negotiations were deferred until June of 1982. In view of the changes of the 1970s, however, it was not possible for the United States simply to return to the policies pursued in the bipolar world of the 1950s when America had nuclear superiority. Managing relations with Moscow and Peking, dealing with economic tensions among the developed countries, maintaining the cohesion of the NATO alliance, responding to North-South issues, and coping with crisis areas such as the Middle East and Central America are complex tasks that require a level of intelligence and coordination in decision making that has been notably absent in recent administrations.

The essays in this book are designed to explore in detail the complex agenda of American foreign policy in the early 1980s. It is an agenda characterized by demands arising from *both* North-South and East-West issues as well as challenges stemming from competitive relations among the Western democracies.

New problems will arise. But the problems discussed in this book are not likely to disappear in the near future. We hope that these essays will inform our readers and give them historical and analytical perspectives for evaluating future events.

chapter 1

The United States and the Soviet Union

ROBERT C. GRAY

While the Bicentennial captured the attention of Americans during the election year of 1976, another anniversary of great importance went almost unnoticed. Thirty years before, in 1946, American policy that would culminate in the Truman Doctrine, the Marshall Plan, and the North Atlantic Treaty Organization began to take shape. In February of 1946, George Kennan sent his "long telegram" from the American embassy in Moscow that set forth the principal rationale for, and elements of, the containment policy. In September, Clark Clifford, then a special assistant to President Harry Truman, prepared a key report reflecting the emerging consensus of civilian officials and military officers that the United States should respond to Soviet postwar behavior with a tough policy. A complex pattern of Soviet-American interaction had led to the cold war, and basic postulates of American foreign policy were established that persisted into the 1970s.

It is difficult fully to understand contemporary U.S.-Soviet relations— or to project future options—without keeping in mind the U.S.-Soviet fixation upon each other. This mutual preoccupation has taken, alternately, the form of proxy war (Korea, Vietnam), nuclear confrontation (Cuban missile crisis), and efforts at limited accommodation (Test Ban Treaty of 1963, Strategic Arms Limitation Treaty (SALT) agreements of 1972 and 1979).

The purpose of this chapter is briefly to review détente as it emerged in the Kissinger years, to describe and assess U.S.-Soviet relations under the

1

Carter administration, and to discuss policy shifts under Ronald Reagan. (Because it is dealt with at length in Chapter 2, SALT will not be discussed here, except where necessary to understand the broader fabric of U.S.-Soviet relations.)

DÉTENTE UNDER KISSINGER

An event that to many symbolized the end of the cold war occurred in 1972, when Leonid Brezhnev and Richard Nixon met in Moscow to sign a number of documents that were to formalize a new relationship. These documents included SALT I agreements; a statement of "Basic Principles" on avoiding confrontations and the exploitation of tensions to gain unilateral advantage; and a number of bilateral agreements on the environment, space, and economic-technical cooperation. From 1972 to 1974, further agreements were reached on cancer research, the use of the ocean's resources, the prevention of nuclear war, and the Apollo-Soyuz joint space mission of 1975.

By the mid-1970s, other negotiations also symbolized the new relationships. The status of Berlin, long a site of cold war confrontation, had been clarified in a 1971 agreement; the Mutual and Balanced Force Reduction (MBFR) talks between NATO and the Warsaw Pact were inching along in an effort to reduce the level of forces on the central front; and the Conference on Security and Cooperation in Europe (CSCE) was meeting as a wide-ranging forum between East and West. Despite these promising developments, the continuation of cooperation and competition was assumed to be an unavoidable dimension of the new Soviet-American relationship. These two dimensions of détente were addressed by the concept of linkage, whereby acceptable Soviet behavior toward the Middle East or Indochina would be a precondition for SALT or economic cooperation. It was only Soviet international behavior that was to be "linked," however, for Presidents Nixon and Ford and Secretary of State Kissinger believed it counterproductive to try to bring public pressure to bear on the internal policies of the Soviet regime.

A key element in American policy toward the Soviet Union was the American opening to the People's Republic of China. Although Kissinger was understandably restrained when describing the new trilateral relationship among America, Russia, and China, it was explicit administration policy to have better relations with the USSR and the People's Republic of China than either had with each other. Such a policy, which probably looked like encirclement to Soviet leaders, was designed to provide additional leverage in dealing with the Soviets.

The hope engendered by the Moscow Summit of 1972 dwindled as the election of 1976 approached, partially because the administration exaggerated what could realistically be expected, especially in the midst of Watergate. Other factors were congressional action that angered the Soviets and Soviet actions in Angola.

The exaggerated hopes for U.S.-Soviet relations resulted from the overselling of détente in 1972. President Nixon proclaimed nothing less than "a century of peace" shortly before Watergate crippled his ability to deal authoritatively with foreign or domestic policy. In his memoirs, Henry Kissinger blames Watergate for preventing "the full fruition of the prospects then before us, not only in nurturing U.S.-Soviet relations, but more generally in developing a new structure of international relations."

While this observation is beyond proof, it is fair to say that the election campaign of 1972 led President Nixon to make exaggerated claims and that Watergate made him search ever more frantically for a foreign policy success. Furthermore, the general weakening of American presidential authority, when coupled with the congressional efforts described in the following paragraphs, probably made Kremlin leaders feel even less constrained than they otherwise would have by the American concept of détente.

Kremlin leaders must have been angered, and were probably puzzled, by the inability of the Nixon administration (or that of Gerald Ford or Jimmy Carter) to obtain congressional passage of economic agreements made in 1972. The agreements involved the reciprocal granting of Most Favored Nation (MFN) status and the provision of Export-Import Bank credits to stimulate U.S.-Soviet trade.

Congress, responding to Soviet limitations on Jewish emigration, passed the Jackson-Vanik Amendment, which linked MFN status to emigration, and the Stevenson amendment, which drastically limited the amount of Export-Import Bank credits that could be extended to the USSR. Because of these actions, the Soviet Union renounced the U.S.-Soviet trade agreement in January of 1975, and the number of Jews allowed to leave the Soviet Union fell. The Soviets made it clear that they would resist public pressure of this kind.

In this instance, congressional intervention in foreign affairs was harmful. American negotiating reliability was called into question. One important aspect of "positive inducements" was removed from détente. And the upward trend in Jewish emigration was reversed.

In Angola, where several internal factions fought for power after the collapse of Portuguese colonial rule, the United States and the Soviet Union backed different sides. In the winter of 1975 to 1976, Congress forbade aid to Angola, stopping administration efforts to assist those opposing the Cuban forces there. The involvement of the Soviets in providing support for the Cubans led to severe criticisms of the policy of détente, including charges of appeasement. The issue became so sensitive that President Ford, facing a challenge from his right by Ronald Reagan for the Republican presidential nomination, stopped using the word *détente* in March of 1976.

Secretary of State Kissinger placed the aborted American effort in an East-West context in a speech in San Francisco: "Angola represents the first time that the Soviets have moved militarily at long distance to impose a regime of their choice. It is the first time that the United States has failed to respond to Soviet military moves outside the immediate Soviet orbit." The Soviets correctly calculated that, in the aftermath of Vietnam, they could move in southern Africa with a minimum of American opposition.

As the election year began, there was a mixed pattern, for U.S.-Soviet relations had begun to deteriorate. In retrospect, Soviet involvement in Angola appears to have been something of a watershed in the decline of détente, for it symbolized the failure of the Kissinger policy of restraining Soviet expansionism. William Hyland, a Kissinger assistant and an astute observer of Soviet-American relations, has concluded that Angola, more than any other development of 1975, "made it impossible to salvage détente."

At the Twenty-Fifth Congress of the Communist Party of the Soviet Union in February, Leonid Brezhnev defended détente *and* the Soviet role in Angola. If it was not clear before, it could scarcely be ignored after this Congress, that the Soviet concept of "peaceful coexistence" did not preclude Soviet participation in the ongoing "class struggle" in the developing countries. Henry Kissinger no doubt understood this all along, and his speeches had addressed both cooperative and competititive aspects of détente. But the dominant message from President Nixon had been a "generation of peace," and it is against such inflated expectations that the backlash against détente in 1976 must be seen.

CARTER'S CRITIQUE OF DÉTENTE

It was in the context of a troubled détente that the presidential campaign of 1976 took place. Although the campaign speeches of challengers are seldom blueprints of policies to be followed when in office, several themes in Jimmy Carter's speeches were reflected in his behavior as president.

Carter's criticism of détente came from both the left and the right. He argued that American intervention in the political processes of other countries had weakened "the moral heart of our international appeal" and had undermined the public confidence in government necessary for the effective pursuit of détente. But he also charged that "to the Soviets, détente is an opportunity to continue the process of world revolution without running the threat of nuclear war," and that Kissinger was "giving up too much and asking for too little."

Noting the coooperative and competitive aspects of détente, Carter advocated making the Soviet-American relationship "broader and more reciprocal," and he placed special emphasis on the necessity for reducing the nuclear arsenals of the superpowers. Secretary Kissinger was singled out for criticism. Carter charged him with having a personal investment in détente, thus failing to hold the Soviets to the human rights provisions of the Helsinki Accords. Kissinger was also criticized for the secrecy of his foreign policy-making and, implicitly, for concentrating power in his hands alone.

These comments were to foreshadow a number of actions that Carter would take as president. The emphasis on arms reduction and human rights would loom large in the first months of his presidency, and he would go to great lengths to avoid the concentration of power in foreign affairs in a single subordinate. Equally clear, however, was a dilemma that persisted at least until the invasion of Afghanistan. Having abjured American intervention, what would halt continuing *Soviet* involvement in the affairs of other nations?

If there was one characteristic of Jimmy Carter more important than any other to an understanding of his foreign policy until the Soviet invasion of Afghanistan, it was his position on American intervention abroad. In the same speech quoted above, he said, "We have learned that we cannot and should not try to intervene militarily in the internal affairs of other countries unless our own nation is endangered." Underscoring the relevance of his noninterventionist stance to East-West rivalry, Carter stated early in his administration that the United States was "now free of . . . inordinate fear of Communism."

In Jimmy Carter the nation had found a president who had learned one of the lessons of Vietnam. But he seemed to bring a personal passion to the principle of nonintervention that transcended the Vietnam experience. American policy toward the Soviet Union would be the result of a reassessment of détente by this new president, who thought so differently from his predecessors. Innovation is no guarantee of success, however, as President Carter was to find out early in 1977.

MANAGING CONTRADICTIONS

Writing in *Foreign Policy* in the summer of 1978, Thomas L. Hughes commented that "the essence of foreign policy is the management of contradictions." Carter was to learn the complexity of this problem, particularly in four areas: promoting human rights and maintaining détente; strengthening defense and maintaining détente; reconciling American nonintervention in Third World conflicts with the continuation of Soviet intervention; and promoting "multiple advocacy" in foreign policy formulation without allowing it to degenerate into contradictory signaling of U.S. intentions. The failure to deal effectively with these contradictions made it impossible for the Carter administration to implement fully its laudable goals.

Jimmy Carter came to the presidency with the intention of deemphasizing the Soviet-American relationship and developing a "world order" foreign policy that would fill the void left by the collapse of the cold war consensus. For a number of reasons, the centerpiece of this new policy was to be human rights. First, Carter's personal convictions inclined him toward internationalizing Western norms of justice.

Second, the issue had already been raised in the context of the Conference on Security and Cooperation in Europe and the 1976 election campaign. The Soviets wanted an all-European summit conference to legitimize the borders of Europe, since no overall peace treaty had been signed at the end of World War II. The Western price for the 1975 summit was the inclusion of what came to be called Basket Three, a set of principles to promote the freer movement of people and ideas between and within nations. As a consequence, during 1976 President Ford had begun to talk about human rights, and candidate Jimmy Carter had elevated the issue to one of prominence during the campaign.

Third, Carter's principal adviser on national security, Zbigniew Brzezinski, had for some time been advocating the inclusion of "moral issues" on the agenda of East-West relations. In criticizing American policy in a Radio Free Europe interview in the mid-1970s, Brzezinski said that Nixon and Kissinger had "elevated amorality to the level of principle. This is not in keeping with fundamental American traditions. It denies American foreign policy an asset, which had made that policy so appealing to many people throughout the world."

The new administration began to implement its human rights policy even before taking office. Although the human rights policy was eventually applied to all countries—allies, neutrals, and adversaries—it took an anti-Soviet cast at the beginning. In late December of 1976, Secretary-of-State designate Cyrus Vance met with Soviet dissident Andrei Amalrik. In February of 1977, a presidential letter to Andrei Sakharov in the Soviet Union reiterated the U.S. commitment to human rights; in March, a meeting was held at the White House with Soviet dissident Vladimir Bukovsky. In May, President Carter spoke at Notre Dame University and, although noting "the limits of moral suasion," he argued that "we can already see dramatic worldwide advances in the protection of the individual from the arbitrary power of the state."

The Soviets had been responding verbally throughout the spring. Brezhnev himself had charged interference in Soviet internal affairs, and he hinted that U.S.-Soviet relations would deteriorate further if the United States kept pressing on human rights. Perhaps to underscore their defiance of the American campaign, the Soviets charged Anatoly Shcharansky with treason for his human rights activities. In August of 1977, Carter admitted that his foreign policy advisers were surprised by the Soviet response to the human rights campaign.

More surprises were to come. In the summer of 1978 Shcharansky was tried, as were Yuri Orlov and Alexander Ginzburg. All were convicted and sentenced to prison. In retaliation, the White House imposed new controls on technology transfers to the USSR and cancelled several high-level Soviet-American meetings. Linkage, which the Carter administration had criticized, was now practiced with reference to Soviet *internal* policies.

Although the administration kept SALT formally insulated from the human rights campaign, Soviet treatment of dissidents—highlighted by administration criticism—worsened the domestic climate for détente and for ratification of SALT II. The administration eventually moved away from frontal assaults on Soviet internal policies, but bilateral and domestic consequences remained.

The Carter administration believed it could challenge the Soviets on the issue of internal control of their society without seriously damaging the policy of détente. The lesson of the Jackson-Vanik amendment had not been learned. While there will certainly be occasions calling for the public articulation of Western principles, the record suggests that the Soviets are unlikely to yield to direct, public pressure to make fundamental alterations in their internal policies.

The issue of defense and détente is so complex that it can only be sketched briefly here. The principal challenge to American policy has been to seek arms control agreements in the face of growing Soviet strength. For a time this task was manageable, for it seemed plausible that the Soviets were merely trying to catch up to the United States in strategic weapons and in across-the-board military power. But the trends had become so adverse that, during the years of the Carter administration, significant action was taken to bolster American defense. (For SALT-related actions and new strategic weapons, see Chapter 2.)

In response to a long-term buildup and improvement of Soviet-Warsaw Pact conventional forces, President Carter encouraged NATO to undertake the Long-term Defense Program and agreed, along with the other NATO governments, to increase annual defense spending by three percent annually (discounting inflation). Through the combination of increased cooperation among alliance members, increased defense expenditures, and continuing arms control negotiations aimed at reducing forces on the central front, NATO's policy of deterrence, defense, and détente was to be strengthened.

Growing European concerns about improved Soviet theater nuclear forces such as the mobile multiple warhead SS-20 missile and the Backfire bomber made the administration take further action. With parity at the strategic level and impressive Soviet power at the conventional level, it was felt that the imbalance in long-range theater nuclear systems would disadvantage NATO both militarily and politically. In December of 1979, the Carter administration succeeded in getting a NATO consensus on the need to deploy new American theater nuclear forces in Western Europe and to conduct arms control negotiations on such weapons.

The actions taken with respect to strategic programs, NATO, and the defense budget might have enhanced the prospects for ratification of SALT, but they—like the human rights campaign—also had bilateral and domestic implications. Bilaterally, the Soviets might well respond with actions that would worsen relations. Domestically, some Americans found it difficult to reconcile ratification of the SALT II treaty with the various military programs underway.

The dilemma for U.S.-Soviet relations posed by these events was real and possibly insurmountable. SALT II was defended on its own terms as in the national interest. But the Senate committee hearings on SALT in 1979 produced a growing consensus in favor of higher defense spending and the acquisition of new weapons.

Although there is nothing inherently contradictory in simultaneously pursuing arms control and arms modernization, this is a very delicate task. The Carter administration never found a conceptual framework embracing both policies that commanded wide support.

The Carter administration's handling of the conflicts in southern Africa differed markedly from that of the Ford administration. The attempt to decouple regional conflicts from the East-West balance was in contrast with the policies of the Nixon, Johnson, and Kennedy administrations as well. The Carter administration responded in a restrained way to continuing Soviet-Cuban involvement in Angola and to Soviet support for an anti-American regime in Ethiopia. Although Carter, Brzezinski, and others criticized the Soviets in strong terms (with the president arguing that the Soviets would fail in Africa because of their "innate racism"), there was no attempt to mount a military response to Soviet policy in Africa. Nor was there a serious alteration of what remained of the détente process in 1978 when the Vietnamese invaded Cambodia (Kampuchea) with Soviet help, or in 1979 when South Yemen attacked North Yemen with Soviet assistance.

In marked contrast, the Soviet invasion of Afghanistan in December of 1979 and the overthrow of its pro-Soviet leader for an even more compliant one led, in the first week of 1980, to a wide-ranging American response. President Carter, in a speech that basically applied the domino theory to Southwest Asia, announced a number of measures designed to "make it clear that the Soviet Union cannot behave this way with impunity."

Specifically, the president postponed Senate consideration of the SALT II treaty; embargoed 17 million tons of wheat earmarked for sale to the USSR; and began to organize a boycott of the 1980 Summer Olympics in the Soviet Union. Most significantly, for a president who had previously stressed nonintervention, Carter declared that "an attempt by any outside force to gain control of the Persian Gulf region will be regarded as an assault on the vital interests of the United States of America, and such an assault will be repelled by any means necessary, including military force."

Secretary of Defense Harold Brown was, by coincidence, scheduled to visit the People's Republic of China early in January. He used the occasion to announce that the United States was prepared to transfer technology, some of which might have military uses, to China. And he laid the foundation for closer cooperation on defense issues and for strengthening "other nations in the region."

Although these actions fell short of military counterintervention, in their totality they constituted the most significant event in U.S.-Soviet relations since the 1972 summit meeting between Nixon and Brezhnev. And for President Carter, they seem to have been a watershed in his views on the Soviet Union. This was the first time Soviet troops had ventured beyond the limits of the sphere of influence they established at the end of World War II. The president told one interviewer at the end of December that, "the action of the Soviets has made a more dramatic change in my opinion of what the

Soviets' ultimate goals are than anything they've done in the previous time that I've been in office." A week or so later he characterized the Soviet invasion as the gravest threat to world peace since World War II.

Unlike previous Soviet interventions of the Carter years (in which proxy forces had been used), the invasion of Afghanistan was placed firmly in the context of East-West relations. And, ironically, in view of the hopes for détente and nonintervention that Jimmy Carter had in 1976, he reacted more strongly than Presidents Eisenhower or Johnson had during the Soviet invasions of Hungary in 1956 and Czechoslovakia in 1968.

It is impossible to know if a stronger American response to Soviet actions in Angola or Ethiopia would have deterred the Soviets in Afghanistan, for the circumstances of each conflict were so different. And it was not obviously incorrect, especially in Zimbabwe and Namibia, to try to deal with conflicts in local rather than East-West terms. The task facing any administration is the difficult one of sorting out those Third World conflicts that should be treated on their own terms from those that involve a Soviet presence (or Soviet proxy) *and* a vital American interest, both sufficiently significant to merit more than a rhetorical response.

Throughout much of the Carter administration, observers commented on the seeming disorganization of foreign policy-making. In the area of Soviet-American relations, attention focused on the rivalry between National Security Affairs adviser Zbigniew Brzezinski and Secretarys of State Cyrus Vance and Edmund Muskie. Brzezinski, it was argued, offered hard-line advice, while Vance and his Special Adviser on Soviet Affairs, Marshall Shulman, counseled moderation. Press attention to this subject was so rampant in the summer of 1978 that the president had to announce that *he* was the chief spokesman on foreign affairs.

Dr. Shulman confirmed and defended the existence of differing views in the administration in congressional testimony in the fall of 1979:

> It appears to me . . . that there are some positive advantages in the president having available to him a diversity of views . . . I would say the diversity of views is not always as characterized in the public prints. . . . In a sense the administration is really representative of a spectrum of views in the country about the Soviet Union.

Having deplored the concentration of power in Kissinger's hands, President Carter sought to maintain access to differing views. This is to his credit. But multiple advocacy in foreign policy-making, coupled with indecision at the top, eventuated in contradictory signaling of U.S. intentions.

Two speeches in 1978 illustrate the point. In March, the president gave a tough speech at Wake Forest University. He reviewed the growth of Soviet military power and noted that the Soviets had shown "an ominous inclination" to use that power to intervene in other countries. He stated that the United States was willing to cooperate with the Soviets across the range of issues usually considered part of détente, but that if the Soviets did not exercise restraint in increasing their military power and supporting interventions abroad, "popular support in the United States for . . . cooperation with the Soviets will certainly erode."

In June, President Carter spoke at the Naval Academy. Prior to his speech, numerous newspaper articles indicated that its purpose was the proclamation of a coherent policy that would end the speculation about policy differences between Vance and Brzezinski. One stark passage got headlines: "The Soviet Union can choose either confrontation or cooperation. The United States is adequately prepared to meet either choice." But, in reality, the speech was a mixture of hard-line and prodétente language that led some to conclude that alternate sections had been sponsored by Brzezinski and Vance. Although the speech elicited stern reactions in Moscow, it was hardly an unambiguous statement from which Soviet leaders—or American citizens—could deduce U.S. intentions.

Such illustrations of contradictory signaling were also evident in U.S. normalization of relations with the People's Republic of China. Dr. Brzezinski favored using relations with the People's Republic of China as direct leverage over the Soviets. Secretary Vance, on the other hand, was inclined to pursue normalization without so stark a tilt toward China.

In the abstract, multiple advocacy may be preferable to the concentration of power and information in the hands of one key aide. And President Carter's desire for an "open" administraton was understandable in the wake of Vietnam and Watergate. But the Carter administration was too open in foreign policy, and multiple advocacy was allowed to go beyond the point of the final decision. The result was the projection of an image of disagreement, confusion, or both at the top echelons of the American government.

Jimmy Carter's goals were admirable: the enhancement of human rights among allies as well as adversaries; the balanced pursuit of arms control where possible and arms modernization where necessary; the attempt to decouple local conflicts from superpower rivalry; and (in comparison with the Kissinger years) the creation of an open administration that drew upon numerous sources prior to decision making. But the Carter foreign policy was flawed in execution. Most notably, it failed to manage adequately the contradictions outlined above.

In the aftermath of the Soviet invasion of Afghanistan, Jimmy Carter adopted a harsher view of the Soviet Union than he previously held; yet his administration still seemed committed to a moderate course in 1980. In particular, Carter remained committed to arms control as an important task in the nuclear age. It is reasonable to suppose that, if reelected, he would have pressed forward with the SALT process while negotiating with the Soviets on theater nuclear forces. (In fact, the first U.S.-Soviet talks on theater nuclear weapons were underway on election day, 1980, only to be put on hold after Carter's defeat.)

A second Carter administration would no doubt have built on the first one, with adjustments for the post-Afghanistan environment. This would most likely have involved the pursuit of moderate policies that necessitated balancing numerous contradictory forces. The defense budget would have been increased and new weapons would have been deployed while arms control negotiations were being pursued. The Rapid Deployment Force would have been further developed for use in Third World contingencies, although not all Third World conflicts would have been viewed in East-West terms.

It is not easy to gauge the extent to which the pursuit of these and other policies would have been tempered by the experience of the first term. Would discipline have been imposed on the factions within the administration? Would Carter have succeeded in forging a new consensus based on a concept of an interdependent world characterized by challenges from many different sources, including the Soviet Union? What is clear is that Carter's failure to forge a new consensus helped pave the way for the election of Ronald Reagan.

THE REAGAN ADMINISTRATION AND THE SOVIET UNION

It is difficult to exaggerate the differences between the world views that Jimmy Carter and Ronald Reagan brought to the Oval Office. Carter was committed to deemphasizing the Soviet-American relationship and to pursuing a "world order" foreign policy. But, committed as he was to eliminating nuclear weapons from the earth, Carter continued arms control negotiations with the Soviets. Ronald Reagan, on the other hand, entered office with a fixation on the Soviet Union and with open hostility toward the arms control efforts of the previous decade.

At the beginning of the Reagan administration, the complexities of a multidimensional world seemed to have given way to the simplicities of cold war containment. As Reagan told an interviewer in the spring of 1980, "The Soviet Union underlies all the unrest that is going on. If they weren't engaged in this game of dominoes, there wouldn't be any hot spots in the world." Although opinions expressed by a presidential candidate do not necessarily become policy when he takes office, there is little doubt that this statement captured Reagan's fundamental instincts.

In the first weeks of the Reagan administration, the president observed in a news conference that the Soviet leaders "reserve unto themselves the right to commit any crime, to lie, to cheat." In the same week, Secretary of State Alexander Haig charged the Soviets with "training, funding and equipping international terrorism." The defense budget was projected to rise sharply, having been exempted from the cuts affecting major social programs. Arms control was placed low on the agenda of the new administration, and any negotiations were to be linked to Soviet behavior in the world. As part of the East-West struggle, the human rights policy of the Carter administration was altered to eliminate public criticism of friendly "authoritarian" regimes. Finally, the new administration's portrayal of conflicts in

Central America, the Middle East, and southern Africa was dominated by the East-West dimension. As Haig put it in March, "the emphasis today is on the Soviet problem".

The actions taken in the initial months of the Reagan administration succeeded in altering the tone of U.S. foreign policy and the rhetoric on U.S.-Soviet relations. But the results were mixed and the problems, many. Leonid Brezhnev responded to the criticisms of Soviet policy (and Soviet leaders) with a carefully crafted though self-serving call for a "dialogue" with Washington. The CIA apparently had some difficulty in providing evidence of Soviet support for terrorism on the scale charged by Secretary Haig. Under pressure from its NATO allies, the United States agreed to begin preliminary talks with the Soviets on theater nuclear weapons in the fall of 1981. The harsh anti-Soviet rhetoric was undercut by the lifting of the grain embargo and then underscored by an announced willingness "in principle" to sell arms to China. The Reagan administration was discovering how difficult it was to translate ideological positions into effective policies.

Just as the Carter administration faced the task of managing contradictions, so has the Reagan administration confronted a number of difficult problems. A brief discussion of four areas will serve to illustrate the range of these problems.

First, the Reagan administration has sought to place a number of conflicts in the Third World in an East-West rather than a regional context. Yet the administration has underestimated the difficulty of persuading other nations to view problems in these terms. The moderate Arabs were not convinced that the Soviets posed the most serious threat in the Middle East. There has been little enthusiasm in Latin America for the administration's estimate of the Soviet-Cuban threat. And a number of European allies of the United States have made it clear that they do not share the Reagan view that the Soviets are the cause of most international instability.

Second, the administration's lack of clarity in its policies toward Taiwan and the People's Republic of China threatens to undermine continued improvement in Sino-American relations at a critical juncture in U.S.-Soviet relations. With the collapse of détente and positive incentives to help structure Soviet behavior, the "negative" levers constructed under Kissinger have become more important. Conspicuous among these is the unpleasant prospect (from Moscow's viewpoint) of ever closer ties with the People's Republic of China.

A third area is the administration's desire to adopt a hard line against the Soviet Union on military, political, and economic issues without rupturing the Atlantic Alliance. Differences between Europe and the United States have been particularly apparent over events in Poland. Having consulted about what collective actions to take in the event of a Soviet invasion, the NATO governments were apparently unprepared for the suppression of Solidarity by the Polish army. The Europeans were more reluctant than the Reagan administration to impose sanctions on the Soviet Union, especially in view of the absence of an American grain embargo.

Some have come to question the future of the Atlantic Alliance. A significant number of people in Western Europe fear that war will come about as a consequence of the continued East-West nuclear buildup. There is a real tension between the need to bolster actual and perceived military power and the need to reassure European allies that the United States does not seek war—especially a nuclear war limited to Europe. The several statements on nuclear war by the president and his secretaries of state and defense inflamed public sentiment in Europe, where the roots of antinuclear sentiment go far deeper than some in the administration choose to recognize. Thus, governments in the Netherlands, Belgium, and the Federal Republic of Germany are under pressure to abandon the deployments promised in the NATO decision of December 1979, while the opposition Labour party in the United Kingdom has adopted a resolution favoring unilateral nuclear disarmament.[1] Also, the European nations have shown little inclination to undertake a defense buildup similar to the one proposed by President Reagan for the United States.

In terms of trade, the links built up between Western Europe and the East during the decade of détente will not be easily abandoned, particularly in the midst of such difficult economic times. This point has been made quite clearly by the failure of American sanctions to stop construction of the Urengoi-Pomary-Uzhgorod pipeline from Siberia to Western Europe.

Frustration with the attitudes of European allies on security and trade issues has led some in Washington to wonder aloud whether America is paying too much to defend an ungrateful and excessively timid Europe. If the Europeans do not share the Reagan administration's view of the Soviet threat, should the United States remain as committed to the defense of Europe as it has since World War II?

In the view of most analysts of U.S. relations with the nations of Western Europe, the attitudes of one administration should not be allowed to undermine the long-standing U.S. support of NATO Europe. Indeed, the differences between Europe and America, which seem so great now, are partly a function of the views of one faction in the Reagan administration. Describing the split in the administration between pragmatic conservatives and ideologues, William Pfaff has pointed out that the predominant American view since the Eisenhower administration has been that "the Soviet-American rivalry functioned within negotiable limits, and need not lead to war." With the election of Ronald Reagan, however, "this view of the Soviet Union has been seriously challenged within the highest levels of government for the first time since the mid-nineteen-fifties."

The ideologues, according to Pfaff, are

> committed to the proposition that no negotiations with the Soviet Union on basic questions can be profitable and no agreements trusted. They believe that . . . it is sentimentality to think that coexistence can be anything other than a mask by

---

[1] For a discussion of the NATO decision and its implications for U.S.-Soviet and U.S.-European relations, see Stanley R. Sloan and Robert C. Gray, *Nuclear Strategy and Arms Control: Challenges for U.S. Policy*, Headline Series no. 261 (New York, N.Y.: Foreign Policy Association, 1982).

which the Soviet Union continues [to wage conflict] . . . These Americans recommend that the United States resume the cold war, applying economic and political pressures that might cause the Soviet system to crack.

To some ideologues, the period of disarray as Yuri Andropov settles in as Brezhnev's successor is an ideal time to increase the pressure on the Soviet Union. In referring to the ideological school of thought, former President Richard Nixon said, at the end of 1982, that although he wished that American pressure would lead to changes in the Soviet Union, " . . . it's just not going to happen. The Soviets have proven over the years that they can always squeeze their people enough to keep up their military strength."

The ideologues will not necessarily prevail. A number of pragmatic officials in the Reagan administration share Nixon's assessment that the Soviet system will endure. Secretary of State George Shultz has had a moderating influence on the Reagan administration, and some of the most notable ideologues at the National Security Council (such as Richard Allen and Richard Pipes) have left government. The United States is negotiating with the Soviet Union at Geneva on intermediate range nuclear forces and on strategic nuclear weapons. And the door has been kept slightly cracked so that President Reagan can, if he chooses, explore the possibilities of improving relations with the new Soviet leadership.

The critical question is whether the Reagan administration is equipped to deal with the serious issues that it faces. After two years in office the administration seemed less well-equipped to deal with foreign policy than its much-criticized predecessor. The fourth area to be discussed here, then, concerns organization for decision making. By denying his first national security adviser, Richard Allen, the policy-coordinating role and direct access to the president that advisers in previous administrations had enjoyed, Reagan sought to avoid two problems. One was the "Kissinger problem" of an NSC adviser who overshadowed a secretary of state. The second was the "Brzezinski-Vance" problem of disagreements between NSC and State leading to contradictory signaling. President Reagan discovered a third option. Without a strong national security adviser or a president inclined to perform this role himself, and with strong personalities at State and Defense, the public bickering naturally developed between Alexander Haig and Caspar Weinberger. The Reagan administration has attempted to resolve the organizational problem by replacing Richard Allen with Judge William Clark (and upgrading the role of the NSC adviser) and by replacing Alexander Haig with George Shultz as secretary of state. Whether these changes will permit the formulation and execution of coherent policies remains to be seen.

CONCLUSION

American problems have been stressed in this chapter. But however somber American perceptions may be, the view from Moscow must be even more grim. The death of Leonid Brezhnev occurred at a time when serious economic, demographic, military, and foreign policy problems faced the USSR. The rise of Solidarity in Poland indicated the failure of Communist ideology and economic policy in Eastern Europe. Despite some friendly noises toward the Soviet Union, China still seems inclined to forge closer ties with the West. The Soviet Union remains bogged down in Afghanistan. The United States is increasing its military power, and, judging by their rhetoric, Reagan officials give little indication that they are restrained by the "Vietnam syndrome." Toward the end of 1983, new American nuclear weapons capable of striking targets in the USSR are scheduled to be deployed in Western Europe. There is general agreement that the Soviet Union faces serious problems in the years ahead. What remains unclear, however, is whether these problems will restrain Soviet leaders or incite them to undertake foreign adventures.

There is no lack of policy guidance for the Reagan administration. George Kennan distanced himself still further from a policy of containment, commenting in the *New Yorker* that he saw Soviet leaders as less interested in aggression than in increasing "their influence among Third World countries." This did not disturb him, for "most great powers have similar desires . . . and what has distinguished . . . Soviet efforts historically viewed, seems to be . . . their lack of success." These views of the architect of containment were singularly out of step with the direction of American policy, whose "central goal" Robert E. Osgood has described as "the revitalization of containment."

Numerous authors outside of government offered rationales for a policy of modified or selective containment. William Hyland called it "selective neo-containment." Dmitri Simes called it "disciplining Soviet power." And the Council on Foreign Relations Commission on U.S.-Soviet Relations stated that "the United States must care about the growth of Soviet influence in any quarter of the globe. But we need to establish priorities among our interests and concerns. The priorities must involve geography as well as the kinds of influence it is reasonable to try to counter."

That the instincts of the Reagan administration lie in the direction of a resurrection of containment is clear. But key officials of the Reagan administration seem to recognize that the containment policy as outlined in the late 1940s cannot be revived unchanged. There is indeed a legacy of détente, particularly among American allies in Western Europe. After the suppression of Solidarity, the Reagan administration continued talks with the Soviets on intermediate-range nuclear forces in Geneva, spoke of a possible summit meeting between Reagan and Brezhnev, and forestalled declaring Poland in default on debts owed to American banks.

A policy of "selective containment" could be complemented by continuing contacts with the Soviets in such areas of mutual interest as arms control negotiations. A return to the stark simplicities of the cold war seems unlikely in today's world.

In the first volume of his memoirs, Henry Kissinger described the task facing the United States as follows:

> For as far ahead as we can see, America's task will be to re-create and maintain the two pillars of our policy toward the Soviet Union that we began to build in Moscow: a willingness to confront Soviet expansionism and a simultaneous readiness to mark out a cooperative future.

This remains the task facing the United States in the 1980s. Whether the Reagan administration was conceptually or organizationally prepared to construct a coherent set of policies that will achieve these goals in such troubled times for East and West remained unclear at the beginning of 1983.

FOR FURTHER READING

Books and Monographs

Barnet, Richard J. *The Giants: Russia and America*. (New York, N.Y.: Simon & Schuster, 1977).

Council on Foreign Relations, Commission on U.S.-Soviet Relations. *The Soviet Challenge: A Policy Framework for the 1980s*. (New York, N.Y.: Council on Foreign Relations, 1981).

Gaddis, John Lewis. *Russia, the Soviet Union, and the United States: An Interpretive History*. (New York, N.Y.: John Wiley & Sons, 1978).

Hoffmann, Stanley. *Primacy or World Order: American Foreign Policy Since the Cold War*. (New York, N.Y.: McGraw-Hill, 1978).

Hyland, William G. *Soviet-American Relations: A New Cold War?* (Santa Monica, Ca.: Rand Corporation (R-2763-FF/RC), 1981).

Kissinger, Henry. *White House Years*. (Boston, Mass.: Little, Brown, 1979).

Szulc, Tad. *The Illusion of Peace: Foreign Policy in the Nixon Years*. (New York, N.Y.: Viking, 1978).

Articles

Bialer, Seweryn and Afferica, Joan. "Reagan and Russia," *Foreign Affairs*, 61 (Winter 1982–83), 249–271.

Brzezinski, Zbigniew. "A Deal for Andropov," *The New Republic* (December 13, 1982), 11–15.

———. "What's Wrong with Reagan's Foreign Policy?", *New York Times Magazine* (December 6, 1981).

Drew, Elizabeth. "Brzezinski," *The New Yorker* (May 1, 1978).

Hughes, Thomas L. "Carter and the Management of Contradictions," *Foreign Policy*, 31 (Summer 1978), 34–55.

Hyland, William G. "Clash with the Soviet Union," *Foreign Policy*, 49 (Winter 1982–83), 3–19.

———. "U.S.-Soviet Relations: The Long Road Back," *Foreign Affairs: America and the World 1981*, 525–550.

Kaiser, Robert G. "U.S.-Soviet Relations: Goodbye to Détente," *Foreign Affairs: America and the World 1980*, 500–521.

Kennan, George. "Two Views of the Soviet Problem," *The New Yorker* (November 2, 1981).

Kissinger, Henry A. "How to Deal with Moscow," *Newsweek* (November 29, 1982), 30–37.

————. "Poland's Lessons for Mr. Reagan," *New York Times* (January 17 and 18, 1982).

Maynes, Charles William. "Old Errors in the New Cold War," *Foreign Policy,* 46 (Spring 1982), 86–104.

Osgood, Robert E. "The Revitalization of Containment," *Foreign Affairs: America and the World 1981,* 465–502.

Seabury, Paul. "George Kennan vs. Mr. X," *New Republic* (December 16, 1981).

Simes, Dmitri. "Disciplining Soviet Power," *Foreign Policy,* 43 (Summer 1981), 33–52.

chapter 2

The United States and Arms Control

ROBERT J. BRESLER

"We will move this year," said President Jimmy Carter in his 1977 Inaugural Address, "toward our ultimate goal—the elimination of all nuclear weapons from this earth." President Carter was soon to learn that noble intentions and hopeful statements are not the stuff of policy. Rhetorical commitments must be translated into substantive achievements. Nowhere did Carter find this translation more difficult than in his search for a SALT II Treaty.

While the path to arms control has been strewn with difficult technical problems, the most difficult barriers have been political. From John F. Kennedy to Jimmy Carter, American presidents have discovered that arms control involves a complex three-cornered negotiation. In one corner is the president, concerned about the hazards of an unlimited nuclear arms race and aware of the political benefits of concluding an arms control agreement. In the second corner is the Soviet Union, a conservative, heavily militarized society, suspicious of American intentions and anxious to preserve its favorite military programs, while also eager to be recognized as the political and military equal of the United States. In the third corner are the domestic skeptics of arms control. This powerful configuration of forces includes much of our military leadership, their numerous supporters in Congress, and the anti-arms control lobbies. Out of this process has come a series of arms control agreements that has failed to achieve major reductions in nuclear weaponry.

The examples are numerous. The Outer Space Treaty (1967) outlawed nuclear weapons in orbit, and the Seabeds Treaty (1971) banned mass-destruction weapons on the ocean floor. Yet these treaties served only to eliminate weapons that neither the United States nor the Soviet Union was seriously considering. Other agreements contained loopholes of greater significance than the agreements themselves. The Limited Test Ban Treaty (1963) allowed underground nuclear testing; the Biological Weapons Convention (1972) ignored the problem of chemical weapons.

By mid-1970 the United States and the Soviet Union were finally dealing with central systems in the SALT talks, but even SALT I (1972) disregarded any limits on the qualitative improvement of offensive missiles, particularly on MIRVs (Multiple Independently Targeted Reentry Vehicles). This comprehensive agreement consisted of two separate parts. The first comprised an Anti-Ballistic Missile (ABM) Treaty restricting each side to two ABM sites. This was later amended in July 1974 to allow only one ABM site. The second part was the Interim Agreement on Offensive Missiles—an executive agreement in force from July 1, 1972 to October 31, 1977. It froze construction of land-based Intercontinental Ballistic Missiles (ICBMs). This left the United States with 1054 ICBMs and the Soviet Union with 1618. The number of submarine-based systems was limited to 710 missiles and 44 submarines for the United States and 950 missiles and 62 submarines for the Soviet Union. These Soviet advantages were balanced against an American advantage in nuclear warheads as a result of our more advanced MIRV program. In 1974, at the midpoint of SALT I, the United States had 7200 warheads and the Soviet Union, 2300.

These agreements were further diluted, in some cases, in order to secure their ratification by the Senate. After the Limited Test Ban Treaty was signed, President Kennedy agreed to military and congressional demands that underground nuclear testing be intensified, thus paving the way for the development of MIRV technology. Secretary of Defense Melvin Laird and the Joint Chiefs of Staff (JCS) sought, as the price for their support of SALT I, the acceleration of the cruise missile, the B-1 bomber, and the Trident submarine programs. Beyond that, President Nixon agreed to the demand of a powerful member of the Senate Armed Services Committee, Senator Henry M. Jackson (D. Wash.), that the pro-arms control SALT I negotiating team be dismantled. This brought into the one agency in government responsible for developing an arms control perspective—the Arms Control and Disarmament Agency (ACDA)—a group of people, led by Agency Director Fred Ikle, whose views closely reflected those of the Pentagon.

FORGING THE BASIC AGREEMENT: GERALD FORD, HENRY KISSINGER, AND SALT II

Within months of succeeding Richard Nixon, President Gerald Ford, with the assistance of Secretary of State Henry Kissinger, appeared on the verge of completing a SALT II Treaty. Ford and Kissinger, meeting with Soviet President Leonid Brezhnev at Vladivostok in November 1974, agreed on the essential parameters of a treaty. The Vladivostok Agreement called for a 10-year treaty, lasting from 1975 to 1985. The treaty would bear these elements: an identical United States/Soviet ceiling on strategic nuclear delivery vehicles (heavy bombers and long-range missiles) of 2400; and a sublimit on missiles armed with MIRV warheads of 1320.

The understanding at Vladivostok was deceptively simple for it involved a somewhat complex formulation of strategic parity. This diplomatic equation was first developed in SALT I. Under the SALT I Agreement on Offensive Strategic Arms the Soviet Union was allowed to maintain an advantage in numbers of Intercontinental Ballistic Missiles (ICBMs) and Submarine-Launched Ballistic Missiles (SLBMs). This offset an American advantage, not explicitly stated in the agreement, in the number of warheads, in the accuracy of those warheads, and in the bombers capable of hitting Soviet targets from bases in Europe and from aircraft carriers in the Mediterranean Sea—the so-called Forward Based Systems (FBSs).

Vladivostok modified this rough definition of strategic parity in appearance only. Ford and Kissinger prodded Brezhnev to accept the principle of "equal aggregates" in bombers and missiles and to drop his insistence that our FBSs be included in these aggregates. In exchange, Ford and Kissinger agreed to an overall ceiling (2400) that would allow the Soviet Union to keep its force largely intact. (The 2400 limit was much closer to the USSR proposal for 2500 than to the U.S. proposal for 2100.)

At two high-level meetings, one between Kissinger and Soviet Foreign Minister Andrei Gromyko at Vienna in May 1975 and another between Ford and Brezhnev at Helsinki in July 1975, another compromise was discussed. The Soviet Union would accept our counting rules for MIRV missiles, that is, any missile tested with a MIRV warhead would be included under the MIRV ceiling. The United States, in return, would allow the Soviets to keep their heavy missiles, the SS-18, at their existing level—308.

But the uncertainties of military technology and domestic politics intervened, and President Ford was never to conclude a SALT II agreement. Two technological developments complicated Vladivostok: one was the Soviet Backfire, a new bomber which fell into a category between medium bombers (not covered by SALT) and heavier ones such as the U.S. B-52. The other was the United States cruise missile program.

This new weapon, a descendant of Germany's World War II V-1 "buzz bomb," was a small, continuously powered, pilotless vehicle that flew through the atmosphere like an aircraft. Its range was well over 2000 nautical miles. It could fly at only subsonic speeds but could carry a W-80 nuclear warhead with the destructive power of about 250 kilotons (tons of TNT). Although much slower than ballistic missiles, cruise missiles, by flying at treetop heights, could penetrate the existing sophisticated Soviet air defense systems. What made a cruise missile particularly deadly was its terrain contour guidance system, known as TERCOM, which could achieve accuracies of between 30 and 50 feet. While too slow to serve as a first strike weapon, cruise missiles could be an effective second strike counterforce weapon against nontime urgent targets such as command and control bunkers and submarine bases.

The Pentagon was planning three types of these weapons: the air-launched cruise missiles (ALCMs), which could be launched from a heavy bomber; the sea-launched cruise missiles (SLCMs), which could be launched from submarines and from surface ships; and the ground-launched cruise missiles (GLCMs), which could be deployed upon a landmobile launcher such as a truck. The Soviets were insistent that all cruise missiles with a range of over 600 kilometers be counted in some form under SALT II. Originally considered as a bargaining chip by Henry Kissinger, the cruise missile program was gathering considerable support among the military, and they were reluctant to give it up in SALT. "How was I to know," Kissinger lamented, "the military would come to love it?"

Brezhnev and Kissinger, while meeting in Moscow during January 1976, came close to a compromise that fit both Backfire and cruise missiles into the Vladivostok framework. The Soviets would be allowed 275 Backfires beyond the overall ceiling until 1981. From 1982 to 1985 there would be no limits on the number of Backfires. The Soviets would agree, however, to certain operational restrictions on Backfire (where based, refueling capacity, and so on) in order to reduce its potential as a strategic weapon. The United States would then count each heavy bomber armed with 12 to 20 ALCMs against the 1320 MIRV ceiling. Strategic cruise missiles would be barred from submarines, but we would be allowed to deploy 250 SLCMs on more than 25 surface ships. Finally, the overall ceiling on launchers would be reduced to 2200.

Kissinger returned to Washington optimistic about the chances for an agreement. However, Secretary of Defense Donald Rumsfeld and the Joint Chiefs of Staff (JCS) raised strong objections. Ford, facing a serious primary challenge from Ronald Reagan and the right wing of his party, confessed in his memoirs that Rumsfeld and JCS "held the trump card." Consequently, Ford rejected the Kissinger/Brezhnev January 1976 compromise and proposed, instead, that the original Vladivostok agreement be accepted with a separate understanding that talks on the Backfire-cruise problem continue. During these talks the Soviets would maintain their present production rate on Backfire, and the United States would not deploy cruise missiles until January 1979. When Brezhnev rejected this offer, SALT negotiations were, for all practical purposes, suspended for the remainder of the election year and, as it turned out, for the remainder of the Ford administration as well. The task of completing an actual SALT II treaty would have to await the new president.

CARTER AND SALT II: SORTING OUT THE OPTIONS

The problems that faced President Carter were familiar. Could he negotiate a treaty that satisfied both the Soviet Union and our own domestic hawks? Would such a treaty make any substantive contribution to ending the nuclear arms race? Would this three-cornered diplomacy result in arms control agreements that were a complement to the arms race rather than an alternative—a vehicle for its rational management and virtual institutionalization?

While Carter's problems were similar to those of his predecessors, they were also more complex. For example, Richard Nixon, in 1972, had the natural political allegiance of many conservative Republican senators, who were otherwise instinctively hostile to arms control and innately suspicious of agreements with the Soviet Union. Most of these senators were reluctant to oppose an incumbent president of their party and were, in a sense, compelled to support the ratification of SALT I. Liberal Democratic senators, generally hostile to Nixon, were, nevertheless, so committed to arms control that their support for SALT I was virtually assured. The SALT I treaty was ratified by a vote of 88 to 2. No such political logic would be at work for Jimmy Carter.

As the Carter administration approached the issue of SALT and arms control, it had essentially five options:

Option 1: Complete SALT as soon as possible. Carter could move to conclude the SALT talks early in his administration on terms similar to the Kissinger/Brezhnev compromise of January 1976. Such an agreement, having been largely negotiated by the previous administration, would have the potential for broad bipartisan support. Still in the midst of the political honeymoon, Carter might have a relatively easy time getting the agreeement through the Senate. Such a quick resolution of the SALT II issues would get Soviet-American relations off to a constructive start under the new Carter administration. With SALT II out of the way early in the life of his administration, Carter would then have the opportunity to move on a more ambitious arms control agenda, for example, a Comprehensive Test Ban Treaty (CTB), Mutual and Balanced Force Reductions in Europe (MBFR), the demilitarization of the Indian Ocean, and what would inevitably be a more complex SALT III treaty.

On the other hand, the JCS did raise serious objections to the January 1976 compromise, and it was ultimately rejected by Gerald Ford. Thus, serious opposition could threaten such an agreement. In addition, this compromise did not resolve two issues of increasing importance in SALT: the qualitative improvements on ballistic missiles and limits on the number of MIRV warheads on each missile (missile fractionation). Any treaty that failed to deal with these questions would be open to criticism from both hawks and doves.

Option 2: Renegotiate SALT II. Rather than settle for the limited understandings carved out by Ford and Kissinger, Carter could immediately propose a new and more comprehensive SALT II treaty. Such a proposal might call for deep cuts in strategic forces of both sides, a freeze on all new missiles, restrictions on cruise missiles and Backfire, and new qualitative controls on all existing missiles.

This option offered tempting political advantages. It might gain the support of hardliners like Senator Jackson, who were becoming impatient with the slow process of SALT and regarded it as only legitimizing a major Soviet strategic arms buildup. It might also gain the support of doves such as Senator George McGovern (D.S.D.) who were anxious to get on with the task of actually reducing strategic arsenals on both sides.

Yet this approach would involve kicking over the traces of three years of tedious negotiations. The Soviet leadership under Brezhnev had invested a considerable amount of political capital in these negotiations. Brezhnev had conceded three vital points to Ford and Kissinger: the principle of "equal aggregates," the exclusion of FBS under the SALT limits, and the acceptance of our MIRV counting rules. Having already gone this far, the Soviet leaders might not be ready for a new diplomatic departure.

Option 3: Downgrade SALT but not arms control.   Recognizing that major obstacles lay in the path of a quick agreement of SALT II, the Carter administration could put its greatest negotiating efforts into other forms. An early agreement of CTB, MBFR, or a plan to demilitarize the Indian Ocean would dramatically affect the nature of détente and could eventually create a more hospitable political setting for the resolution of SALT II.

But this option would be difficult to pursue. Serious issues remained unresolved in the other areas. Verification uncertainties presented a real problem in the CTB talks; and the scientists working in the nuclear weapons laboratories were articulate opponents of any such agreement. MBFR was not simply a Soviet-American issue. It involved negotiations between the Warsaw Pact and NATO nations and required time-consuming intra-alliance discussion. For a variety of reasons, these talks held out little promise for a quick agreement. With oil supplies in the Middle East an issue that touched the vital interest of many nations, neither the United States nor the Soviet Union was likely to forego a naval presence in an area (the Indian Ocean) so close to the Persian Gulf. In short, the closer one looked at each set of arms control negotiations, the more complicated they appeared. SALT II was not the only vexing problem.

Option 4: Continue SALT but hold out for our terms while accelerating strategic weapons programs.   The Carter administration could offer the Soviet Union SALT II on a take-it-or-leave-it basis. Carter could call for steep reductions in Soviet heavy missiles, deep cuts in the overall ceiling on missiles and bombers, and strict limits on Backfire. In the likely event that the Soviet Union would reject such an offer, the Carter administration could begin accumulating more bargaining chips. The mobile MX missile, the B-1 bomber, and the cruise missile programs could be accelerated. Then, from a position of strategic superiority, the Carter administration could dictate the terms of SALT II.

While such a position had a certain superficial appeal, few in or out of the Carter administration were making an effective case for it. This strategy would surely presage a return to cold war politics. Since their humiliation during the Cuban missile crisis, the Soviet leadership has been determined to avoid negotiating with the United States from a position of strategic inferiority. Any acceleration of our strategic programs would likely be matched by a similar Soviet effort. A return to cold war policies would also pose difficult domestic choices for Carter. He had campaigned for the presidency as a fiscal conservative and had promised early in his term to produce a balanced budget by fiscal year 1981. Dramatic increases in defense spending would require painful choices: either the reduction of spending on social programs or the abandonment of the goal of a balanced budget.

Option 5: Seek arms control through unilateral restraint.   Rather than return to the tangled state of the SALT negotiations, Carter could, by taking one or more of the following steps, challenge the Soviet Union to show its seriousness: curb the B-1 bomber program, put a freeze on accuracy improvements for Minuteman III missiles, and place the cruise missile and MX programs on hold. Such a dramatic series of steps might, by galvanizing world opinion, put pressure on the Soviet Union to take corresponding steps.

Yet, serious pitfalls awaited such a policy. The domestic climate was changing in 1977. The humiliation in Vietnam had scarred American pride. For the first time in almost a decade, a majority of Americans was opposed to reductions in defense spending. A powerful new defense lobby was being formed, the Committee on the Present Danger, which was made up of some influential citizens: General Maxwell Taylor, Lane Kirkland, Saul Bellow, and Admiral Elmo Zumwalt. Its chief spokesman was Paul Nitze, a former member of the SALT II delegation and a knowledgeable critic of arms control. These voices were added to those who were already calling for a dramatic increase in defense spending in the wake of a new Soviet military buildup. Carter would undoubtedly face severe criticism if he were to undertake such unilateral initiatives. Carter's decision to have the pro-arms control lawyer, Paul Warnke, head both the ACDA and the SALT delegation was a sign of the times. Warnke was severely criticized for his views from Senate hawks, and he was confirmed as leader of the SALT delegation by a Senate vote of only 58 to 40.

THE MARCH 1977 PROPOSALS

Nevertheless, the initial proposals that the Carter administration brought to the SALT talks were far more comprehensive and ambitious than those presented by the Nixon or Ford administrations. They largely represented the approach of Option 2. Secretary of State Cyrus Vance led the American delegation to Moscow in March 1977 and brought with him proposals that went beyond the conceptual understanding of SALT I and Vladivostok.

The proposals included measures which would: reduce overall nuclear ceilings, severely restrict weapons that could pose a first-strike threat, and weaken the reliance of both sides on the more vulnerable land-based missiles. Specifically, Carter and Vance were offering the Soviet Union this swap: the United States would refrain from building its new MX missile (which could have a first-strike capability) if the Soviet Union would reduce the number of its heavy SS-18s from 308 to 150; the United States would also forego the development of all cruise missiles with ranges over 2500 kilometers if the Soviet Union would agree to a set of measures limiting the range of the Backfire bomber.

The overall ceiling on launchers would be reduced from 2400 to between 1800 and 2000; the ceilings on all MIRV missiles would be between 1100 and 1200, down from the Vladivostok limit of 1320. In addition, there would be a new sublimit on land-based MIRV missiles of 550, and flight testing of ballistic missiles would be limited to six per year for ICBM and six per year for SLBM.

Should the Soviet Union demonstrate no interest in this comprehensive approach, Carter offered simply a slight modification of Vladivostok: The Vladivostok ceilings would remain intact, and the resolution of the Backfire cruise issue would be postponed to SALT III. Should the Soviet Union demonstrate some interest in the comprehensive approach, Vance came prepared to bargain. President Carter had given Vance a set of fallback positions, the contents of which were known only by a select few in the American delegation.

Senator Jackson, who had been informed in advance of the comprehensive proposals, lauded the plan as a "gigantic step." Jackson had long felt that the Soviet SS-18 could eventually threaten a first strike against our land-based Minuteman force. Jackson was particularly pleased with the provisions that reduced the SS-18 to 150 and restricted land-based MIRV missiles to 550.

The Soviets, on the other hand, shared none of Jackson's enthusiasm. In fact, Brezhnev and Gromyko greeted these proposals with outright hostility. Carter had taken two largely symbolic actions in the area of human rights, which apparently infuriated the Soviet leadership. He had, soon after his inauguration, sent a sympathetic letter to Andrei Sakharov, a leader of Soviet dissidents. And just weeks before the Vance delegation arrived in Moscow, Carter received the exiled Soviet dissident, Vladimir Bukovsky, in the Oval Office. What Carter may have considered an expression of American ideals in foreign policy, the Soviet leaders interpeted as unwarranted interference in their internal affairs.

Adding to this suspicion of him, Carter violated the Soviet penchant for secrecy. The day before Vance was to arrive in Moscow, Carter gave the press a general outline of his new arms control proposals. This public unveiling of the March proposals, combined with the new human rights offensive, may have led the Soviet leadership to dismiss Carter's initiative as part of a propaganda offensive.

But apart from this troubled political climate, the proposals themselves upset what the Soviets had considered to be a carefully crafted understanding at Vladivostok. In suggesting that the ceiling on their SS-18 be reduced to

150, Carter had reopened an issue the Soviets considered settled. The United States, by offering to limit missile test flights, was seen to be simply protecting its advantage in missile accuracy. The proposals to limit land-based MIRV missiles to 550 not only paralleled the present size of the American force but also would complicate Soviet plans to make most of its land-based missiles MIRV. The United States was planning to add its additional MIRVs only to its submarine force.

The Soviets were building a heavier and more extensive land-based missile force to compensate for the American advantages in weapon accuracy, in sea-based missiles, and in forward-based systems. SALT I and Vladivostok were essentially conservative formulas, based upon the understanding that both sides would keep their advantages. The Carter administration was now asking the Soviet Union to give up those advantages by cutting back on its SS-18 and by restricting its land-based MIRVs to American levels. Carter was not offering, in exchange, to relinquish any weapon system under production. The cruise missile and MX programs were only in a very early stage of development. As David Aaron, a senior staff member of the National Security Council, put it, "We would be giving up future draft choices in exchange for cuts in their starting lineup."

In retrospect, the Societ rejection of the March 1977 proposals may have been unavoidable. But what came as a shock to the administration was the categorical nature of the rejection. Both the comprehensive proposals and the modification of Vladivostok were summarily rejected. Brezhnev and Gromyko were not even willing to accept them as a basis for negotiations. Secretary Vance was never given the opportunity to present the fallback position, although he had previously communicated to Brezhnev through Soviet Ambassador Anatoly Dobrynin that the United States was prepared to compromise.

Leslie Gelb, then Director of the State Department's Bureau of Politico-Military Affairs, was later to reflect that "the real tragedy was that the Soviets simply turned down the comprehensive idea *in toto* instead of bargaining. If the Soviets had begun to bargain they would have found that President Carter was prepared to make far-reaching decisions about American forces as well. The opportunity would never come again." Carter's first venture in SALT diplomacy was to end in failure.

The Carter administration cannot bear the complete burden for this debacle. Blame can be parceled out on both sides. The Soviets were suspicious to the point of paranoia and dismissed a serious attempt to break out of the narrow confines of SALT I and Vladisvostok. Had Brezhnev and the other Soviet leaders read their hopes rather than their fears into Carter's initiative, agreement on genuine reductions in strategic nuclear weapons may have been reached. Instead, the Soviets served only to weaken an American administration genuinely interested in arms control. Returning from Moscow empty handed, the Carter administration was to gain a reputation for incompetence, a reputation that would hinder its ability to deal with the domestic critics of SALT. Henry Jackson, Paul Nitze, and other hardline critics would judge future SALT proposals against a new public yardstick, the March proposals.

PICKING UP THE PIECES

SALT II was not to be signed in the honeymoon stage of the Carter administration, when the path to ratification might have been smooth. As it was, SALT II consumed practically the entire four years of the Carter administration. These negotiations were conducted against a background of increasingly turbulent Soviet-American relations. The emergence of pro-Soviet governments in Ethiopia, Angola, and Afghanistan; the use of Cuban forces in southern Africa; and the continual buildup of both Soviet conventional and strategic forces did little to improve this climate.

On the American side, the development of new weapons, particularly MX and cruise missiles, continued. Ironically, these programs only hindered the future flexibility of Carter's arms control policies. The closer they came to actual production, the more difficult it was for the military to see them bargained away. In early 1977 military interest in MX and cruise was not clearly focused. The Air Force was, in fact, suspicious of the ALCM program, for they saw it (and rightly so) as an alternative to their penetrating bomber, the B-1. Nor was there a strong congressional demand for MX. The path was clear for Carter to use them as bargaining chips. Relinquishing (or reducing) these programs in exchange for deep cuts in Soviet strategic forces was a bargain the military might well have accepted in early 1977. As the negotiations were to extend into 1978 and 1979, these weapons programs would gain momentum. The military and its supporters in Congress would eventually see an important role for them.

In June 1977, Carter made a startling decision. He canceled the B-1 bomber program. Plans had called for building 244. It was to be the biggest weapons acquisition program in history. Clearly this decision was not framed as a unilateral arms control initiative (see Option 5). The rationale was purely military and managerial: Cruise missiles were better suited to penetrate Soviet air defenses than the manned bomber, and ALCMs could be better deployed on the modified B-52 than the B-1.

Cheered by arms control advocates, the decision may have worked to reduce the president's maneuverability in SALT. One member of the Carter administration was quoted as saying, "the B-1 cancellation put additional pressure on us to treat the cruise missile as some sort of holy thing." Secretary of Defense Harold Brown made it clear just how directly the B-1 decision had magnified the importance of the cruise missile program, especially the ALCM. Brown told a House Committee, "We have to continue to assure that our position (in SALT) on cruise missiles does not interfere in any serious way with our plan for the incorporation of cruise missiles into the strategic bomber force."

During the spring of 1977, Carter curtailed two other strategic programs that had been scheduled by Ford and Rumsfeld. Carter closed the production line of Minuteman III missiles, freezing the force at 550. He canceled a program to improve the accuracy of the 450 single warhead Minuteman II missiles. Since no effort was made to put even an arms control gloss on these decisions, they engendered no response from the Soviet Union. The response came from American military leaders who clung all the more tenaciously to those remaining strategic programs.

THE SEPTEMBER 1977 BREAKTHROUGH

When the SALT talks resumed in September 1977, it appeared that at least Carter's comprehensive approach had made some impact. The Soviet Union was willing to discuss the issues of missile modernization and of limits on land-based MIRVs. Whatever precise form SALT II would take, it was becoming clear that its scope would exceed Vladivostok. Carter had, in the March 1977 proposals, retracted a key concession made by Ford and Kissinger: granting the Soviet Union permission to keep their 308 SS-18 in exchange for their acceptance of our MIRV counting rules. Carter apparently had greater expectations for SALT II, and he was willing to bargain hard for them. This fact was not lost entirely on the Soviet leaders. Carter was telling the Soviets implicity in the March proposals that he would expect even more concessions for their SS-18s.

Consistent with the diplomatic pattern under Nixon and Ford, the breakthroughs in SALT II came during discussions at the highest level. Carter, Vance, and Gromyko, after a series of September meetings in Washington, agreed on the essential framework of a new agreement. SALT II would consist of three separate understandings: an eight-year treaty, a three-year protocol, and a statement of principles to guide SALT III.

The eight-year treaty included some important modifications of Vladivostok. The 2400 ceiling on launchers would be reduced to either 2250 (the Soviet position) or 2160 (the U.S. position). The ceiling on MIRV launchers would remain at 1320, but it now included two additional sublimits: a 1200-to-1250 limit for all missiles equipped with MIRV and an 820 limit for all land-based missiles equipped with MIRV. Heavy bombers armed with ALCMs would be counted under the 1320 ceiling. The Soviet Union would be allowed its 308 heavy SS-18.

The treaty contained two major concessions by the United States and five, by the Soviet Union. The United States had withdrawn its demand for reductions in the Soviet heavy missile force and had agreed to count its heavy bombers armed with ALCMs under the 1320 MIRV ceiling. The five Soviet concessions were as follows.

1. The Soviets agreed to a lower ceiling on launchers that would require the actual dismantling of some of their forces, which numbered over 2500. Since the United States forces were below 2100, the overall ceiling had no effect on American strategic forces.

2. They also agreed to a new subceiling on the land-based MIRVs. This is where most additional Soviet missile forces were to be placed. The United States had no plans to expand beyond 550 the land-based MIRV force, the Minuteman IIIs.
3. They would restrict their MIRVed ICBMs to either 1250 or 1200, below the 1320 agreed to at Vladivostok.
4. The Soviet Union would allow the United States to have 120 heavy bombers armed with ALCMs above the MIRV missile ceiling. The Soviet Union lagged far behind the United States in this area, and they were unlikely to develop a comparable ALCM program during the life of the treaty.
5. The Soviets would count all their missiles in the ICBM fields near the towns of Derazhnya and Pervomaisk as MIRVs. (The Soviets had mixed their single warhead SS-11 missiles at these sites with their MIRVed SS-19. The United States had insisted that silos for the two missiles were indistinguishable.)

The three-year protocol dealt with new weapons systems. It placed a freeze on the deployment of mobile ICBMs (such as our MX and the Soviet SS-16); it forbade the deployment of SLCMs and GLCMs with ranges over 600 kilometers; and it banned the testing and deployment of any new missile system (this provision was later refined and elevated in the treaty by the negotiators in 1978). The concessions the United States had granted here were more apparent than real. The protocol would have no immediate effect on American force posture. Neither MX, SLCM, nor GLCM would be ready for deployment until after the protocol was to expire.

THE CONSENSUS IS FRAYED

On October 21, 1977, in a moment of carelessness and euphoria, Carter told an audience in Des Moines, Iowa that, "within a few weeks, we will have a SALT agreement that will be the pride of the country." Carter's aides had to caution reporters immediately that the president was being too optimistic. Both Henry Jackson and Paul Nitze had expressed serious doubts over the bargain Carter and Vance had struck with Gromyko in Washington.

Carter's problem was simply this: the agreement was not being judged against Vladivostok nor even the 1976 Kissinger/Brezhnev compromise, but against Carter's own March proposals. Carter had not been able to gain Soviet acquiescence in restricting their land-based MIRVs to 550 or in reducing their SS-18 force. Jackson and Nitze were also concerned that the three-year protocol, barring the deployment of MX, SLCM, and GLCM would establish an unfavorable precedent for SALT III. They argued that the Soviet ICBM force, unless curtailed, would threaten our Minuteman force within the lifetime of SALT II.

An attack eliminating the ICBM force would leave the United States with only its SLBM force, its strategic bombers (some of which would be armed with ALCMs), and its FB-IIIs deployed abroad. These weapons are deemed to be far less accurate than the Minuteman IIIs and would, as Jackson and Nitze saw it, leave an American president in an untenable position. His alternatives would be exceedingly distasteful. He could either launch an all-out attack on Soviet cities, risking a similar attack on American cities—or he could do nothing, allowing such aggression to go unanswered and unchallenged. The mobile, allegedly invulnerable MX was thus perceived as the only realistic American response to this problem.

While many felt alternatives to the highly accurate MX were available (such as placing more missiles on smaller submarines), the Jackson-Nitze critique had considerable political force. On the issue of SLCM and GLCM another influential voice was heard. Senator Sam Nunn (D. Ga.), a powerful member of the Senate Armed Services Committee, felt that these weapons would eventually be of special interest to NATO as a counter to the new Soviet SS-20, a mobile medium-range missile with MIRV, aimed at Western Europe.

Carter was also having problems within the administration. Lieutenant General Edward Rowny, the representative of the JCS on the SALT delegation, who had been given the post in 1973 at Jackson's behest, began to criticize publically the emerging shape of SALT II. Rowny told reporters in Geneva in December 1977, that U.S. negotiators were rushing into an agreeement. "We tend to offer more," Rowny said, "and telegraph our position more and move more quickly to a fallback position." (Rowny later would resign from the administration and oppose ratification of the treaty.)

To compound matters further, the Carter administration learned, in the winter of 1977 to 1978 of a major Soviet technical breakthrough. The Soviet Strategic Rocket Corps had achieved the ability to deliver its warheads within a few hundred yards of our land-based missiles. The question of Minuteman vulnerability and the critique of Jackson and Nitze gained new force and importance. Carter had to negotiate for new restrictions on the Soviet missile force. He would have to negotiate new limits on warheads and more precise restrictions on new types of missiles; he would have to do this without foreclosing the MX or the cruise missile options. In short, Carter, faced with serious domestic opposition to the agreement and a potential Soviet threat to Minuteman, had to raise the ante with the Soviet Union.

NAILING DOWN THE DETAILS

If SALT II were to have any chance of Senate ratification, Carter would have to build in as many restrictions on Soviet forces as possible without closing down American options. The specific restrictions were as follows.

1. Limit the number of warheads that can be placed on each type of missile (missile fractionation).
2. Pin down the precise limits on the Backfire bomber.

3. Reduce, somewhat, the length of the protocol so that MX and cruise would not be delayed beyond the mid-1980s.
4. Clarify the definition of new types of missiles so as not to preclude MX but to prevent the Soviet Union from building a new generation of missiles to replace their SS-17s, SS-18s, and SS-19s.
5. Modify the range limitations on ALCM, which had been 2500 kilometers, so that they could be launched from distances far beyond the reach of Soviet air defenses.

Eventually, Carter was to gain all of these points in the final agreement. It would require, however, two additional years of agonizing negotiations, which Leslie Gelb described as "eye-crossingly complicated." The breakthroughs were to come in driblets.

April 1978   During a series of meetings between Vance and Gromyko in Moscow, a compromise was struck on missile ceilings. The United States agreed to the Soviet figure of 2250 for the overall ceiling; the Soviet Union, in turn, agreed to the 1200 figure on MIRVed missiles. In a major concession, the Soviets also agreed to language in the eight-year treaty that did not preclude the deployment by the United States of long-range GLCMs and SLCMs in Western Europe, after the protocol had expired.

July 1978   In Geneva, Gromyko offered Vance a deal on missile fractionation. The Soviets would agree to freeze all warheads per missile at those levels already tested. The United States would have to agree, however, to limit the number of ALCMs allowed on a heavy bomber to 20 (bomber fractionation). While the precise numbers in the fractionation limits were not settled at the time, the basic exchange was established. The Soviets would agree to a freeze on missile fractionation in return for an American agreement on bomber fractionation.

September 1978   The United States negotiators wanted to redefine range limits on cruise missiles as encompassing the distance between launch point and target. This would allow the missile to follow its TERCOM guidance system on a circuitous route to its target. In technical language this was known as *delta overages*. In the language of the negotiators it was known as the *wiggle factor*. The Soviets had insisted that range meant simply the total distance covered by cruise missiles. In addition, the United States wanted an exemption from SALT for all conventionally armed cruise missiles (a distinction that was difficult if not impossible to verify).

During a series of meetings in New York and Washington, Gromyko offered to remove the 2500-kilometer limit on ALCM in exchange for a strict definition of the 600-kilometer range for SLCM and GLCM, eliminating delta overage or the wiggle factor. This compromise became part of the final agreement and constituted a major gain for the United States. The restrictions on SLCM and GLCM were bound only by the protocol, which would expire before these weapons were ready for deployment.[1]

December 1978 Vance and Gromyko, meeting in Geneva, put what the Carter administration anticipated would be the final touches on the agreement. The precise nature of the missile fractionation limits was settled. Both sides would limit each missile to the maximum number of warheads with which it had been flight tested as of May 1, 1979. The exception was the untested MX, which would be equipped with the same number of warheads (10) allowed for the SS-18.

Carter dropped his insistence upon allowing conventionally armed ALCMs outside the limits of SALT. The Soviets then agreed to ease the task of verification by agreeing not to impede telemetry signals from missile tests (an evasion technique known as *telemetry encryption*). Both sides agreed that each side would be restricted to one new type of ICBM, either MIRVed or non-MIRVed. Thus, the United States would be allowed to go forward with the MX, and the Soviet Union would be allowed to develop a possible replacement for its single warhead SS-11 or a new MIRVed missile. The Backfire issue would not be handled in the SALT agreement per se. Limits on its range, production, and development would be specified in a separate letter from Brezhnev to Carter. The Air Force had come to terms with this concession, after Carter had made it clear to Gromyko that we reserved the right to deploy a comparable aircraft, perhaps a modified FB-111.

The remaining issues were close to resolution. Both sides were only nine months apart on the expiration date of the protocol. The precise definition of a new type of missile was also unsettled. But the differences here and on minor technical points were narrow. Vance expected that he and Gromyko would confirm an agreement in principle. The permanent delegation could then resolve the remaining points, and a date for the Carter-Brezhnev summit and treaty signing ceremony could be announced.

At the last minute, Gromyko informed Vance that all remaining points would have to be settled before either a summit date or an agreement in principle could be announced. This sudden Soviet reluctance was perhaps a reaction to Carter's announcement a few weeks earlier that the United States and the People's Republic of China had agreed to normalize diplomatic relations. This postponement of SALT II may have been an example of Soviet linkage: a way of indicating its displeasure with the warming Sino-American relationship. If this were the Soviet motivation, it was another self-destructive act. By delaying SALT II, the Soviets pushed the timetable for Senate ratification closer to the next American presidential election. And given the record of delay in 1976, SALT and presidential politics were an

[1]The Soviets were clearly hoping that the protocol would establish a precedent for SALT III. The United States continued to stress that it would not consider itself bound by the protocol after the expiration date. Perhaps only when the Soviet Union developed a modern cruise missile program of its own would the United States take a serious interest in its restriction.

uncertain mix. As John Newhouse, a senior ACDA official put it, "The clock became the enemy of the process."

Between January 1 and May 1, 1979, Secretary Vance and Ambassador Dobyrnin met over 25 times in Washington to resolve the remaining differences. A compromise date, December 31, 1981 was established for the termination of the protocol that would coincide with a reduction in the overall ceiling from 2400 to 2250. With the exception of the one new type allowed, neither side could modify, plus or minus, the length, diameter, launch weight, or throw weight of its ICBMs by more than 5 percent. The Soviets accepted the American figure of 28 as the average of ALCMs on a cruise missile carrier, while the United States agreed to a limit of 20 ALCMs on its force of B-52s.

THE TREATY IS SIGNED

With these issues and a number of other technical points settled, the long awaited Carter/Brezhnev summit was announced for mid-June in Vienna. After years of protracted negotiations, the summit conference was almost anticlimactic. The substantive issue remaining for Carter and Brezhnev was the production rate of the Backfire bomber. Carter wanted to commit Brezhnev to an exact figure, 30 a month. And in the elliptical world of international diplomacy, a "noncontradiction" is tantamount to assent.

On June 18, 1979, the document finally was signed. Three hundred pages long, it represented almost seven years of painstaking diplomacy. Carter had negotiated an agreement which went considerably beyond SALT I and Vladivostok. When compared to the vast magnitude of the problem, however, SALT II was only a modest step. The expectations created by Carter in the inaugural pledge and by his March 1977 proposals worked to dampen the enthusiasm for the agreement.

In fact, neither side was giving up any of its major strategic programs. During the lifetime of the treaty, even with its fractionation limits, each side would be able to increase its number of warheads. Estimates called for an increase by the Soviet Union from 5,000 to almost 10,000 deliverable warheads. The United States arsenal would increase from 9,200 to about 13,000. Yet without the treaty the nuclear arsenals of the superpowers would be multiplied even further, perhaps getting out of control.

Carter and Vance had bargained hard and, on the whole, effectively. The United States had made only two major concessions: on the SS-18 and on Backfire. Both concessions were less important than they appeared. The SS-18s presented no greater threat to the United States land-based missiles than did the SS-17s or SS-19s. In any event, the United States had only 24 percent of its warheads on ICBMs (the Soviet Union had 70 percent of its warheads on its land-based force). The remaining American force of SLBMs, heavy bombers, and cruise missiles could not be threatened during the lifetime of the treaty nor, in all probability, beyond then.

The Backfire bomber added little to the Soviet strategic force and could only reach targets in the United States by flying at high altitudes and at subsonic speeds. It was primarily intended for use against Western Europe, China, and naval targets. The United States had 160 F-llls, based in Britain and equipped with nuclear weapons, that could hit Soviet targets. Leaving Backfire out of the SALT II limits was the price for also excluding American forward-based systems—not to mention the British and French nuclear forces.

SALT II: TECHNICAL SUCCESS/POLITICAL FAILURE

SALT II, unlike previous arms control agreements, failed to engender public enthusiasm. The humiliating defeat in Vietnam, the holding of hostages in Iran, the declining dollar, and the increasing dependence on foreign oil all dramatized American vulnerabilities. Those reminders of our frailty did not produce an atmosphere conducive to arms control. The NBC/AP poll showed support for the SALT II agreements falling from 62 percent in March 1979 to 43 percent in September 1979.

Steering the agreements through the Senate appeared to require as much patience and skill from the Carter administration as was demonstrated in negotiations with the Soviet Union. In order to secure the support of Senate Majority Leader Robert Byrd (D. W.Va.), President Carter personally assured him in a letter of October 26, 1979, that the MX, SLCM, and GLCM would be deployed, once the Protocol expired, and these weapons would not be bargained away for Soviet reductions in a SALT III agreement.

This concession, significant as it appeared, was not enough to secure broad bipartisan support for SALT II. Gerald Ford and Henry Kissinger, while careful not to criticize an agreement which bore much of their work, conditioned their support for SALT II upon substantial increases in defense spending. Ford told an audience at the Army War College that, "I am against the treaty unless the necessary defense spending decisions have been made and have been written into law. I don't believe vague, short-term, or revocable assurances are enough." Kissinger testified at the Senate Foreign Relations Committee hearings on SALT II that ratification of the agreement should be conditioned upon, "the accelerated development of MX and Trident II, air defense against Backfire, immediate steps to beef up our capacity for regional defense, including accelerated modernization and expansion of our Navy."

Reflecting the mood of Ford and Kissinger, the Senate voted on September 18, 1979, 55 to 42, for a 5 percent increase (over and above the inflation rate) in defense spending for fiscal years 1981 and 1982. Such an increase would bring defense spending to $170 billion by 1982, nearly doubling the spending levels of 1976. After the Soviet invasion of Afghanistan on Christmas Day 1979, Carter, in January, asked the Senate to delay consideration of SALT II until a more propitious time.

REAGAN AND START

The victory of Ronald Reagan over Jimmy Carter and the defeat of 10 pro-SALT senators in the 1980 election sealed the fate of SALT II. Mr. Reagan had campaigned against the treaty, calling it "fatally flawed." Reagan's appointments and subsequent policy statements underscored his intention to stick to his campaign position. Eugene V. Rostow, a Yale law professor who was a leading spokesman for the Committee on the Present Danger as well as a vociferous opponent of SALT II, was appointed ACDA director. General Rowny was designated as Chief Arms Control Negotiator.

But, the shift from Carter to Reagan had implications for arms control that went beyond the fate of SALT II. Richard Perle, a former aide to Senator Jackson who became an Assistant Secretary of Defense under Reagan, proclaimed "a fundamental change in the focus on arms control as a way of moderating our [military] requirements." President Reagan, in a June 1981 commencement address at West Point, made the point more emphatically. "The argument," Reagan insisted, "if there is any, will be over which weapons [to build], not whether we would forsake weaponry for treaties and agreements."

Arms control policy underwent a fundamental review during the first year of the Reagan administration. Rostow told the Senate Foreign Relations Committee that the administration had, "reached no conclusions on this subject beyond the conviction that the SALT II Treaty is deeply flawed and should not be ratified." Paradoxically, the Reagan administration stated its intention to observe the SALT II provisions as well as the SALT I interim agreement on offensive forces.

Rostow expressed an interest in perhaps a more ambitious treaty and wondered if it would be feasible, "to negotiate and verify a dramatic and equitable cut in each side's arsenal—to achieve a real breakthrough in the mad spiral of arms accumulation." General Rowny, in Senate testimony, cited the March 1977 proposals as a model agreement and lamented that the Carter administration, "didn't have the will power to stick by it." Had the Carter administration given up too easily on the March 1977 proposals? Could Reagan, Rostow, and Rowny succeed where Carter, Vance, and Warnke failed?

Between 1980 and 1982 American public opinion made a dramatic reversal. Fear of nuclear war and resentment over high defense spending replaced public concerns about the Soviet arms buildup. A Harris Poll taken in October 1982 showed only 17 percent of the public supported increases in the defense budget, a decline from 71 percent in the fall of 1980. In addition, a proposal for a bilateral freeze on nuclear weapons testing, deployment, and production generated impressive support in the 1982 elections. Resolutions endorsing the freeze carried in 8 out of 9 states plus the District of Columbia and in 29 localities. In Chicago, Philadelphia, and New Haven, the margins of support were over 70 percent.

Perhaps sensing this new public mood, President Reagan announced his new arms control proposal during an address at Eureka College on May 9, 1982. Renamed START (Strategic Arms Reduction Talks), the proposal called for substantial reductions in nuclear arms to take place in two phases. In the first phase, both superpowers would reduce their number of missile-launched warheads to 5000. (Under a sublimit, land-based missiles could carry no more than 2500 warheads.) The number of land-and sea-based missiles would be reduced to 850. These reductions would be phased over a 5 to 10-year period.

In the second phase, Reagan proposed that aggregate missile throw-weight on each side be reduced to levels below the present U.S. ICBM force. Reagan administration officials argued that START would promote strategic stability by reducing the Soviet threat to our ICBM force—the so-called window of vulnerability. Clearly, the requirements for a reduction in both the number of land-based warheads and in the overall throw-weight were directed at the Soviet MIRVed ICBM force, especially the SS-18s. The first phase of START, alone, would require a reduction of over 2400 Soviet land-based missile warheads.

Critics such as former CIA Deputy Director Herbert Scoville, Jr. argued that START would widen, rather than close, the window of vulnerability. Scoville contended that, although START would reduce the total number of Soviet warheads targeted against our ICBMs, the reduction to 850 launchers would result in a disproportionate decrease in American ICBM sites. Thus, the ratio of accurate weapons to silos would, in fact, increase under START. This, the critics charged, was not thoughtful arms control. In any event, the omission of any limits on either land-range bombers or strategic cruise missiles made it unlikely that the Soviet Union would accept the proposal in anything close to its original form.

CONCLUSION

As each side refined its missile accuracies and its threats to each other's land-based force, the arms control process was confronting a moment of truth. The new talks would produce either significant controls on first strike weapons and meaningful reductions in overall forces, or the technology of destruction could leap beyond our grasp. Cruise missiles produced in the tens of thousands could overwhelm the techniques of verification. Pressure to protect land-based missiles with ABM could lead to the abrogation of the ABM treaty, undoing the entire arms control process.

The Reagan approach did contain a troubling contradiction that would have to be resolved if any arms agreements were to be concluded. The commitment to accelerate arms spending was difficult to square with genuine reductions in nuclear weapons. Reagan found it difficult to move in opposite directions simultaneously.

The arms control process was in serious political and technical jeopardy, closely tied to the general state of United States-Soviet relations.

Soviet behavior such as was exhibited in Afghanistan made it difficult for any American president to gain either public or congressional support for future arms control agreeements, not to mention SALT II itself. New agreements would inevitably, by the nature of the technologies they would have to control, be more elaborate and complex. Technical advances in verification techiques would not be enough, standing alone, to sustain such agreements. A level of civility and restraint would have to mark the relations of the superpowers.

The United States would have to demonstrate clearly to the Soviet Union both the advantages of détente and the severe costs of confrontation and aggression. SALT I was achieved against a background of rising expectations for détente. But SALT II was negotiated during a period of great uncertainty and flux in Soviet-American relations. If we were to get to START, Soviet-American relations would have to be reconstructed.

The arms control process had reached a crossroad. Agreements that merely ratified previous deployment decisions had little chance of containing these frightening technologies. Incremental agreements appeared inadequate to guide the superpowers over what one poet called, "this cosmic minefield."

The prodigious effort that produced SALT II would not be enough for the future. Agreements to constrain the arms race were not consistent with the policy that all weapons not specifically prohibited be built. A bolder vision was required for the 1980s: Political leaders needed to be reminded of John Stuart Mill's adage that, "Against a great evil a small remedy does not produce a small result, it produces no result at all."

FOR FURTHER READING

Bresler, Robert J. "The Tangled Politics of SALT," *Arms Control: The Journal of Arms Control and Disarmament,* 3 (May 1982), 3–12.

Carnegie Endowment for International Peace. *Challenges for U.S. National Security: Defense Spending and the Economy—The Strategic Balance and Strategic Arms Limitation* (Washington, D.C.: 1981).

Jodal, Jan M. "Finishing START," *Foreign Policy,* 48 (Fall 1982), 66–81.

Moynihan, Daniel Patrick. "The SALT Process," *The New Yorker* (November 19, 1979), 104–180.

Nye, Joseph S., Jr. "Restarting Arms Control," *Foreign Policy,* 47 (Summer 1982), 98–113.

Schell, Jonathan. *The Fate of the Earth* (New York, N.Y.: Avon, 1982).

Sigal, Leon. "Warming to the Freeze," *Foreign Policy,* 48 (Fall 1982), 54–65.

Sloan, Stanley R. and Gray, Robert C. *Nuclear Strategy and Arms Control: Challenges for U.S. Policy,* Headline Series #261 (New York, N.Y.: Foreign Policy Association, 1982).

Stockholm International Peace Research Institute. *The Arms Race and Arms Control* (Cambridge, Mass.: Oelgeschlager, Gunn & Main, 1982).

Talbott, Strobe. *Endgame: The Inside Story of SALT II* (New York, N.Y.: Harper & Row, 1979).

Wolfe, Thomas W. *The SALT Experience.* (Cambridge, Mass.: Ballinger, 1979).

chapter 3

The United States and China

MICHAEL L. BARON

More than a decade has passed since President Richard M. Nixon announced that he would travel to China, a journey that broke through 22 years of accumulated hatred and vitriol. Although American dealings with the People's Republic of China (PRC) were placed on a more regular diplomatic footing after Nixon's visit, the two nations approached each other gingerly, shaking hands but maintaining a healthy distance. The last month of 1978 and the first month of 1979 saw the tentative reacquaintance of long-feuding friends bloom into a warm embrace. By early 1980, the Soviet invasion of Afghanistan had driven the two nations even closer together, but the passion cooled almost immediately. What is remarkable about this change is the two decades of sharp and acrimonious history that preceded the Nixon visit.

With the establishment of the PRC on October 1, 1949, Chiang Kai-shek, leader of the Kuomintang (Nationalist Party), fled with his remaining troops from the mainland to his island refuge of Taiwan. Despite Chiang's defeat, American officials were reluctant to halt financial and diplomatic support to the isolated and discredited regime because of the long-standing policy of support for the Nationalists and the intense pressure on the Truman administration from congressional critics. President Harry Truman and his aides generally came to the view that Mao Zedong and his Communist supporters were mere puppets on a string pulled by Kremlin masters, a perception that was seemingly confirmed when Mao vowed that China would "lean to one side," that is, toward the Soviet Union, in world politics.

The Korean War and the direct involvement of Chinese "volunteers," as United Nations-American troops neared the Chinese-Korean frontier, cemented this identification of China with a monolithic Communist menace directed from Moscow. The military conflict shattered any lingering hopes that the United States might soon recognize the Peking government, carry on normal diplomatic relations, or encourage trade. By judging all events around the globe in a black-and-white cold war context, however, American leaders missed significant signs that the Sino-Soviet honeymoon was less than perfect. Thus, in its treatment of China as an appendage of the Kremlin, the United States left Chinese strategists no choice but to put their eggs in Stalin's basket.

President Dwight D. Eisenhower and his Secretary of State, John Foster Dulles, were equally convinced that the Chinese leaders had forged the tightest of bonds with the Soviet Union, selling out their nationalism for a dominating foreign ideology. Quickly moving to expand the containment policy, Dulles initiated a series of defense pacts with nations surrounding China in an attempt to reduce China's political influence in the area and restrain it from military action against its neighbors. Taiwan (the Republic of China, ROC), the Philippines, and the nations of Southeast Asia—among others—joined the defensive scheme. With the creation of these alliances, Chinese diplomats feared that American aggressors, spurred by Chiang and his entourage on Taiwan, would ultimately choose to seek to roll back Communism in China using military means, possibly even nuclear weapons. This deeply held fear induced Chinese planners to rely on an implicit Soviet nuclear umbrella. By pushing the two Communist states closer together, rather than playing on existing tensions to pull them apart, the United States failed to recognize its long-run interests.

In the 1950s, Communist military probes of Western intentions with regard to Quemoy and Matsu, islands held by the Nationalists in sight of the mainland, brought a firm American response. While the American government agreed to begin official contacts with Chinese representatives in Geneva in 1955 in order to reduce the danger of war, no progress resulted from the talks. Dulles, in fact, refused publicly or privately to shake hands with Communist Zhou Enlai at the Geneva Conference and was unwilling to compromise on the issue of the safety of Taiwan.

In 1960, disputes between Peking and Moscow spilled into the public realm. Disagreements about nuclear sharing arrangements, policy toward the United States, ideology, and intra-Communist block affairs fueled the split. With American analysts unsure of the best ways to take advantage of this cleavage, President John F. Kennedy adhered to the containment policies formulated by his predecessors. Faced with intense domestic opposition against any conciliatory maneuvers (by the so-called China Lobby) and locked into a cold warrior mentality himself, Kennedy's foreign policy sought to maintain China's isolation while reducing outstanding tensions to manageable proportions.

One of the original motives for American involvement in Vietnam was to block Chinese expansionism. Escalation of that war during the Johnson administration made the Chinese even more implacably anti-American and ensured that American distrust of China would remain widespread. Meanwhile, during the height of the conflict in Vietnam, China was convulsed with an extended period of anarchy: the Great Proletarian Cultural Revolution. Chinese ambassadors were recalled from foreign posts. All Sino-American contacts were suspended. Chinese relations with Moscow drastically deteriorated. Approaching the 20th anniversary of the founding of the PRC, Chinese-American enmity continued unabated. Peking found itself without allies, cornered, deserted by Communists and non-Communists alike. Its only ally was tiny, powerless Albania.

FRAGILE FRIENDSHIP: THE NIXON-FORD YEARS

Suddenly, a combination of international and domestic events created an atmosphere conducive to Sino-American reconciliation. First, the Chinese were frightened by the Soviet invasion of Czechoslovakia in 1968, which was followed immediately by the buildup of Soviet military strength along the Sino-Soviet border. Second, President Lyndon Johnson's Vietnam peace initiatives and President Nixon's deescalation of American involvement in South Vietnam reduced the worry among Chinese that the United States posed a short-term threat to China. Third, from an American perspective, Washington's relations with Moscow seemed to be frozen. Soviet-American negotiations to limit nuclear arms were stalemated and no solution to the impasse was in sight. Fourth, Nixon, a conservative Republican, anticipated that opposition to opening relations with China would be muted by his impeccable anti-Communist credentials. Finally, in China, moderates controlled the reins of power. In light of their diplomatic isolation, the military threat of Russian troops to the north, and the economic distress caused by the radicalism that was rampant during the Cultural Revolution, the Chinese government perceived a need to open channels to the most powerful military and economic rival of the Soviet Union: the United States.

The United States carefully signaled its interest in rapprochement with Peking. It lifted travel restrictions, ended American naval patrols in waters separating Taiwan and the mainland, eased trade restrictions, and resumed direct diplomatic contacts. Chairman Mao expressed his willingness to have President Nixon visit China even if no formal diplomatic relations existed between the two nations. American spokesmen, in making public statements, suddenly began to refer to the People's Republic of China, abandoning the once obligatory pejorative terms "Communist China," "Mainland China," or "Red China." In April 1971, an American Ping-Pong team played exhibition matches in China and received wide media coverage.

In July 1971, Richard Nixon stunned a nationwide audience with the announcement that he soon would visit the PRC. Nixon's gambit, arranged by National Security Adviser Henry Kissinger during secret trips to Peking, sought to improve ties with China in order to prompt Soviet policy makers to cooperate with American plans for détente. A direct result of the changed climate was the admission of the PRC to the United Nations, while the ROC was expelled at China's insistence.

At the conclusion of Nixon's heralded journey, a joint statement was issued. The Shanghai Communiqué promised that both sides would work to improve relations and to reduce the dangers of military conflict. Firm opposition was pledged against "efforts by any other country or group of countries to establish . . . hegemony. . . ."

Because hegemony was used by the Chinese as a code word for Soviet expansionist designs, this was an important signal to Moscow that Sino-American rapprochement had implications for U.S.-Soviet relations. However, the Taiwan issue blocked complete normalization. Peking asserted that the "liberation" of the island was an internal affair in which no interference was acceptable. American spokesmen responded somewhat ambiguously by admitting that there was only one China, but they avoided recognition of Peking's claim that the PRC was the sole government of China. American negotiators promised to withdraw military forces from Taiwan, but no mention was made of timing. In June 1972, Secretary of State William Rogers said of the commitment to Taiwan, "Our new relationships will not be achieved by sacrificing the interests of our friends . . . ."

The communiqué served as the basis for the relationship for the next six years. Both powers needed a peaceful, stable environment. The United States wanted to extricate itself from the Vietnam quagmire without too great a "loss of face" while China sought to proceed with economic modernization programs. Their common aim was to prevent Soviet penetration in Asia and around the world. American foreign policy makers sought to scare the Russians with visions of a Chinese-American alliance so they would be more willing to cooperate on other matters. Chinese officials wanted to counterbalance Soviet power by intimating that the United States would interfere if Moscow exerted pressure on Peking. The Chinese adapted two historic adages: "Use barbarians to control other barbarians"; and, "The enemy of our enemy is our friend."

The China connection yielded quick dividends for the United States. On the heels of his visit to China, President Nixon traveled to Moscow where SALT I was initialed. The arms agreement was interpreted by administration analysts as a direct payoff of the strategy of playing China against Russia to gain better relations with both.

From 1973 through 1976, Sino-American relations were stagnant. The Chinese were noticeably impatient with American foot dragging on Taiwan. They also interpreted American policy toward the Soviet Union as dangerous appeasement, viewing the Vladivostok Accord signed by President Gerald Ford and the 25-nation Helsinki Accords, which guaranteed Soviet borders, as signs of American weakness and lack of resolve. To ameliorate Chinese concerns Ford made a pilgrimage to China in December 1975. At that time Vice-Premier Deng Xiaoping told his guest that Peking was primarily interested in a strong American stand against Moscow. Taiwan, according to Deng, could wait, provided the United States stood up to Soviet leaders.

For China, 1976 was a momentous year. Revered Zhou Enlai, the foreign policy director highly respected in the West as well as in China, died. His moderate policies were immediately challenged by radical leaders, and his protegé Deng was purged for the second time in a decade. Leftists adopted a militant foreign policy line including a renewal of anti-American propaganda. In September, the "Great Helmsman," Mao died. His death was followed unexpectedly by a purge of the radical "Gang of Four," a group of high-ranking leftists led by Mao's widow Jiang Qing. Hua Guofeng was named Chairman of the Communist party and was joined by a revived Deng. Policy focus shifted from class struggle and ideological purity to rebuilding the economy and restabilizing the political situation. Modernizing rapidly would mean that China must import technology and capital from the West and neutralize its biggest military threat—the Soviet Union.

THE CARTER ADMINISTRATION AND CHINA

Upon taking office, Jimmy Carter and his Secretary of State, Cyrus Vance, affirmed their intention to move toward normalization of relations as specified in the Shanghai Communiqué. The major stumbling block continued to be the legitimacy, security, and economic well-being of Taiwan. To break the deadlock, Vance went to Peking proposing that liaison offices in Washington and Peking set up to handle diplomatic and commercial problems be upgraded in status to official embassies. The embassy designation of diplomatic offices in Taipei would be downgraded to liaison status. Vance also suggested that China issue a unilateral statement vowing not to use force to settle the Taiwan problem. The Chinese angrily rejected both proposals and made it clear that they were extremely unhappy with the foreign policy of the new administration.

This obvious setback in Chinese-American relations was matched by a sharp deterioration in Soviet-American relations. Carter's human rights pronouncements and his public advocacy of far-reaching reductions in nuclear arsenals without first discussing his ideas with Russian officials perturbed Moscow. Soviet-sponsored Cuban military adventures in Africa brought oral protests from the United States and further soured the atmosphere. Within the president's foreign policy staff, especially in the National Security Council, there were growing demands to use Nixon's technique of threatening to improve Washington-Peking links at the expense of the Soviet Union. It was argued that the specter of a Sino-American alliance would compel the paranoid Russians to be more cooperative.

An overt signal of change in American policy came in May 1978, when National Security Adviser Zbigniew Brzezinski, during a visit to the PRC, stressed the parallel strategic interests shared by the United States and China. He simultaneously downplayed differences over Taiwan. In a toast to Chinese leaders, at one of their gala banquets, he remarked: ". . . We recognize . . . and share . . . China's resolve to resist the efforts of any nation which seeks to establish global or regional hegemony. . . . Only those aspiring to dominate others have any reasons to fear the further development of American-Chinese relations. . . ."

At another point, in a direct reference to Soviet aggression, Brzezinski said: ". . . Neither of us [the PRC or the United States] dispatches international marauders who masquerade as nonaligned to advance big power ambitions in Africa. Neither of us seeks to enforce the political obedience of our neighbors through military force . . . ." In other informal remarks, he repeatedly referred to the danger posed by the Soviet Union, leading some Chinese to dub him "the Bear tamer."

Additional steps were taken that affected the triangular relationship. An agreement to sell American advanced computers to the Soviet news agency Tass was postponed while similar equipment was sold to China. An American delegation of top-level scientists and technology experts traveled to China to exchange information and expand opportunities. An equivalent group, although scheduled to visit the Soviet Union, protested the trials of prominent dissidents by refusing to make the trip. The United States also goaded the Japanese into signing the Sino-Japanese Treaty, which contained an antihegemony clause directed against the Soviet Union. The Japanese, always cautious, long resisted including such a clause in any treaty, but with American encouragement they proceeded despite Russian warnings. Finally, the administration gave verbal support to Chairman Hua's unprecedented trip to Eastern Europe, thus further upsetting the edgy occupants of the Kremlin.

NORMALIZATION AND ITS AFTERSHOCKS

On December 15, 1978, President Carter announced that the United States and the PRC would normalize diplomatic relations on January 1, 1979. Washington would sever diplomatic ties with Taipei, recognizing Peking as the sole legal government of China. Second, the United States would terminate its defense treaty with Taiwan. According to the terms of the treaty, either party could withdraw after one year's notice was given. Carter gave such notice and said the treaty expired on December 31, 1979. Third, administration leaders agreed to withdraw all American troops from Taiwan.

The president alleged that breaking formal links with the government of Taiwan did not mean the end of cultural, commercial, and other nonofficial business. He pointed out that after Japan and Canada broke relations with Taiwan, the amount of business, investments, and cultural exchanges actually increased. Congressional leaders, in Carter's words, took the decision "with mixed response." Many were angry that the administration failed to consult Congress before acting (as it had previously pledged to do and as a Senate resolution passed in July 1978 requested). Senator Barry Goldwater joined with others in Congress to begin an ultimately unsuccessful court action designed to overturn the president's decision to cancel the defense treaty. Prominent Democrats as well as Republicans criticized the administration for failing to gain Chinese assurances that no military force would be used against Taiwan. Senator Howard Baker summed up the opinion of several colleagues: "The Taiwanese have been a good and faithful ally, and we certainly owe them more than this."

To bolster the normalization process Vice-Premier Deng visited the United States. His well-publicized comments often zeroed in on the Soviet menace, and he made repeated calls for Sino-American cooperation to contain the "hegemonists." Bilateral agreements relating to science and technology and cultural exchanges were signed. Understandings on collaborative efforts in agriculture, space exploration, education, and high-energy physics were also reached. Deng's efforts to project a favorable image in the United States—capped by his appearance in an oversized ten-gallon cowboy hat in a Texas rodeo—were partially offset upon his return to China when the Chinese army marched into Vietnam in mid-February 1979. The "counterattack," as the Chinese called their military action, was aimed at teaching Vietnam a lesson. For a while the fighting threatened to spread to the Soviet-Chinese border area when Moscow warned Peking to halt its "aggression" against Vietnam, a Soviet ally. The possibility of a direct Chinese-Soviet clash sobered Washington policy makers still basking in the glow left by Deng's visit to the United States.

The timing of the Chinese attack implied that the United States had approved the military action during Deng's visit, but, although displeased by this implication, America did not back off from its new friend. To promote trade and commercial intercourse, Treasury Secretary Michael Blumenthal went to Peking, soon followed by Commerce Secretary Juanita Kreps. These efforts resulted in the solution of a major, long-standing problem. Since the Korean war, Chinese assets in the United States had been frozen pending payment of debts allegedly owed Americans. Until assets were unblocked and American claims satisfactorily settled, any Chinese ship that called at an American port or any property that the Chinese government bought could be seized by a court acting on behalf of American claimants. The resolution of the frozen assets question thus cleared the way for unhindered trade and commercial interactions. But another economic problem arose when the Chinese rebuffed Robert Strauss, President Carter's special trade representative, who went to Peking to gain Chinese acceptance of "voluntary" limits on their exports of textiles to the United States.

When Vice-President Walter Mondale visited China in August 1979, the Chinese were delighted with his frequent assertions that the United States and China shared a wide range of "parallel strategic and bilateral interests." In a speech at Peking University that was televised throughout China, Mondale again pleased his hosts with his accounts of the rationale behind the new relationship.

. . . any nation which seeks to weaken or isolate you in world affairs assumes a stance counter to American interests. This is why the United States normalized relations with your country, and that is why we must work to broaden and strengthen our new friendship. . . . Above all, both our political interests are served by your growing strength in all fields, for it helps to deter others who might seek to impose themselves on you. . . . Let there be no doubt about the choice my country has made. The United States believes that any effort by one country to dominate another is doomed to failure. . . .

Everyone listening understood that the Vice-President was referring to the Soviet Union in his comments. He again calmed Chinese fears that they were alone in recognizing the threat of Soviet expansion. On a more concrete plane, during Mondale's sojourn a number of additional bilateral agreements were initialed. These agreements were intended to bolster China's modernization drive, foster cultural and scientific exchanges, and enhance the position of moderate leaders within the Chinese government.

These developments confirmed a remarkable transformation in the international system. China, in the span of one decade, moved from an ostracized, lonely international outcast to a position as semi-ally of its most implacable former enemy. At the same time, the United States found itself wooed by both China and the Soviet Union, thereby able to play one Communist power against the other. But the enviable bargaining position of the United States did not mean that all problems would disappear or that American leverage could easily manipulate either or both of the two nations.

"TILTING" TOWARD CHINA: PROBLEMS AND PROSPECTS

According to most observers, American foreign policy makers have consciously "tilted" toward China. In this context, *tilting* simply means allowing the PRC to derive certain substantive benefits from its relationship with Washington, but denying Moscow similar benefits. The alternative to a lean-to-one-side policy is an even-handed policy in which China and the Soviet Union are treated in precisely the same way.

The argument in support of abandoning an even-handed policy runs as follows: Peking is measurably weaker economically and militarily than Moscow. China also lags far behind in technological know-how. Therefore, a policy that treats the two states as equals in reality discriminates against China and favors the Soviet Union. Without help the Chinese will fall further behind the Soviets; this, in turn, will give Kremlin tacticians influence over their weaker neighbor to the south. If the United States does not move to aid China in its development, China will astutely understand that it is condemned to permanent inferiority. Then China might negotiate an end to the Sino-Soviet conflict in order to reduce the Soviet threat to its national security. Détente between the long-warring nations might, it is feared, lead to renewed pressures on Japan and the independent states in South-East Asia.

Those who want to assist China assume that its strength and independence are in America's best interest. They argue that a powerful China complicates life for the Kremlin. Soviet troops would have to remain in the

Far East instead of being redeployed to Europe. The Kremlin's decision makers would retain their preoccupation with China. Hence the PRC is viewed as a useful de facto ally serving to confuse and limit Soviet freedom of action.

Evidence that advocates of tilting in the American government were in ascendance in 1979 and 1980 comes from several actions taken by the Carter administration. Examination of these activities, however, illustrates the pitfalls of the tilt strategy and highlights the dangers lurking in the future.

In the trade arena, President Carter's request to Congress to grant China most-favored-nation (MFN) status was approved. The Chinese received substantial tariff reductions from rates that dated back to 1934. China also was given access to credits from the Export-Import Bank that had previously been denied under the restrictive terms of the Jackson-Vanik amendment to the 1974 Trade Act. This amendment was designed to block such benefits to nonmarket societies (particularly the USSR) unless a liberalization of emigration policies was adopted. Deng Xiaoping reportedly told leading congressmen that the United States could have as many million Chinese as it wanted.

Senator Henry Jackson (D. Wash.), among others, wanted to continue to withhold trade privileges until Russian authorities gave clear assurances on free emigration. President Carter had earlier pledged that he would only consider lifting trade restrictions on both nations at the same time so that neither the USSR nor PRC would benefit more than the other—a key tenet of even-handedness. Soviet leaders were quite unhappy that China received favored trade consideration while they were denied similar concessions. The Soviets have argued, with some justification, that Senator Jackson and National Security Adviser Brzezinski favored lifting trade restrictions on China not as a reward for Chinese emigration policies, but as a political maneuver designed to punish the Soviet Union. In fact, congressional sentiment against the Soviet Union over perceived inequities in SALT II virtually precluded the president from granting Moscow equal benefits.

American political leaders were caught in a dilemma. Granting trade privileges to China without equal treatment for the Soviet Union angered the Soviets, perhaps reducing chances for further arms agreements or even jeopardizing the basis for détente in general. Some members of the Carter foreign policy team, reportedly including Secretary of State Vance, felt that an unbalanced MFN decision would damage critical Soviet-American relations. However, if trade benefits to China were stymied the Chinese would feel slighted, if not betrayed. And China would quickly search elsewhere for trade and economic assistance, with Japan being China's probable alternative source for capital, equipment, and markets. In December 1979, Peking and Tokyo reached an agreement providing China with large, low-interest loans. Total trade surpassed $10 billion in 1981. In comparison, American-Chinese trade was less than half that amount.

Another arena where observers saw a tilt toward China was the strategic military realm. This took on added significance with Secretary of

Defense Harold Brown's unprecedented visit to China in January 1980. This journey took on new meaning after Soviet troops were sent into neighboring Afghanistan, thus upsetting the Persian Gulf balance of power. Brown and his party of top military planners and technology experts discussed strengthening "other nations in the region" such as Pakistan, consulted with leading Chinese officials, and visited Chinese military installations. It was announced that a satellite ground station would be sold to China, and it was clear that the United States was willing to transfer technology that might have military uses to the PRC. Soviet leaders, by their invasion of Afghanistan, virtually guaranteed the creation of closer relations between America and China.

The United States, although not yet willing to sell arms to the Chinese, permitted its Western European allies to sell China advanced military hardware. Peking negotiated to acquire French anti-tank guided missiles, surface-to-air missiles, and radar equipment. Britain sold advanced plane engines, and there were rumors of deals with Italy. Any purchases of military technology by China profoundly upset Moscow officials who wanted to maintain their huge advantage along the Sino-Soviet border.

CARTER'S LEGACY TO RONALD REAGAN

American recognition of the People's Republic of China is likely to be the most enduring foreign policy achievement of the Carter administration. By putting relations on a normal diplomatic footing, Carter finally carried out the promise of the Shanghai Communiqué, which itself heralded a historic shift. Though cries of outrage reverberated throughout the halls of Congress and in Taiwan, in every aspect except formal diplomatic contact, the American relationship with that island actually prospered.

The Carter foreign policy team, dominated by Brzezinski and his National Security Council staff, constructed the Sino-American agenda in such a way that President Reagan's options were significantly narrowed. Despite his well-publicized remarks during the campaign that called for official ties with the "Republic of China," Reagan has yet to rock the boat. Trade with both China and Taiwan rapidly expands as cultural interchanges grow. China has become the fourth largest purchaser of American agricultural products. Taiwan remains a major supplier as well as a consumer of American products, the eighth largest exporter to the United States, and the tenth largest importer of American goods.

Just how closely the Reagan administration is following the Carter blueprint was revealed in the results of a visit to China by former Secretary of State Alexander Haig. During his talks in Beijing in June 1981, Haig and current Chinese leaders concurred on their assessment of the Soviet Union and the need to cooperate to limit its perceived expansionist drive around the world. Haig promised to let the Chinese make military purchases in the United States, although he specifically downplayed the potential for substantial arms deals. Then the secret existence of a CIA listening post in

China that bordered the Soviet Union was made public through leaks to the press. Perhaps this was to mollify, in advance, critics in Congress who bridle at the idea of supplying Communist "Red China" with military equipment. Presumably, one of the benefits of helping China build a capable military force is an installation that enables the United States to better monitor Soviet missile developments.

Although not yet allies in a formal sense, the United States and China were no longer mere friends. Now they were "buddies" who collaborated to frustrate the designs of the neighborhood "bully." Although they did not necessarily share the same interests, they were united against their mutual foe. Their policies toward Korea, Israel, and South Africa remain among the few areas where serious differences exist.

In effect, Reagan has been locked into a strategy toward China by the promises and commitments of his predecessor and by the logic of his anti-Moscow posture. If, as his conservative supporters had hoped, he revoked or modified existing obligations to Taiwan, arms sales to China, or trade and credits, the Chinese-American connection would appear to backslide and be downgraded. Because it perceives the Soviet Union as a dangerous, provocative challenger to peace, the Reagan administration is compelled to keep the Chinese in the Western camp and provide concrete incentives to maintain an anti-Russian position. Beijing, after all, ties down millions of Soviet troops in Asia, thus diverting Moscow's resources from the more critical European theater. China, recognizing the strategic importance of Europe, repeatedly emphasizes that Europe is the primary concern of Soviet planners, and Asia is secondary.

Despite the agreement to contain the Soviet menace, several fundamental problems inherent in the Sino-American relationship have yet to be resolved.

Although American benefits from closer cooperation with a stronger PRC are emphasized, a significant question is frequently ignored: Could helping China create a powerful military machine be dangerous? Growing Chinese strength might provoke Soviet action against China now, before the gap narrows. If another Vietnamese-Chinese clash erupts, Soviet military specialists may convincingly argue that unless Soviet troops move quickly, future Chinese military abilities will foreclose Soviet military options. American and Western European policy makers must ponder what their reaction would be to a Sino-Soviet war.

Second, a mighty China, with military power nearly equal to that of the Soviet Union, would be compelled to reduce the level of tension with Moscow to lessen the chance for war. Paradoxically, a stronger China might well be a China willing to negotiate with a current enemy from a position of equality rather than inferiority. A Sino-Soviet rapprochement would undoubtedly make Washington analysts nervous, since Chinese troops now massed along the Soviet frontier might be moved to the Taiwan straits area or along the borders of its South-East Asian neighbors. China, if armed with the latest technology imported from the West, could easily be viewed as a threat to American friends.

Finally, the Soviet Union will assume the worst regarding Sino-American military ties. Soviet leaders may read into Haig's bluster and continuing Western arms and technology sales to China a spreading Western encirclement of Soviet territory. Indeed, some have argued that Sino-American friendship was one of the many factors that led the Politburo to invade Afghanistan.

American policy seems to be predicated on a defensive assumption that the United States can manipulate the Sino-Soviet relationship to American advantage. But if policy makers do not agree on the specific forms of behavior they want to modify, there is no hope that events can be molded to fit American predilections. Specifically, decision makers must ask themselves: Do we want the Chinese (Russians) to implement a new policy direction? Are we trying to induce a shift in the composition or policy preferences of the leadership group? What kinds of changes in the regime or society would be in the interests of the United States?

Even if such goals are specified, the implementation of a policy deliberately aimed at producing changes in behavior will be quite difficult, and even risky. Different factions in elites abroad are likely to interpret signals from the United States in conflicting ways. Therefore, to expect a policy initiative to have an anticipated effect is foolhardy. Since the processes by which the PRC and USSR make foreign or domestic policy are obscure at best, it is shortsighted to think that specific aspects of these states' policies can be readily manipulated in directions that can be forecast in advance.

The principal problems in trying to manipulate the triangular relationship are uncertainty, unanticipated consequences, and undefined or ambiguous policy. The inability to determine precisely the factional divisions within Soviet and Chinese leadership makes uncertainty an inevitable feature of American foreign policy. Which coalition is in command, which groups favor which policies, who belongs to which group, and the relative strength of various groups are usually unknown.

American policy toward other areas, for example Africa or the Middle East, frequently has unanticipated consequences on interactions among the three major nations. If America does not take stern action against Soviet-Cuban involvement in Africa, China protests American weakness. If the United States opposes attempts to seat the Vietnamese-backed government of Cambodia in the United Nations, the Soviets charge Sino-American collusion on behalf of the pro-Chinese Pol Pot/Prince Sihanouk coalition.

Yet, without a solid consensus among American foreign policy makers, policy will be ambiguous or undefined. While having advantages in terms of flexibility, an ambiguous policy will be interpreted in conflicting ways by competing factions in foreign capitals. Misunderstandings and miscalculations will be hard to avoid. Internal dissension and bureaucratic conflict will ensue at home.

The primary practical problem in making American policy toward China and the Soviet Union is the difficulty in devising a strategy that maximizes American interests in dealing with both countries simultaneously. If the United States tilts too far toward China, the turbulence in Soviet-American relations could escalate to a dangerous level of confrontation. If no tilt occurs, the Chinese, who are far behind the Soviet Union in all spheres, could take offense and rethink their policy toward the United States. For now, Afghanistan has dictated a solution to this problem, and Sino-American cooperation seems as clearly in the interest of both nations as does opposition to Soviet expansion. In the long run, however, the problem of how to deal with the PRC and the USSR will resurface more clearly, and the dilemma is unlikely to go away.

In addition to the broad dilemmas facing American policy makers, two bilateral issues pose major problems for Chinese-American relations. The first trouble spot is trade, specifically Chinese textile exports to the United States. Without large exports of manufactured products, the Chinese will be unable to earn enough foreign exchange to finance their ambitious development schemes, which depend on importing advanced technology and equipment. Congress, always sensitive about competition from abroad, has demanded that the Chinese limit their exports to the United States so as not to damage American industries. Chinese political leaders, not fully understanding the independent role of Congress, wonder why the United States refuses them the opportunity to sell the one product for which a ready market exists in the United States. Moderate Chinese officials who favor closer relations with the United States may well feel disappointed by what they see as insensitive American actions that give the PRC smaller quotas than those given to Taiwan. A top Chinese trade official commented after the failure of textile negotiations in August 1982, "China is strongly dissatisfied with the treatment it is receiving."

Even without the textile problem, China faces the prospect of a serious imbalance in its trade with the United States. There are, of course, only two ways the Chinese can reduce this imbalance without sacrificing modernization plans. They can export more textiles and cheap manufactured goods to the United States—which is unlikely because of intense political pressures exerted by powerful lobbies in Washington—or they can export that most precious of all commodities that is so much in demand: oil. However, the rapid pace of domestic economic modernization, coupled with long-term exchange deals involving Japan, make it very unlikely that China would, even if willing, send large quantities of petroleum to the United States.

The long-range time bomb clouding the future of Sino-American relations is Taiwan. The recognition of Peking as the legitimate seat of Chinese government meant the end of official American ties with the Republic of China, the withdrawal of remaining American troops from Formosa, and the termination of the Mutual Defense Treaty. To handle continuing commercial, cultural, and tourist activities, the United States set up a nongovernmental entity, the American Institute in Taiwan, while Taiwan established a similar organization in Washington. Despite the political changes, trade between Taiwan and the United States has flourished, being up over 100 percent in 1981 from 1978, which was itself a record year. Investments by Americans in Taiwan also rose to new record levels.

But American involvement in the island extends beyond commercial and cultural interactions to security matters. Despite President Carter's termination of the defense treaty, a bill passed by Congress in 1979 stated that the United States would "consider any effort to resolve the Taiwan issue by other than peaceful means a threat to the peace and security of the Western Pacific area and of grave concern to the United States."

Peking immediately indicated its displeasure over the American stand. An article in the *People's Daily* in Peking gave a fair reading of leadership opinion on the issue. The author wondered about what "appears to be a coordinated effort to undermine the developing normalization of relations between China and the United States."

In August 1982, the crisis provoked by American arms deals with Taiwan was partially, and perhaps only temporarily, defused. In a joint communiqué issued by the Chinese and United States governments, the U.S. side stated that:

> . . . it does not seek to carry out a long-term policy of arms sales to Taiwan, that its arms sales to Taiwan will not exceed, either in qualitative or in quantitative terms, the level of those supplied in recent years since the establishment of diplomatic relations between the United States and China, and that it intends to gradually reduce its sale of arms to Taiwan, leading, over a period of time, to a final resolution.

For their part, the Chinese promised to adhere to the *fundamental policy:* to strive for peaceful resolution of the motherland. The accord alleviates but does not dispose of the crisis. The Chinese immediately made clear that the fundamental policy toward Taiwan was certainly not a pledge to forswear the use of force forever. A spokesman for China's Ministry of Foreign Affairs pointedly noted, "On this issue, which is purely China's internal affairs, no misinterpretation or foreign interference is permissible." China simply refused to abandon the possibility of using force and rejected the idea that the American cessation of arms sales was in any way linked with a Chinese pledge to use peaceful means to resolve the Taiwan issue.

Top officials in the Reagan administration, including the president, thought that the Chinese had publicly committed themselves to the peaceful means approach. However, the Chinese are adamant that the United States unconditionally stop those activities, such as arms sales, which encourage Taiwanese intransigence. The issue will undoubtedly reappear in the near future.

In any case, China vows to incorporate Taiwan into mainland administration. Chinese diplomats hope for peaceful accommodation on the part of forward-looking Taiwanese, but warn that unless Taiwan soon agrees to serious negotiations, the situation could change. How the United States would respond to a direct Chinese attack or a naval blockade is uncertain. What is certain is that a clash between the United States and China would be difficult to avoid in the event of an attack on Taiwan by China.

CONCLUSIONS

The 1980s mark the second decade of renewed Sino-American friendship. Long-term trends over the past decade and recent events in Southwest Asia suggest that a framework of stable cooperative relations may be created. However, the possibility that the relationship will deteriorate cannot be ignored. The danger in the short run revolves around economic problems between the two countries; in the longer run it involves Taiwan. As for the strategic triangle, much remains to be clarified as the world absorbs the impact of Soviet moves in Asia.

An extensive and probing public debate over American-Chinese policy has yet to occur. What, in the long run, does the United States stand to gain from better relations with China? Where would the United States like the relationship to lead? The basis of the United States-China connection must be clarified and American interests spelled out. Equally important to the future is a frank assessment of the risks inherent in triangular diplomacy. One element makes it difficult, if not impossible, to carefully plot a course: leadership instability in China and the difficulty of predicting Soviet behavior in post-Brezhnev Russia.

Putting Sino-American relations on an even keel means ending, once and for all, the dramatic swings between euphoria—seeing China socially as another United States with a market of unlimited potential—and hatred—seeing China as the epitomy of evil and aggression. American leaders need to discuss openly what the United States hopes to get from China, and vice versa. Without a careful evaluation, American policy toward China is like a rudderless ship with no set destination, drifting aimlessly in constant danger of crashing into unforeseen obstacles.

FOR FURTHER READING

Books

Fairbank, John K. *The United States and China* (Cambridge, Mass.: Harvard University Press, 1979, 4th edition).

Hsiao, Gene T. and Feeny, William R. *Sino-American Normalization and Its Policy Implications* (New York, N.Y.: Praeger, 1982).

Solomon, Richard H., ed. *The China Factor: Sino-American Relations and the Global Scene* (Englewood Cliffs, N.J.: Prentice-Hall, 1981).

Starr, John Bryan, ed. *The Future of U.S.-China Relations* (New York, N.Y.: Columbia University Press, 1981).

Government Publications

Department of State. *Selected Documents, No. 9. The United States Policy Toward China, July 15, 1971–January 15, 1979* (Washington, D.C., 1979).

Senate Committee on Foreign Relations and the Congressional Research Service. *The Implications of U.S.-China Military Cooperation.* (Washington, D.C., 1982).

Sutter, Robert G. and Baron, Michael L. *"Playing the China Card": Implications for U.S.-Soviet-Chinese Relations* (Washington, D.C.: Congressional Research Service, Library of Congress, 1979).

chapter 4

The United States and the Middle East

JEROME SLATER

The United States has three major interrelated national interests in the Middle East: the preservation of basic security, territorial integrity, and political independence of Israel; continued access, at reasonable prices, to Middle Eastern oil; and the containment of actual or potential Soviet expansionism.[1] These national interests are partially conflicting and partially converging. They arise out of four separate but intertwined and interacting conflicts in the Middle East: the Arab-Israeli conflict; the great power rivalry between the United States and the Soviet Union; the indigenous Arab conflicts between radicalism/communism versus traditionalism/anticommunism; and the conflict between the oil-producing states of the Middle East and the oil-consuming states of the West, led by the United States. Each of these conflicts would exist even if the others did not. Yet, each is exacerbated by the others. Because of the complexity of these conflicts in their own terms and the manner in which they have become intertwined, the task of formulating and implementing a consistent policy that maximizes the realization of all three major U.S. national interests is enormously complicated. Indeed, the complexities may simply be too great to allow a consistent U.S. policy. Still, both policy makers and citizens have to try. What follows is a

---

[1]My discussion here parallels, and is in part based on, the similar analysis in William B. Quandt, *Decade of Decisions* (Berkeley, California: University of California Press, 1977).

description of how recent U.S. government policy makers have sought to unravel these complexities, along with some prescriptions for the future.

THE AMERICAN COMMITMENT TO ISRAEL

Why is the United States committed to the preservation of the state of Israel? The most fundamental reason for U.S. support of Israel is the widespread, genuine, and deeply felt belief, shared by American policy makers and the public, that the United States has a moral obligation not to allow Israel to be overrun by its Arab enemies. Opponents of Israel, or those who are excessively cynical about the importance of moral principles in foreign policy, have had a difficult time understanding or accepting the consistency and depth of U.S. support for Israel. Even when U.S. support apparently ran counter to other "national interests," it could only be explained in terms of a *sense of fundamental moral obligation*. At its root, this sense of obligation stems from Western Christian guilt over the failure to prevent the Nazi Holocaust—or even to mitigate its effects by accepting large numbers of Jewish refugees from Nazism in the late 1930s and early 1940s—as well as the failure to make the survival of European Jews one of the major priorities of World War II. Beyond that, Israel has captured the imagination and sympathy of American public opinion. The history of Israel has been that of a people striving to survive. They have succeeded, against all odds, while simultaneously creating and maintaining a liberal democracy in an area dominated by either feudalistic authoritarian reaction or mob-based radical demagoguery.

The sense of moral obligation that underlies U.S. policy toward Israel stems from the fact that prior to 1970 (at the earliest) the fundamental reason for the continuation of the Arab-Israeli conflict was that no Arab state would accept the existence of Israel. This was at the root of Arab violence against Israel—from the anti-Jewish mob riots beginning in Palestine in 1919 through the major interstate wars of 1948, 1956, and 1967. All the other Arab-Israeli conflicts—over territory and borders, refugees, the rights of the Palestinians, symbolic issues (for example, Jerusalem)—were either pretexts or exacerbating factors. The conflicts were more symptoms than causes.

This is not to say that the origins of the Arab-Israeli crisis are entirely the responsibility of the Arabs. On the contrary, the initial establishment of a Jewish homeland in Palestine, which was later to become a state, clearly disregarded both the rights and the sentiment of the Arab residents. Reduced to its central components, the Jewish or Zionist case for the establishment of a Jewish homeland in Palestine in 1917 was this:

1. Historical world mistreatment of the Jews can only be ended by the establishment of a Jewish homeland.
2. Palestine is the appropriate location for that homeland because of the religious ties of Judaism to the area and the fact that Jews occupied the land for hundreds of years before they were forcibly expelled during the Roman empire.

3. A more contemporary legal basis for a Jewish homeland was established by the 1917 British commitment to a Palestinian homeland for the Jews. The Balfour Declaration became an international commitment when it was incorporated in the League of Nations mandate to Britain in the Middle East following World War I.
4. In any case, the Arabs were not being asked to sacrifice very much. The Jewish area of Palestine amounts to only one percent of the Arab Middle East. Moreover, the establishment of a Jewish homeland also benefited the Arabs because the Jews brought Western science, health, technology, and organization to a backward area.

However, in response to these arguments, Arab spokesmen make the following points:

1. World anti-Semitism was far more a Western Christian phenomenon than an Arab Moslem one. Jews had lived without major problems in Arab countries for centuries prior to 1917. If anti-Semitism was essentially a Western phenomenon, its solution should be found in the West.
2. The religious ties of Islam to Palestine are no less strong than those of Judaism. The Jewish historical claim to the area, based on previous occupation some 2000 years ago, has no basis in either law or common sense and is outweighed by the fact that Arabs had lived on the land for 1300 consecutive years.
3. The Balfour Declaration was simply a colonialist imposition by Britain. It was a direct violation of British (and French) promises to Arab leaders that the Arab Middle East would gain independence if the Arabs rose against Turkish rule in World War I. The fact that the Balfour Declaration was incorporated into the League mandate adds nothing to Jewish claims, since the League was dominated by the major colonialist powers of the era and was, in part, *designed* to perpetuate Western rule over large parts of the globe.
4. The claim that Jewish immigration brought economic, political, and cultural benefits to the Arabs is irrelevant. This is the classic argument of colonialism and, even when it is partially or largely true, it is psychologically unacceptable. Nationalist goals and sentiments far outweigh purely utilitarian ones.

It is hard to deny the overall force of the Arab argument: The *origin* of the Arab-Israeli conflict lies in the imposition of a Jewish settlement in a land that was already occupied. The occupants were not consulted about this decision, had no effect on it, and (rightly or wrongly) were unwilling to accept such a Jewish settlement. Nonetheless, the assessment of moral responsibility for the continuation of the Arab-Israeli conflict over the past 67 years is entirely another matter. The moral balance has shifted over the years, especially since the 1930s. To see the matter differently, one must accept a rather grotesque argument that is implicit in the Arab position and remains so precisely because it could not stand the light of day. The greatest evil imaginable—justifying violent resistance regardless of the human cost to both sides—is to take away a people's territory, no matter how small the territory or what the circumstances may be. In this case, the circumstances were not merely 2000 years of anti-Semitism and Jewish suffering, but the immediate situation of the 1930s. In light of the Holocaust, the Arab argument that they should not be made to "suffer" or "pay" for Hitler's crimes is unpersuasive (to put the matter mildly), even though it is absolutely true that the Western states were prepared to do very little themselves to mitigate the effects of Nazism. The key point is that the Arabs were "suffering" or "paying" only in a purely symbolic sense. In this context, the Zionist argument takes on new force. It *does* matter that only one percent of the Arab Middle East was at issue and that only in a tiny sliver of land were the Arabs being asked to give up their sovereignty. And, moreover, it is relevant to note that whatever the damage to the Arab psyche, Jewish immigration *did* produce concrete economic (and other) benefits for all the inhabitants of Palestine—Arab as well as Jewish.

Beyond that, the deeper question is whether the Arab means were justified by their grievances, whatever the exact degree of legitimacy that inhered in those grievances over time. The human consequences of the diehard, fanatical, uncompromising Arab resistance to a Jewish homeland, and then a Jewish state, in Palestine made a mockery of their claim to be in the right. The moral balance sheet has been eloquently summed up by a well-known Israeli writer, Amos Elon: "The Arabs, it is true, bore no responsibility for the breakdown of civilization in Europe. Yet their opposition to Zionism grew so ferocious, their insensitivity to Jewish sentiments so great, their refusal of all compromise so absolute, their violence so indiscriminate, and their policies, finally, so genocidal—that the original balance between right and wrong was lost. In time it was entirely superseded by fresh concerns, by a new balance of rights and wrongs within the framework of an entirely new existential situation."

As long as the Arab goal was the literal destruction of Israel (as it remained for all Arab states until the death of Nasser in 1970), a sense of moral responsibility to Israel was bound to play a major role in U.S. policy. This is not to say that the sole basis for U.S. support of Israel has been moral. On the contrary, Israel's survival and continued power has increasingly become linked to U.S. strategic interests in the Middle East. A strongly anti-Communist, pro-American, stable, and militarily powerful Israel could help prevent the spread of Soviet influence and/or radical, anti-Western regimes in an area that is critical to the very survival of the West.

As oil has become more important, the general U.S. commitment to stability and anti-Communism in the Middle East has been reinforced and made more urgent. It is only in the last fifteen years that the Middle East has become truly vital to the United States in terms of its strategic interests. As late as 1965, the United States imported only about three percent of its oil from the Mideast. It did so more as a convenience than a necessity, as the world surplus of oil ensured that other sources were available. However, today most of the world's proven oil reserves are located in the Persian Gulf states, principally in Saudi Arabia.

American dependence on oil imports from the Gulf rose dramatically through the late 1970s, despite efforts to reverse this dependency after the 1973 Arab oil embargo. In the last several years this dependency has begun to decline. However, it is too soon to know if this is a temporary effect of economic recession in the West (reducing the demand for oil), or if it represents a permanent structural shift. The latter would result from greater conservation of energy and the development of new oil sources (as in Mexico and the North Sea) as well as new alternatives to oil.

THE SOVIET UNION AND THE MIDDLE EAST

To what extent does the Soviet Union threaten U.S. objectives to maintain the security of Israel and access to oil? The Soviet role in the Middle East expanded considerably from the mid-1950s through the 1973 war. The Soviets have provided the arms and military assistance that enable the Arabs to go to war. The Middle East is perhaps the most dangerous area in the world because it is one of the most likely sites for a direct Soviet-American confrontation. Still, the nature of Soviet objectives is not at all clear, despite the growing acceptance of some simplistic assessments in the West. The prevalent interpretation (particularly in the Reagan administration) is that the Soviet Union is following a policy of planned aggressive expansionism. Soviet aims, according to this interpretation, are to eliminate Western influence from the Middle East, to establish itself as the dominant power in the area, to "outflank NATO" and thus put severe pressure on Western Europe, and perhaps even to deny Middle Eastern oil to the West (especially in the next decade when the Soviet Union itself will probably need to import oil).

The Soviet invasion of Afghanistan has obviously exacerbated all of these fears. However, a closer look at the history of Soviet involvement in the area makes it more likely that Soviet objectives have been and remain considerably less ominous. The pattern of events strongly suggests that Soviet policy has been driven by two factors.

1. *Defensive cold war strategies* (rather than those that are aggressive or offensive). It is now clear that the invasion of Afghanistan was motivated primarily by traditional Soviet sensitivity to unfavorable changes in the political status quo along its borders, rather than by grandiose objectives to seize the oil fields of the Persian Gulf. And elsewhere in the Middle East, the cold war between the United States and the Soviet Union can be best understood as a pattern of action-reaction-counteraction, a cycle of conflict involving both sides. Each genuinely views its own actions as necessary defensive responses forced by the aggressive or threatening actions of the other.

2. *Russian nationalism* (rather than Soviet ideological expansionism). In the past the Russians have always sought warm-water ports in the Mediterranean for both military and commercial purposes. (Many of the Russian Atlantic and Pacific outlets to the sea are ice locked most of the year.) More recently, Russian geopolitical nationalism has been supplemented by a desire to achieve recognition as a superpower that is equal in status and influence to the United States. The Soviet naval buildup and the acquisition of military base rights in the Mediterranean and Persian Gulf area can be interpreted, then, as simply an emulation of the United States. It is an effort to acquire superpower status by following the path taken by the United States (and other states before it) to gain recognition as superpowers. In this interpretation, psychology is at least as important as substance, and one cannot infer expansionist objectives from the acquisition of military capabilities.

An examination of the role of the Soviet Union in the Middle East lends more credence to the latter two interpretations than to the notion of Soviet aggression and expansionism. In the early 1950s, the United States decided to complete a ring of Western alliances and military power around the USSR. This was both a reaction to earlier Soviet pressures on Iran and Turkey and part of its general cold-war strategy of military containment of the Soviet Union. The key to this strategy was to have been the Baghdad Pact, an American-sponsored military alliance modeled on NATO. The pact included the pro-Western states of Turkey, Iraq, Iran, Pakistan, and Britain, and they were armed and financed by the United States. In order to forestall what would turn an area directly on its borders into an anti-Soviet military bastion, the Soviets issued repeated warnings against the militarization of the area. On several occasions they proposed to demilitarize the entire Middle East through a mutual arms limitation agreement with the United States. The West rejected the proposal and proceeded to establish the Baghdad Pact and arm the member states. The Soviets countered by forming a political-military alliance with Egypt, the leading anti-Western state in the area. This culminated in the Soviet-sponsored Czech-Egyptian Arms Pact of 1955. This action—clearly a reaction to Western moves—brought the Soviet military into the Middle East for the first time. More by the structure of the situation than by design, the Soviets aligned with the Arabs in the Arab-Israeli conflict.

From the mid-1950s through the 1973 war, the Soviets were increasingly drawn into the Arab-Israeli conflict. Their involvement was usually a result of events over which they had only limited influence rather than part of a deliberately expansionist strategy. It is generally agreed that in 1967 the Soviets were not consulted on Nasser's decision to force UN forces out of the Sinai. Nor were they consulted before Nasser reestablished a blockade against Israeli shipping in the Gulf of Aqaba and decided to escalate the conflict to one that threatened the very existence of Israel. However, once war came the Soviets felt obliged to support Nasser diplomatically and militarily. The United States and Israel were warned of possible direct military intervention if Israel failed to accept a ceasefire and sought to press its military victory to the point of a full-scale invasion of Egypt or Syria.

After the war ended, the Soviets replaced all Egyptian and Syrian losses with newer, more sophisticated arms. They sent thousands of advisers and technicians into Egypt and Syria to help operate advanced weapons systems, particularly surface-to-air missiles. The Israelis responded to Egyptian artillery bombardments across the Suez Canal with a heavy increase in air attacks, extending by the summer of 1970 to industrial targets in the heartland of Egypt. The Soviets countered by sending their own pilots to fly Soviet Migs with Egyptian markings. This process of escalation led to direct Soviet-Israeli air combat just prior to a new ceasefire in August 1970.

Strong evidence shows that the Soviets neither desired nor encouraged the 1973 war. For several years Moscow had pressed Sadat to seek a political settlement with Israel and had withheld heavy offensive weapons from Egypt. Perhaps Moscow did so because it had a low opinion of the military prowess of the Arabs and feared that in the event of another debacle it would be pressured to rescue its clients through direct military intervention, thus risking a confrontation with the United States.[2] Still, once the war began the Soviets again felt obliged to support Egypt and Syria. They did so through the resumption of major arms shipments and by pressing other Arab states to help Egypt and support the Arab oil embargo against the West. And, once again, a complete Egyptian collapse and the possible occupation of large parts of Egypt beyond the Sinai by the Israeli army was averted by Soviet threats to intervene. Israel reluctantly accepted a ceasefire.

Since 1973 the Soviets have evidently disengaged somewhat from the Arab-Israeli conflict. They have ended major arms shipments to Egypt, refrained from providing Syria with the kind of weapons that might lead to offensive action against Israel, and remained entirely on the sidelines during the 1982 Israeli invasion of Lebanon. It is generally accepted that the Soviets prefer a settlement to continued war. However, they have clearly resented domination of the peace process by the United States for the past 10 years.

The pattern that emerges is an unplanned, and to a considerable degree, unwanted but growing Soviet involvement, primarily in reaction to events over which it has little control. Soviet behavior in the Middle East may be compared with the American predicament in Vietnam in the late 1950s and early 1960s. Each new step has further engaged Soviet prestige and broadened its commitment. The Soviets were led reluctantly into a quagmire from which they have found it difficult to emerge without a presumptively devastating loss of credibility and an undermining of their superpower status. This is not to minimize the danger of continued Soviet involvement, as the Vietnam analogy ominously suggests. However, it does have different implications for U.S. foreign policy than the simplistic image

[2] This assessment of Soviet policy in the Middle East from the 1973 war onward is based primarily on Galia Golan, *Yom Kippur and After* (London: Cambridge University Press, 1977).

of planned, aggressive, unrelenting Soviet expansionism seeking the destruction of Israel and the domination of the entire area by the Soviet Union.

DOMESTIC POLITICS AND U.S. POLICY IN THE MIDDLE EAST

U.S. support of Israel traditionally has focused on moral and strategic factors. To what extent is support of Israel by every American government since Harry Truman also a function of domestic politics—the Jewish vote, Jewish political contributions, Jewish influence in the mass media? There is no doubt that domestic politics do indeed play a significant role. Pro-Israel groups (by no means exclusively Jewish) are among the best organized and are well financed, highly active, and sophisticated in American politics. Their influence is felt both in elections and in the daily policy-making process in Congress and the executive branch. The Jewish vote has influenced key elections, particularly in states with substantial Jewish populations like New York and California. The influence of Jewish groups and their many supporters in Congress has deterred several presidents from putting pressure on Israel during peace negotiations by cutting back on U.S. economic and military assistance. In recent years, Presidents Nixon, Ford, and Carter have all considered and even publicly threatened reassessments of U.S. policy. They have done so in response to perceived Israeli intransigence, only to back down because of the domestic reaction, particularly in Congress.

Still, the impact of domestic politics should not be overstated. The Jewish vote is relatively insignificant. Therefore, the overwhelming support of U.S. public opinion and Congress cannot be explained by this vote, let alone by alleged Jewish influence in the mass media. Evidence suggests that the support of Israel by such presidents as Truman, Johnson, Nixon, and Reagan has been based more on their conviction that it was morally right and in the U.S. national interest than on political expediency. Indeed, the most unambiguously pro-Israeli presidents have been Richard Nixon and Ronald Reagan, both of whom received only a small proportion of the Jewish vote!

To recapitulate the argument so far: the major objectives of the United States in the Middle East are to ensure the survival of Israel, maintain access to Arab oil, and contain any Soviet expansionism (actual, potential, or merely feared) in the area. The U.S. commitment to Israel is first and foremost a moral commitment. However, it is increasingly congruent with the objective of maintaining access to Arab oil and containing the Soviet Union. A militarily strong Israel could deter the spread of Soviet influence or indigenous radicalism (or fanatic nationalist fundamentalism), especially in Saudi Arabia and perhaps in other Persian Gulf sheikdoms.

THE NIXON ADMINISTRATION AND THE MIDDLE EAST

During the first few years of the Nixon administration, oil was not yet a central concern, and the focus of U.S. policy was on preserving the general status quo in the area. Initially, the Nixon administration's position was that Israel should withdraw to the pre-1967 boundaries in exchange for peace and security guarantees. Several American proposals were made that embodied these principles. However, the matter did not appear to be urgent in light of the overwhelming defeat of the Arab confrontation states in the 1967 Arab-Israeli War. When Israel uncompromisingly rejected the principle of complete withdrawal, the United States did not press the issue. Nasser then turned to direct Soviet assistance in the form of 10,000 to 15,000 Soviet military advisers and technicians stationed in Egypt. The Nixon administration reacted by seeking to maintain the military predominance of Israel as a means of containing Soviet influence.

The key event in reinforcing and solidifying the perceptions of the Nixon administration was the brief Jordanian-Syrian conflict of 1970, when the Soviet-armed Syrians attacked the pro-Western Hussein regime in Jordan. For a while it appeared that the Syrians might succeed in overrunning Jordan, but they were forced to withdraw when the United States and Israel devised a joint plan. The plan called for Israeli intervention on the ground to prevent a Syrian victory, and U.S. carrier forces stood by to provide air cover if the Soviets threatened any counterintervention. The success of these pressures convinced Nixon and Kissinger that Israel was of strategic importance to the United States. American interests therefore required all-out military support of Israel, with a minimum of pressure on it to be more forthcoming in its negotiating position vis-a-vis Egypt and Syria. From 1970 through 1973 there was a major increase in U.S. economic and military assistance to Israel and an effective end to any proposals for settlement of the Arab-Israeli dispute on the basis of Israeli withdrawal. Thus, the United States had clearly accepted the Israeli position that the status quo was stable, that time was on the side of Israel, and that Sadat and the rest of the Arabs had no real choice—despite their rhetoric to the contrary—but to accept "new facts," that is, the territorial status quo.

In early 1973 Sadat suddenly and shockingly announced that all Soviet military advisers were to be expelled. His publicly stated reasons were the failure of the Soviets to provide Egypt with offensive weapons that would make possible effective military pressures against Israel and nationalist resentment at general Soviet heavy-handedness in its relations with Egypt. However, it later became clear that the more important factor in Sadat's dramatic reversal was his conclusion that only the United States had sufficient leverage with Israel to pressure a withdrawal from the Sinai. Sadat had repeatedly been told by Washington, though, that it would not seriously press the Israelis for any concessions as long as Egypt continued its military alliance with the Soviet Union. Thus, the Egyptian expulsion of the Soviets paved the way for a shift in U.S. policy and a resumption of earlier U.S. efforts for a settlement based on Israeli withdrawal from the Sinai and, perhaps, other areas captured by the Israelis in the 1967 war.

Sadat, however, had miscalculated—or had been misled. Despite the implicit promise of the Nixon administration that U.S. policy would be reevaluated if Egypt ended its military alliance with the Soviet Union, there was no change in American policy. On the contrary, the expulsion of the Soviet military advisers seemed to confirm the Nixon administration's view that unconditional backing of Israel was the best way both to check the expansion of Soviet power and to preserve the status quo in the Middle East. Sadat's actions were seen as vindicating U.S. policy rather than suggesting the need for reassessment. With Washington reacting in this manner, there was even less reason for Israel to seriously consider making any concessions.

The outcome of this stalemate was the 1973 war undertaken by Sadat as a desperate last resort to break the deadlock and force a reevaluation of both U.S. and Israeli policy.[3] The first indication of a shift in U.S. policy came during the war, when Kissinger put great pressure on the Israelis (perhaps even including the threat to end U.S. military assistance). They were to accept a ceasefire rather than press their military advantage by destroying the Egyptian Third Army on the East Bank of the Suez Canal or by advancing further into Egypt on the West Bank. The American pressures, in part, may have stemmed from indications that the Soviets were considering unilateral military intervention to prevent the complete collapse of Egypt. However, they also reflected Kissinger's own assessment that a total Israeli victory would solve nothing: The Soviets would rebuild Arab armies once again, and another defeat would be just one more devastating blow to Arab pride, to be avenged "at any cost." An imposed stalemate, Kissinger believed, would be the psychological prerequisite and necessary precondition for opening up the negotiating process. The overall strategy was to allow the Israelis enough of a victory to convince the Arabs of the general futility of war against Israel in the future. Yet, the victory should not be great enough to allow Israel to stand pat and refuse to make territorial concessions.

There is no doubt today that Kissinger's assessment was sound and that his strategy was successful. As Sadat had hoped, the 1973 war, for the first time, made a peaceful settlement possible because both sides were given fresh incentives to avoid war. On the Arab side, especially for the Egyptians, the early successes of the war (the later defeats were glossed over and camouflaged from the Egyptian public) relieved the pain of past humiliation and thus made it psychologically possible for them to make concessions. On the other hand, the eventual military victory of Israel (though aborted by superpower action before it came to full dimensions) ended any illusions Sadat or other Arab leaders might have had about going beyond the limited aim of recovering land lost in the 1967 war to their earlier objective of destroying Israel. Not only was Israel itself capable of preventing that, but, if in the future it were not, the Arabs and the Soviets would

---

[3]The preceding assessment of U.S. policy from 1968 to 1973 is based primarily on Quandt, *Decade of Decisions*, and Nadav Safran, *Israel, The Embattled Ally* (Harvard University Press, 1978), ch. 23.

have to assume that the United States would increase its military assistance to Israel, and even, in extremis, directly intervene. A Soviet counterintervention would simply turn the area into a superpower battleground, which would hardly be in the interest of the Arab states.

On the other hand, the war also made a negotiated settlement critical for Israel. The Arab military had proven to be much stronger than expected, and the casualties inflicted on the Israelis were heavy. Even if Israel were eventually capable of decisively defeating any combination of Arab armies—for which there was no guarantee—the 1973 war, like the 1967 and 1956 wars that preceded it, once again demonstrated that the superpowers would not allow a total Israeli victory. Finally, the ominous development of the oil weapon had given the Arabs an entirely new and highly potent means of exerting pressure on the West to draw back from unconditional support of Israel.

Following the war, the Nixon administration—Kissinger, really—succeeded in reestablishing close ties with key nations in the Arab world (primarily Egypt and Saudi Arabia) without abandoning the fundamental commitment to Israel. Just a few years earlier this might have seemed to be the diplomatic equivalent of squaring the circle, but several critical factors had changed. First, Sadat continued to recognize his need for U.S. support to press Israel to make concessions, but he also realized and fully accepted the basic commitment of the United States to the survival of Israel. Beyond that, Egypt was in desperate economic shape and was calling for a Marshall Plan for the Middle East; Sadat knew that only the United States and its Western allies could provide assistance of that magnitude. Finally, the Saudis, though holding the oil card, wanted access to advanced Western civilian and military technology and feared Arab radicalism and expanding Soviet influence almost as much as they hated Israel. For both of those reasons, the Saudis needed U.S. support and goodwill perhaps almost as much as the United States needed Saudi oil. Thus, a kind of tacit American alliance evolved, though it was to remain a tense and mutually suspicious one.

THE CARTER ADMINISTRATION AND THE MIDDLE EAST

By the time the Carter administration took office in 1977, Kissinger had succeeded in negotiating partial Israeli withdrawals from the Sinai and the Golan Heights in return for demilitarized zones policed by UN forces. The choice for the new administration was either to continue pressing for incremental, step-by-step negotiations, or to seek a grand comprehensive final settlement between Israel and all its Arab neighbors in one all-encompassing package. The argument for the gradualist approach was that seemingly intractable problems could only be handled by breaking them down into small components; instilling the habit of negotiations rather than war; and even, hopefully, increasing trust between bitter adversaries. A comprehensive settlement, it was argued, was not within the realm of political reality, and the attempt to achieve it would only give veto power to the most intractable issue or party.

On the other hand, after the last Kissinger-negotiated partial withdrawals, the Arab-Israeli negotiations process seemed to be at a dead end. Syria, Jordan, Saudi Arabia, and even Egypt seemed to be opposed to anything less than a comprehensive settlement that would include complete Israeli withdrawal from the post-1967 occupied territories and the establishment of a Palestinian state. The central issues, it seemed, could no longer be avoided. Accordingly, the major policy makers of the Carter administration entered office committed to an active role in the negotiation of a comprehensive settlement. It would be based on Israeli territorial withdrawal, strong security guarantees for Israel (including joint U.S.-Soviet guarantees), and the establishment of a Palestinian "homeland" or "entity" (these terms deliberately ambiguous about whether they meant a Palestinian *state*).

Within a year, however, the Carter approach was abandoned because of Israeli intransigence and surprising Egyptian flexibility. The election of the Begin government effectively ended any prospect of serious Israeli concessions no matter what security arrangements could be made with regard to Syria and the West Bank. On the other hand, Sadat was willing to reach what amounted to a separate peace between Egypt and Israel. With the benefit of hindsight, we now see that the subsequent Egyptian-Israeli peace treaty, as painfully difficult as it was to negotiate and as fragile as it may yet turn out to be, was the easiest Arab-Israeli agreement that could be reached. Not only did Sadat prove to be an almost incredibly courageous and moderate statesman, but also the strictly Israeli-Egyptian components of the Arab-Israeli dispute were relatively easy to resolve once the will to do so was present. In the West Bank or Jerusalem, Israel had religious or historical claims. However, it had neither in the Sinai: Its overriding concern was simply security. When it became clear that Sadat was willing to provide Israel with very substantial security guarantees in return for Israeli withdrawal, the basis for a settlement became clear. Although it still took several years to overcome a variety of obstacles, an agreement was finally reached in early 1979 under which the state of war between Israel and Egypt was terminated. Furthermore, Israel agreed to withdraw gradually from the Sinai and the Gaza strip over a three-year period; during this time Egypt and Israel would establish full diplomatic, economic, and cultural relations under conditions of permanent peace. This agreement was also facilitated by the following.

1. The willingness of the United States to offer massive new economic and military assistance to both sides over the next decade.
2. A commitment by the United States to guarantee the Israeli oil supply in exchange for Israeli withdrawal from the oil wells of the Sinai.
3. The presence of U.S. technicians and advisers to supplement UN peacekeeping forces in implementing the staged withdrawals.

4. The establishment of demilitarized or limited-force zones in the Sinai.
5. A tacit agreement for an increased U.S. military presence in the area.

It is too soon to know what the lasting effects of the Israeli-Egyptian peace treaty will be. Until the 1982 Israeli invasion of Lebanon things had gone well; not even the assassination of Sadat had derailed the agreement. Israel has completed its withdrawal from the Sinai and there has been a normalization of diplomatic relations between Egypt and Israel. Sadat had promised that "never again" would there be armed conflict between the two countries, and Mubarak has reaffirmed this pledge. If the agreement continues to hold it will be a tremendous accomplishment regardless of what happens elsewhere in the Middle East, because in the absence of Egypt, the Arabs have nearly lost their military option. However, precisely for that reason the rest of the Arab states have bitterly rejected the peace between Israel and Egypt. With Israel remaining adamant on all other issues, the removal of Egypt from the ranks of the confrontation states has clearly eliminated a major incentive for Israel to compromise further. Until now Egypt has weathered the storm of Arab disapproval and the diplomatic and economic sanctions the Arab bloc has directed against Egypt, though the peace with Israel probably cost Sadat his life. Whether Mubarak or *his* successors will indefinitely continue the peace is another matter, especially if Israel continues its pattern of major provocations to the Arab world: the bombing of the Iraqi nuclear reactor, the annexation of the Golan Heights, the continued settlement of the West Bank, and the invasion of Lebanon.

In the long run, continued peace with Egypt probably depends on whether a reasonably satisfactory settlement of the Palestinian issue can be reached. At Camp David, Israel committed itself to serious, good-faith negotiations with Egypt on this issue, but (as shall be discussed later) in effect it has reneged on that promise and is well on its way to simply annexing all the remaining occupied territories. If Israel continues to refuse a reasonable compromise, the real test of the durability of peace with Egypt is yet to come.

THE REAGAN ADMINISTRATION AND THE MIDDLE EAST

The Reagan administration's early policies and actions concerning the Arab-Israeli conflict were most unpromising. The administration began office under the assumption that the central issues of the Arab-Israeli conflict could be avoided and that the "pro-Western" states of the area, including Israel and many of its adversaries, could be drawn into an anti-Soviet, anticommunist military alliance. To this end, the administration sent billions of dollars of the most advanced and lethal American weapons systems into the Middle East, particularly to Israel, Egypt, and Saudi Arabia. At the same time, in various ways the U.S. military presence in the area became most visible, and the first steps were taken to secure permanent bases for an increased U.S. military commitment.

Meanwhile, U.S. efforts to prod Israel into meaningful negotiations for Palestinian autonomy and for Israeli withdrawal from the occupied territories were shelved, as diplomacy was effectively dropped in favor of purely military instruments of policy. Underlying this policy was the administration's belief that the Arab-Israeli conflict was stabilized and that the major Arab states, particularly Saudi Arabia, would agree to subordinate their grievances against Israel in favor of a de facto military alliance among the United States, Egypt, Israel, and Saudi Arabia. However, even prior to the 1982 Israeli invasion of Lebanon the Saudis had given no indication that they shared this view. The Mubarak government in Egypt was coming under increasing domestic and external Arab pressure to move away from its alliance with the United States and even the peace agreement with Israel unless the Israelis showed some flexibility on the Palestinian issue. Yet, precisely because of the nearly unconditional support of Israel by the Reagan administration and its unwillingness to use the ever-growing Israeli dependence on U.S. military and economic assistance as a means of leverage to induce Israeli flexibility and moderation, the Begin government was given no incentive at all for moderation.

Israel's invasion of Lebanon in the summer of 1982 effectively demolished the early Reagan approach. There could no longer be any doubt that the Arab-Israeli conflict continued to overshadow any other issue in the Middle East and that a settlement was the indispensable precondition for stabilizing the area and creating an alliance of status quo anticommunist states. Accordingly, the Reagan administration shifted to a policy of pressing Israel to withdraw from Lebanon and to agree to an American-sponsored plan. As stated in the plan, the Palestinians in the West Bank and Gaza would be given some kind of "autonomy" and self-rule—but explicitly not an independence as a state—in "association" with Jordan. Although the Reagan administration's new diplomatic effort was widely hailed in the Middle East by both the moderate Arab powers and the Labor opposition in Israel, it was rejected out of hand by the Begin government, and it remained to be seen whether it would be acceptable to the PLO or even to the Palestinians. With the Reagan administration (at this writing) still unwilling to bring economic pressures to the Begin government, it seemed unlikely that there would be any movement in Israel, at least until a new government took office. Thus, it was not clear whether the new Reagan initiative would prove to be a promising first step or merely one more in a long line of half-measures that failed to decisively confront the real issues in the Arab-Israeli conflict and, as a result, ended in failure.

THE ISSUES AHEAD

In the judgment of this author, there can be no peace in the Middle East and no success for American foreign policy in the absence of a truly comprehensive peace settlement between Israel and its Arab neighbors. The three remaining major issues between Israel and the Arab states (other than Egypt) are the Israeli annexation and occupation of the Golan Heights in Syria, the status of Jerusalem, and, by far the most important, the Palestinian problem. Despite the seeming complexity and intractability of these issues, the principles that should govern a comprehensive and fair settlement are clear enough: they are those embodied in the 1967 UN Resolution 242. Resolution 242 was essentially a package deal that called for Israeli withdrawal from the "territories" (leaving open whether this meant *all* the territory) occupied in 1967. Stipulations in return were a political settlement based on an end of the state of war between Israel and the Arab countries; an undefined "just settlement" of the Palestinian problem; and respect for the sovereignty, independence, and territorial integrity of all states in the area. Despite the ambiguous language, it is widely accepted that a settlement based on the UN principles required; an Israeli withdrawal from all the territories except for some minor adjustments, the establishment of a Palestinian state on the West Bank and Gaza, a variety of strong security measures to ensure Israel's security, and a final peace settlement between Israel and all the Arab confrontation states. In fact, this has been the objective, however cloaked in ambiguity, of each American president except Reagan since the 1967 war.

The Syrian-Israeli Conflict

The conflict between Israel and Syria is partially over territory—the continued Israeli occupation and, since 1981, the annexation of the Golan Heights. But, more importantly, it is a function of the refusal of Syria to consider a separate peace with Israel that would leave the Palestinian issue unsettled. In principle the dispute between Syria and Israel is easy to settle. Israel should withdraw from the Golan in exchange for demilitarization of the area, which the United Nations or other international forces would observe, acting as a buffer between the military forces of each side. Syria would be responsible for controlling any potential Palestinian terrorism originating on its side of the border, and there should be a peace agreement or, at least, a non-belligerency pact between the two parties. However, Syria will not even consider such an agreement until the Palestinian issue is resolved. Just what would constitute a satisfactory resolution to the Syrians is not clear. On the one hand, Syria's hostility to the Israelis is far more bitter than Egypt's, and President Assad of Syria considers himself a guardian of Pan-Arabism, hence of Palestinian interests. On the other hand, the Syrians themselves have repressed the PLO in Lebanon—violently on occasion—in order to establish their domination there. They have also prevented Palestinian terrorists from operating on Syrian territory since the 1975 partial agreement with Israel. Moreover, Syria has accepted UN Resolution 242, thereby accepting Israel's right to exist. Despite his extremist rhetoric (and his internal repression), Assad is considered by most close observers to be reasonably moderate and pragmatic. Thus, it is not unreasonable to expect that Syria would end its state of war with Israel in return for the establishment of a Palestinian state in the West Bank and Gaza and Israeli withdrawal from the Golan Heights.

At present, even putting aside the Palestinian issue, the Begin government maintains that it will never relinquish the Golan, even in exchange for peace and demilitarized zones, and it is rapidly building settlements in the recently-annexed areas. The security argument of the Israelis, however, is not impressive. The key to Israeli security in the area is not to hold sovereignty over Golan but only that the area not be used by the Syrians for aggressive attacks on Israel. This objective could be realized by guaranteed demilitarized zones patrolled by an international peacekeeping force (and implicitly backed by the Israeli capability of retaking the Golan in the event of serious Syrian violations), a solution that Assad has said he would accept. In any case, the military significance of the Golan is continually declining, for the Syrians, if they chose, could bombard Israel with long-range artillery and Soviet surface-to-surface missiles far beyond the Golan. Thus, the best way for Israel to protect its northern boundaries is not to hold the Golan but to establish a stable peace with Syria.

The Jerusalem Problem

Other than the Palestinian problem, the only major issue between Israel and the Arab states is the status of Jerusalem. Jerusalem was initially divided, as a result of the Arab attack on Israel in 1948, then reunited under Israeli control after the capture of East Jerusalem from Jordan in the 1967 war. Jerusalem is not a territorial or a security issue, but a religious and symbolic one. The status of Jerusalem is regarded by almost all Israelis as nonnegotiable: never again will Jerusalem be divided. It is Jewish in the past, Jewish now, and Jewish forever. Unfortunately, with equal intensity nearly all Arabs fervently insist that the high Moslem shrines in East Jerusalem require Islamic sovereignty. For the Saudis, in particular, this is also a nonnegotiable position.

On its surface the issue appears to be intractable. On the other hand, if other issues should be resolved, particularly the Palestinian problem, it seems reasonable to assume that some kind of ingenious diplomatic device for papering over the seemingly irreconcilable positions can be devised. The Vatican City in Rome has frequently been cited as a potentially useful model: control over Islamic holy places by Arab political and religious governance, given extraterritorial status within an otherwise Israeli Jerusalem. An issue so purely symbolic, one assumes, would not finally block a settlement when all the more concrete issues have been resolved.

The Palestinian Problem

The key to peace in the Middle East, then, is a successful resolution of the Palestinian problem. Because of the centrality of this factor, its historical background as well as its present manifestations should be understood. Palestinian nationalism began developing in the aftermath of World War I, as a consequence of betrayal by the British, who promised the Arabs independence after the defeat of the Ottoman empire. More directly, a Jewish settlement in Palestine was established by a British and Zionist fait accompli, without consulting or regarding the local inhabitants and political leadership. Palestinian nationalism was thus a reaction to Jewish nationalism, or Zionism. In the next 30 years, Palestinian nationalism continued to grow, or fester. As Jewish immigration greatly increased, violence between the two communities became routine, and the Jewish community moved toward establishing itself as a full-fledged independent state.

Palestinian Arab resistance to the establishment of Israel in 1948 and the subsequent major war, intensified Palestinian nationalism. When the Arabs lost the war, some 700,000 Palestinians were displaced from their homes in what became Israel. Most of the displaced Palestinians ended up in refugee camps in the Gaza strip and the West Bank of the Jordan River. How the Palestinians came to be displaced is still controversial, though it is no longer of practical significance. The most convincing assessment is that the displacement came about as a result of three factors. Early in the war, many Palestinians left because the invading Arab armies urged them to leave, despite Israeli efforts to convince them to remain. At this point, the leaders of the new Israeli state were still hopeful that Arabs and Jews could peacefully coexist within a Jewish state; the Arabs intended to prove that they could not. In the latter stages of the war, however, the Israelis changed their position, understandably enough, about the desirability of a large, disgruntled Arab population within the Jewish state. As a result, many thousands of Palestinians were encouraged to leave, intimidated, or driven from Jewish-controlled areas. Finally, though, it is likely that the most important factor in the Palestinian exodus was simply the war itself. Hundreds of thousands fled because they did not want to get caught between the two sides, and they needed neither Arab nor Jewish "encouragement" to reach this conclusion. Since 1948, many Palestinians have resettled and have assimilated into the surrounding Arab countries. But large numbers of them have remained in squalid refugee camps in Gaza and the West Bank, partly as a result of Arab policy and partly as a result of their own fanatical determination to resist resettlement and some day return victoriously to their former land and homes.

There is no doubt that the Arab confrontation states, particularly Egypt under Nasser, deliberately used the refugee issue as a means of exacerbating hatred against Israel and keeping the war option alive. Rather than seeking to assimilate the refugees into Egypt or other neighboring Arab states, Nasser sought to inflame the Palestinians against Israel. He did so by promising them that Israel would soon be destroyed, by arming them, and by providing them with bases and sanctuaries. Under these circumstances Israel was hardly likely to readmit hundreds of thousands of Palestinian refugees, particularly with Nasser openly proclaiming that the effect of such

71

action would be to destroy the Israeli state from within. With this kind of encouragement, it is not surprising that most Palestinians refused to seek new lives elsewhere in the Arab world, and the refugee camps became the spearhead of the most militant and violent form of Palestinian nationalism— the terrorist groups, ranging from the Fedayeen of the 1950s through El Fatah in the 1960s and the Palestinian Liberation Organization (PLO) today.

The final major event that precipitated the emergence of Palestinian nationalism as a potent political force was the 1967 war. Although the responsibility of the war was that of the Arab states, particularly Syria and Egypt, one of the underlying causes (as will be discussed) was the festering refugee problem. One of the most important consequences of the sweeping Israeli victory was the occupation of the West Bank and the Gaza strip by Israel. The occupation added nearly a million new Arabs to Israel or Israeli-ruled territory, about half of whom were Palestinian refugees from the 1948 war. (In the next few years several hundred thousand left the area, either voluntarily or by persuasion, intimidation, or outright deportation by the Israeli occupying forces.) The continuation of Israeli occupation of these areas since 1967 has, of course, dramatically increased Palestinian nationalism, particularly in its most militant form. It remains to be seen whether the Israeli defeat of the PLO in Lebanon, accompanied by yet more severe Israeli repression of PLO sentiment and supporters in the occupied areas, will succeed in its obvious goal of crushing Palestinian nationalism.

In the judgment of this writer, Israeli repression will ultimately fail, and therefore Palestinian nationalism must be accommodated by Israel. To begin with, the Palestinians have repeatedly demonstrated their capacity to disrupt the peace and prevent a settlement of the Arab-Israeli conflict. Palestinian nationalism and guerrilla warfare against Israel have been the most militant expressions that set in motion the chain of events leading to the 1956 Arab-Israeli war. Several years of Palestinian terrorist raids against Israel, mainly from bases in Sinai and the Gaza, led to ever-increasing Israeli retaliatory raids. In 1955, following a particularly devastating and humiliating Israeli raid into Gaza, Nasser turned to the Soviet Union for arms. This large-scale Egyptian acquisition of Soviet arms precipitated the Israeli attack on Egyptian forces and Palestinian base camps in the Sinai in 1956.

Similarly, the 1967 war was set in motion by the same cycle of Palestinian terrorism and Israeli retaliation. By early 1967 El Fatah raids on Israel had increased, this time from bases in Jordan and Syria. The fact that they were primarily armed and supported by Syria led to an Israeli decision to mount a major military operation against Syria. To counter this Israeli threat, the Syrians signed a defense pact with Egypt, and the Soviets encouraged the Egyptians to move major forces into the Sinai. The Soviet (and, initially, the Egyptian) intention was simply to deter a massive Israeli invasion of Syria; however, Nasser quickly escalated his objectives to the outright destruction of Israel. When Israel attacked Syrian and Egyptian forces in June, the primary issue, formerly the Palestinians, was now the survival of Israel. However, the conflict probably never would have reached that point but for the Palestinian problem and the terrorism-retaliation cycle that resulted from it.

It is probable that even after the defeat of the PLO in Lebanon the Palestinians will retain their capacity to block any comprehensive Arab-Israeli settlement that does not accommodate Palestinian objectives. Pan-Arabist sentiments and aspirations have waned somewhat, particularly in Egypt, but they are still forces to be reckoned with elsewhere in the Arab world. The Palestinian cause is presently the focal point of Pan Arabism, and outside of Egypt no Arab confrontation state either wants or feels free to make peace with Israel over Palestinian opposition. The force of the Palestinian issue has been dramatically evident in the policies of Saudi Arabia. Despite fears of PLO radicalism, Saudi Arabia has been the major source of financial assistance to the PLO and has joined with the most rejectionist Arab states in bitter opposition to the Israeli-Egyptian peace treaty and various economic sanctions against Egypt. Under these economic, political, and psychological pressures, it is by no means certain that Mubarak will be able to maintain a separate peace with Israel, particularly in light of the provocative actions of the Begin government.

Thus, a peace without Palestinian support may be no peace at all for Israel. Another reason the Israelis must accommodate the Palestinians is that their current policies for dealing with Palestinian nationalism have been a clear failure in both practical and moral terms. Even before the 1982 invasion of Lebanon, the Israeli policy for dealing with Palestinian terrorism (in fact if not officially), has long been one of massive retaliation—not merely an eye for an eye, but many eyes for one eye. This has been justified on the familiar, dreary assumption that "the only thing the Arabs understand is force." Presumably, what the Arabs are supposed to "understand" is that they have more to lose than to gain through terrorism. Thus, the test of Israeli policy—even in its own terms—must be whether it successfully deters Palestinian terrorism. On this score the evidence is conclusive: terrorism has not been deterred. On the contrary, years of Israeli retaliation have led to an unending and growing stream of new recruits for the PLO, new support from Arab states, a cycle of action and reaction, and attack and counterattack that has always culminated in war. There is little reason to suppose that the crushing Israeli attack on the PLO in Lebanon will, in the long run, end this deadly cycle. Somehow the Israelis have failed to observe that thirty years of massive retaliation have inflamed Palestinian nationalism rather than diminished it; have precipitated Palestinian terrorism rather than deterred it; and have not reduced support among the Palestinian people for the most violent and fanatical nationalists, who, instead, have become Palestinian heroes. Of course, not all Israelis have failed to observe this. Some years ago, the distinguished Israeli philosopher J. L. Talmon wrote of the Arab-Israeli conflict: "If anything has been proved by the fifty years' conflict, it is precisely that it is just not true that the adversary 'understands only the language of force.' Instead of bringing him to his knees, despair goads him into more desperate acts of resistance or aggression."

Yet another reason that the Israelis must accommodate Palestinian nationalism is that failure to do so is rapidly undermining Israeli democracy and forcing Israel into increasingly coercive policies. These policies will undercut the moral legitimacy and distinctiveness of Israel that have long attracted worldwide support, especially in the United States. There are now about 1.3 million increasingly embittered Palestinian Arabs living within Israeli-occupied territory, and a million more live on its immediate borders. Moreover, the heretofore loyal, or at least passive, 500,000 Israeli Arabs increasingly support the Palestinian cause. Without Israeli withdrawal from the occupied territories and the establishment of a Palestinian state, Israel will increasingly have to restrict the rights of all the Arabs over whom it rules and will probably have to resort to increasing repression, simply to maintain the status quo.

Today Arabs make up over 40 percent of the Israeli population, and because of the higher Arab population growth rate, the diminishing rate of Jewish immigration, and the rising rate of Jewish emigration, within less than a decade Israel is likely to be an Arab majority state. An Israel determined to hold onto the occupied territories thus faces two dismal choices: either it ceases to be a Jewish state, thus undermining one of the major *raisons d'etre* of Zionism; or it turns itself into an undemocratic garrison state, thus undermining the other major Zionist aspiration, with the increasingly hopeless task of repressing a nationalism that is bound to grow in direct proportion to Israeli efforts to repress it. Could there be a worse betrayal of Zionism than for Israel to end up as the French did in Algeria or as South Africa today?

Finally, then, Israel must accommodate Palestinian nationalism because it has no other practical or morally legitimate choice. Jewish nationalism has found a home, and Palestinian nationalism cannot be denied one. But Israel will not be able to accommodate Palestinian nationalism unless it deals directly with the PLO. It is an undeniable fact that the PLO is the dominant political organization of the Palestinians. It is a well-organized, well-financed, persistent political force that has survived military defeats in the past and is likely to emerge again as the major military-terrorist arm of Palestinian nationalism. For this reason alone the PLO would have to represent the Palestinians in any negotiations for a Palestinian state. In addition, there is increasing evidence that the PLO truly represents the will of the majority of Palestinians and would likely win any democratic election in a Palestinian state, just as so many other nationalist organizations have successfully led national independence movements elsewhere. About 10 years ago the Israelis might have been able to negotiate with much less militant, violent, radical Palestinians, but their outright refusal to do so—indeed their suppression of even moderate Palestinian political action in the occupied territories—resulted in a growing radicalization of the Palestinians and a vacuum of power in which the PLO has been able to thrive.

It would be a bitter pill for Israel to have to deal with an organization that has relied so heavily on terrorism—"a gang of murderers," as Begin calls it—but the argument for not dealing with it on this score is unpersuasive. Dozens of states, including Israel itself, have come into existence in part or primarily because of successful terrorism: Terrorist movements are brought into the political arena precisely when they are strong enough to resist suppression. Protestations that as a matter of principle one cannot deal with terrorists come with particular irony and lack of persuasiveness from Begin and the Likud, the former leaders of the Irgun, a ruthless, terrorist, pre-independence Zionist organization. Even more to the point, though, are the *current* policies of the Begin government: Israeli counteractions against PLO terrorism are increasingly terrorist themselves and, in strictly numerical terms, far more destructive to innocent lives than PLO terrorism. Even before the recent invasion of Lebanon, Israel had been responding to PLO attacks (against soldiers, as well as civilians) with massive attacks in Lebanon and elsewhere. Israeli use of indiscriminate weapons like artillery, air bombardments, napalm, and antipersonnel devices has predictably resulted in a heavy loss of life among innocent Arab civilians, many of them not even Palestinians let alone fighters for the PLO. For example, in 1978 Israel invaded southern Lebanon in retaliation for PLO terrorism that, in the course of the previous year, had killed 140 Israelis. The Israeli raid, making use of massive firepower, killed at least 2000 people, most of whom were not associated with the PLO. In April 1979, Israel retaliated against a Palestinian terrorist raid with four days of heavy artillery bombardment and air attacks that killed about 50, wounded hundreds, drove people from their homes, and inflicted heavy property damage. In July 1981, Israeli planes bombed an apartment complex in Beirut and killed at least 300 (supposedly in retaliation for PLO attacks on Israel that killed 60), few of them either PLO leaders or even Palestinians. Of course all this pales before the destruction of civilian homes and lives in the 1982 invasion of Lebanon that is estimated to have killed more than 10,000 innocent civilians, maimed tens of thousands more, and made refugees of nearly 1 million people.

Thus, the line between PLO terrorism and what is, in effect, Israeli counterterrorism is becoming increasingly thin. For years Israeli retaliation has been just as indiscriminate as Palestinian terrorism and far more devastating in terms of civilian lives. Moreover, once this deadly cycle takes hold, on what basis can the Israelis persuasively claim they are merely "retaliating"? Even before the Israeli invasion of Lebanon reduced the retaliation argument to mere pretext, the PLO could (and did) increasingly claim that it was only "retaliating" for the latest *Israeli* attack. Assuming, as is only too likely, that the PLO or a successive Palestinian guerrilla movement survives or reconstitutes itself in the aftermath of the attack in Lebanon, the destruction of Palestinian homes, property, and lives—most of them innocent by all standards of modern warfare—will provide grist for the retaliation mill for years to come.

Finally, prior to the Israeli attack on the PLO there were increasingly convincing indications that the PLO was divided about its future strategy. Some of its leaders were prepared to abandon attacks on Israel if the Israelis would allow the establishment of an independent Palestinian state in the West Bank and Gaza. The PLO's official position still calls for the regaining of all of Palestine and the elimination of Israel. Unofficially, however, at least one faction of the PLO (perhaps the majority) has been shifting steadily from such an impossible and illegitimate goal to one that is far more moderate, realistic, and legitimate: the creation of a Palestinian state beside, rather than in place of, Israel. In the last few years, a number of PLO leaders, including Arafat, have dropped talk of "liberating all of Palestine" and have told journalists, U.S. congressmen, and others that they would accept a compromise based on partition and, in that context, would be willing to favorably consider arms limitation, demilitarized zones, peacekeeping forces, joint superpower guarantees, and mutual de facto recognition.

To be sure, PLO flexibility should not be exaggerated. On several occasions over the past decade it appeared as though the PLO might formally agree to language confirming Israel's right to exist, only to back off in the face of vehement opposition by more radical elements within the PLO coalition. Obviously it would be a far more promising situation if the PLO moderates could overcome the rejectionism and fanaticism in their own ranks. Indeed, it is certainly possible that ultimately the Israeli defeat of the PLO in Lebanon might encourage a more moderate rather than a more fanatical PLO policy. On the other hand, the policy of the Begin government offers little incentive for PLO moderation and is probably so designed. As long as Begin continues to proclaim that *under no circumstances* will Israel recognize or deal with the PLO or allow the creation of a Palestinian state—that is, *even if* the PLO formally accepts the permanent existence of Israel—the Palestinians will be reluctant to give away what they consider, wisely or not, to be their major trump card or bargaining chip. Finally, whatever the precise degree of PLO flexibility, now or in the future, both Israeli interests and moral justice would be served by far greater—though, as I shall argue, hardly unlimited—Israeli flexibility.

For a variety of reasons the West Bank and Gaza would be the appropriate place for a Palestinian state. In the first place, no existing state has a clear, unambiguous claim to either area. The Gaza strip, though administered by Egypt for some years, is not Egyptian territory and is not claimed by the present Egyptian government. The West Bank is an integral part of Palestine. After the British defeated the Ottoman Empire in 1917 it became part of the League of Nations mandate to Britain, then was occupied by Jordan in the course of the 1948 Arab attack on Israel. Jordan lost the West Bank to Israel in the 1967 war, and Hussein has since renounced any claim to it in favor of the Palestinians. Israel's sole claim to legitimate ownership of the area is based on the religious ties of Judaism to the area and previous occupation some 2000 years ago. The claim is an embarrassingly bad one, and it has no standing in either international law or common sense. It is far outweighed by the fact that the religious ties of Islam to the area are no less strong than those of Judaism and, of greater importance, by the fact that Arabs have lived on the land for 1300 consecutive years.

Thus, the present status of both Gaza and the West Bank are anomalous, which has the major advantage of making it easier to create a new state there. Secondly, the area is appropriate for a new Palestinian state for symbolic reasons: It is undeniably part of ancient, historical "Palestine." Thus, Arab Palestinian nationalism has focused on it for precisely the same reason that Jewish Palestinian nationalism (Zionism) did. The creation of a Palestinian state on the West Bank and Gaza would amount to a partition, the standard and inevitable compromise solution whenever two diametrically opposed and irreconcilable nationalist movements lay claim to the same area. Finally, the West Bank and Gaza are the appropriate places for a new Palestinian state since the current population of those areas is still (despite the Jewish settlements) overwhelmingly Palestinian, including many refugees from the 1948 Arab-Israeli war.

Of course, no Palestinian state can or should be created unless it is reconcilable with the basic security of Israel. But contrary to Israeli propaganda as well as genuine fears, the establishment of such a state would be more conducive to real peace (and, therefore, real Israeli security) than a continuation of the attempt to prevent it. No Palestinian state could or should come into existence on an unconditional basis. Israel would have both the right and the capability to impose a variety of constraints on that state's policies and actions to ensure that it would not become a base for continued Palestinian war on Israel.

One possible constraint, partially embodied in the 1982 Reagan administration's proposed settlement and favored by the Labor party opposition in Israel, would be a close linkage or federation between the West Bank and Jordan. The premise of this proposed settlement is that Jordan could control or at least exercise a moderating influence on the Palestinians. However, in light of the long conflict between the Palestinians and the Bedouins of Jordan, culminating in the fierce suppression of the PLO by Hussein's Bedouin army in 1970, it is unlikely that the Palestinians would accept anything other than a fully independent state.

However, other constraints would be both essential and politically feasible. A new Palestinian state would have to accept severe limitations on its armaments, would have to refrain from entering into military alliances with other states, particularly the Soviet Union, and would have to prevent extremist groups from using Palestine as a base for continued terrorist actions against Israel. There are a variety of indications that at least some of the PLO leadership understand the necessity for such constraints and would accept them. If they didn't, their case for a Palestinian state would be fatally weakened. The Palestinians are entitled to a homeland and a state of their own, not a base for the destruction of Israel. In any case, the former is the most they can possibly get, and they know it.

Suppose, then, that the PLO agreed to accept a state on the West Bank and the Gaza as the definitive realization of its nationalist aspirations and agreed to a number of measures designed to reassure Israel of its security.

How could such an agreement be enforced once a new state was formed? Would Israel be asked to trust the Palestinians with its future, to exchange land for paper promises? Certainly not. A Palestinian state on the West Bank and Gaza would be tiny, economically dependent on outside support, divided in two by Israel itself, and militarily inconsequential. It would be vulnerable not only to economic pressures but also to being overrun by Israel in a matter of hours. The Israelis cite geography as the basis of their security concerns: the West Bank is only fifteen miles from Tel Aviv. But this is at least as much an Israeli advantage, especially given the disparity of military power between Israel and a prospective Palestinian state. In effect, a Palestinian state would be on permanent notice: Any serious violation of the restrictions that it must accept as a condition for coming into existence would be grounds for reoccupation. Israel could accomplish this on its own with relative ease. In any case, however, Israel would not be the only state in the area that would insist on a Palestinian state that minded its own business and refrained from political or military action not only against Israel but also against its Arab neighbors. On its immediate eastern borders would be Jordan, which has already convincingly demonstrated its willingness and capability to suppress Palestinian radicalism. Not far to the south would be Saudi Arabia, clearly the primary potential source of financial assistance to a new Palestinian state and not likely to be interested in subsidizing a new focal point of radicalism in the Middle East, especially in the context of a general peace settlement with Israel that included some form of Moslem rule over East Jerusalem. Thus, surrounded by far more powerful neighbors determined to ensure that it remain on its best behavior, financially weak and dependent on foreign assistance, a new Palestinian state would have little choice but to strictly concentrate on ensuring domestic stability and development. The logic of that position is not lost on much of the PLO leadership today and, once they were given a real stake in preserving the status quo, the logic would be even more compelling in the future.

Unfortunately, there are few indications that either the Israeli government or the public realize that Israeli security would be far better served by the creation of a limited Palestinian state than by prevention of it through unending repression, violence, and warfare. At this point, Israel can be seriously asked only to agree to the *principle* of eventual withdrawal from the occupied territories, which would take place only gradually and would be conditional upon firm security guarantees that Israel could, in the last analysis, unilaterally uphold. But Israel's position is totally uncompromising. The Begin government has repeatedly affirmed that it will *never* withdraw under *any* conditions, not mainly for security reasons but because it regards "Judea and Samaria" as Israeli territory. The sole concession Israel will make, even in principle, is in reality no concession at all. The Begin government's proposal for "autonomy" for the Palestinian inhabitants of the occupied territories is meaningless for it specifically asserts Israeli sovereignty over the area, retains permanent Israeli political and military control, and continues and expands the policy of Jewish settlement on the West Bank. This "autonomy" proposal gives the Palestinians little more than some highly limited local self-government within the context of total Israeli domination. This is precisely the kind of arrangement that colonial powers in the past undertook: making use of local notables to exercise direct control while seeking to conceal where all the real power lay. This Israeli version of colonial rule will almost certainly prove no more successful in meeting nationalist aspirations than did its unmourned predecessors.

Let us summarize. For both moral and practical reasons, not only because it is the right thing to do but because it is the *only* thing to do in order to maximize Israeli security over the long run, Israel must change its policy from military repression of the Palestinians to political accommodation. That there would be risks in such a policy is evident, but the risks in the continuation of the status quo are far greater. Israel must agree to gradual withdrawal from the West Bank and Gaza and the creation of a Palestinian state accompanied by strict security guarantees for Israel. The alternatives to such an agreement are likely to lead to increased bloodshed and insecurity, the undermining of Israeli democracy and moral distinctiveness, increasing world isolation, the fracturing of the de facto Israeli alliance with the United States, and sooner or later, new wars, which eventually may be nuclear wars, with a reconstituted PLO or the rest of the Arab world.

The last point cannot be overemphasized. If for no other reason, the spectre of a desperate, fanatical Palestinian terrorist group in possession of a nuclear weapon should persuade a rational Israeli government that military suppression of Palestinian nationalism is utterly hopeless. A stateless nuclear terrorist group could well be undeterrable, for the Israelis might not know where or even against whom to retaliate. By contrast, again for this reason alone, a Palestinian state would be subject to the same calculations of deterrence as any other state and thus would be far less a nuclear as well as a conventional military threat to Israeli security.

In short, there would be no serious security threat to Israel from a Palestinian state that had been formally accepted by the Palestinian people and their political leadership as the final realization of their nationalist aspirations rather than as a stepping stone to the destruction of Israel. (And there is every indication that such an acceptance is growing, despite the lack of incentive provided by current Israeli policy.) The new Palestinian state, which would have an inherently weak military and economy, would have to accept a variety of restrictive conditions before independence could be achieved. It would be surrounded by Israel and Arab states that have their own reasons to oppose Palestinian expansionism. Under these conditions, a Palestinian state would not be inconsistent with Israeli security, but only with Israeli expansionism. And it is Israeli security, not expansionism, that is entitled to U.S. support.

THE PROSPECTS FOR PEACE

Is peace possible in the Middle East? There are grounds for either optimism or pessimism. On the one hand, an Arab war against Israel is increasingly impractical because of the removal of Egypt from the ranks of the confrontation states, because of the bedrock support of the United States for Israeli security and, above all, because of the overwhelming power of Israel itself. This power includes not only Israel's powerful conventional forces, but also its nuclear weapons, for it is a near-certainty that Israel has a considerable nuclear force. Israel would use its force for defense or retaliation against leading Arab cities should it ever face imminent danger of being overrun.

The involvement of outside powers in the Arab-Israeli conflict also generally works in favor of peace. The commitment of the United States to a settlement is clear and its influence is substantial; as for the Soviet Union, despite some ambiguity, it is, on balance, probably more of a force for restraint than of provocation. Though arguably the Soviets "want to keep the pot boiling," they clearly do not want another major Arab-Israeli war, and on at least three different occasions since 1972 they have publicly joined with the United States in calling for a peace settlement based on the preservation of Israeli society; the gradual withdrawal of Israel to the 1967 boundaries; the establishment of demilitarized zones along Israel's borders; superpower and UN guarantees; the establishment of peacekeeping forces; a "just settlement" of the Palestinian problem; and full peace and normal diplomatic and economic relations between Israel and the Arab states upon the successful completion of the previous steps. In any case, in the last decade Soviet influence in the Middle East has greatly diminished. Judging from their insignificant role in the Israeli-PLO war of 1982, the Soviets may have decided to substantially cut their losses in the area.

On the other hand, a number of disquieting forces are also at work: (1) the growth of Israeli militarism, religious mysticism, fanaticism, and general intransigence or immobility because of the exigencies of domestic politics; (2) the continued bitter rejection of peace with Israel by most Arab states in the absence of complete Israeli withdrawal to its pre-1967 boundaries and the creation of a Palestinian state; (3) the growth of Arab oil money, a major factor in allowing the Arabs to continue pressuring Israel (Saudi Arabia is currently said to be paying $3.5 billion annually to Syria, Jordan, the PLO, and Palestinian inhabitants of the West Bank and Gaza in return for their refusal to make peace with Israel under the present circumstances); and (4) traditional political instability in the Arab Middle East, now compounded by the revolution in Iran and the Islamic revival, making uncertain the survival of the Mubarak regime in Egypt as well as the "moderate" kingdoms of Saudi Arabia and Jordan.

At present, the prospects for peace in the Middle East would appear quite poor unless Israel agrees to the eventual withdrawal from the occupied territories and the establishment of a Palestinian state. Israel is extremely unlikely to take these actions in the absence of persistent and heavy U.S. pressures. The issue of whether the United States should pressure Israel poses the following questions.

1. Whether it *should* do so: Is it morally right and in the best U.S. national interest?
2. Whether it *can* do so: Does the United States have the leverage to force Israel to adopt policies it considers anathema to its security and its nationalist and religious objectives?

In the past decade, the United States has inconsistently wavered between the beliefs that (1) the best way to induce Israel to make important concessions is to make it feel more secure by providing it with ever-increasing economic and military assistance and closer security ties with the United States, and (2) unconditional U.S. support is leading to an overconfident Israel, whose intransigence is so deep that only severe pressures could force a fundamental reevaluation. For the most part, the policies of the Nixon, Ford, and Carter administrations were based on the first premise, but each also publicly threatened a fundamental "reassessment" of U.S. support of Israel at moments of despair over Israel's policies. However, all of the "reassessments" were, in effect, called off when Israel threatened to ignore them and both the pro-Israel lobby and Congress protested them vociferously. Thus, Israel has learned that it can ignore presidential disillusion and count on the nearly automatic support of Congress and important interest groups no matter how intransigent its policies.

Aside from the problem of domestic politics, the major arguments against the exercise of U.S. pressure against Israel are as follows. Such pressure would be wrong because only Israel can judge its own basic interests; an imposed settlement is bound to fail in the absence of the positive will of the parties to resolve the conflict by mutual agreement; pressures against Israel might mislead the Arabs about the basic U.S. commitment to Israel and encourage them to become more intransigent; and our own national interest requires a militarily strong, pro-American, anticommunist, antiradical Israel, our most reliable and powerful ally in the Middle East. Moreover, it is argued, U.S. pressures would be ineffective. Israel clearly will not be moved on matters it considers crucial, regardless of what the United States does. Alternatively, U.S. pressures might harden Israeli attitudes, perhaps even to the point of causing them to strike out in a desperate preemptive military attack against the remaining Arab confrontation states before they became too weak to do so.

These arguments are serious ones and deserve respectful consideration. Nonetheless, on balance they are not decisive. There is no reason to assume that Israel is really the best judge of its own interests. History is replete with examples of nations that were indeed poor judges of their own best interests (for example, the United States in Vietnam). The most persuasive assessment is that Israeli emotionalism about the Arabs, particularly the

Palestinians, is blocking rational policies and that, therefore, "Israel must be saved from itself."

Secondly, an imposed settlement in principle may be clearly inferior to one reached by the parties to the conflict, but such a settlement is nowhere in sight. The Israelis have so tightly cornered themselves over the future of the Golan Heights, Jerusalem, and the West Bank and Gaza that they are unlikely to be able to extricate themselves on their own. Similarly, as pointed out before, Arafat's hands may be tied by the exigencies of PLO coalition politics. Precisely because both sides have become prisoners of their internal policies, then, it is all the more essential that external pressures make it apparent that there is no choice but compromise. It is possible that the PLO's defeat in Lebanon and its dispersal throughout the Arab world will force it to adopt more moderate policies. But in the case of Israel, only American pressures can protect Israeli political leaders from internal charges of a sell-out by providing the necessary excuse for flexibility.

Third, the argument that Israel is the only ally we have in the Middle East and that our national interests are completely consistent with Israel's is a considerable oversimplification, although it threatens to become self-fulfilling. There is no doubt that our support for Israel is embittering the other states in the region and may eventually have the effect of endangering our access to oil (as indeed it did in 1973) and opening the door for the expansion of Soviet and radical (or reactionary theocratic) influence. In particular, U.S. relations with Saudi Arabia have been seriously undermined by our support of the separate peace between Israel and Egypt. Saudi Arabia has frequently indicated that its willingness to maintain high oil production and hold the line on prices is related to U.S. policies toward Israel, although, of course, its own economic self-interest also plays a major role in its oil policies.

Beyond these factors, Israeli intransigence could once again lead to a general war in the area, raising the possibility of a U.S.-Soviet confrontation. As long as Israel wants—or even demands—major U.S. economic and military assistance, the United States has not only the right, but also the elemental duty to consider its own national interest. It is common sense that the American government cannot be expected to subsidize indefinitely an Israeli policy that blocks progress toward peace, endangers Western access to oil, and could even embroil the United States in a war with the Soviet Union.

Would U.S. pressures such as the slowing down or withholding of economic and military assistance work? There is considerable reason to believe that they would, provided they were sustained and serious and Israel were disabused of its present well-founded belief that it can ride out short-term shifts in U.S. policy and count on the Israeli lobby to force presidents to back down. Israel's economy is now crucially dependent on U.S. assistance. Israel spends over 40 percent of its gross national product on defense and relies heavily on the United States for grants and high technology weapons systems. Without the annual $4 billion in American military and economic assistance, Israel could not maintain its present military edge over the Arab states. Besides this military and economic assistance, Israel relies on the United States as its only reliable and significant source of diplomatic assistance and friendship on the world scene. Without U.S. support, Israel would be almost totally isolated. Finally, Israel implicitly counts on the United States to deter Soviet intervention in the event of war, as may have occurred in the 1967 and 1973 conflicts. These are all highly powerful inducements for Israel to take seriously U.S. unhappiness with its present policies.

There is a widespread myth that Israel will not respond to American pressures. Begin, in particular, is thought to be so adamant as to react to pressure by doing the opposite of what is desired. Evidently in good part because of this myth (carefully fostered by the Israelis, of course), the Reagan administration refused to publicly criticize Israel, let alone threaten the cessation of American aid, during the Israeli invasion of Lebanon. However, the entire history of Israeli-American relations demonstrates the falsity of this myth: The Israelis *do* respond to serious American pressures, and, indeed, that is the *only* thing they respond to. Certainly they do not respond to positive inducements alone or to mild criticism, hand-wringing, or diplomatic appeals.[4] In 1956 Israel withdrew from the Sinai when the Eisenhower administration threatened to cut off all U.S. aid. In the 1973 war Israel agreed to a ceasefire and a halt to its advance into Egypt only after Henry Kissinger threatened to end the American military airlift. In 1975 Israel agreed to a partial withdrawal from the Sinai only after the Nixon administration combined promises of new American aid with the threat of a major "reassessment" of U.S. policy if Israel failed to withdraw. In 1979, similar carrot-and-stick policies by the Carter administration induced a reluctant Begin to agree to the complete withdrawal of Israel from the Sinai in exchange for a peace treaty with Egypt. In July 1981, pressures from American Jewish leaders and close supporters of Israel in Congress convinced Begin to end the bombing of civilians in Beirut—or face a decisive shift in American attitudes toward Israel. Finally, only strong congressional representations as well as entreaties of the Reagan administration that implicitly threatened an end to American support of Israel induced the Israelis to refrain from a massive ground assault against the PLO in Beirut in 1982.

Moreover, along with the unfortunately necessary pressures, the United States can offer positive inducements to elicit Israeli flexibility and concessions. The most important additional step the United States can now take is to offer formally a firm U.S. defense treaty with Israel that commits

[4]For a startling example, consider the fact that in the weeks prior to the Israeli invasion of Lebanon, the Reagan administration tried to talk the Begin government out of the obviously impending attack. The administration offered to revive the strategic cooperation agreement between the United States and Israel, suspended after the Israeli annexation of the Golan Heights. Meanwhile, the Senate Foreign Relations Committee was voting to substantially *increase* U.S. military assistance to Israel and to make the terms of repayment substantially easier. Gratefully, Begin proceeded to authorize the attack on Lebanon.

the United States to guarantee only Israel's pre-1967 borders and territorial integrity. In fact, the United States has been moving closer to such a commitment ever since the mid-1950s, when America became Israel's major supplier of economic and military assistance. As a result of this aid, and of U.S. actions to deter any possible Soviet intervention in the 1967 and 1973 wars, it is now taken for granted by all concerned that the United States will not allow the destruction of Israel. In the last few years, the United States has gone well beyond previous commitments in its efforts to induce Israel to agree to the earlier disengagement agreements with Egypt and Syria and the final peace treaty with Egypt in 1979. As a result, the United States is now committed to providing the most modern armaments; to taking appropriate diplomatic, economic, and military measures if the security of Israel is endangered by Egyptian violations of the peace treaty; and to supporting Israel if its survival or security is threatened by a world power.

In effect, then, the United States already has a de facto military alliance with Israel that remains only to be formalized and institutionalized. To add credibility and value as a deterrent, U.S. troops (at least in symbolic numbers) must be stationed in Israel. Israel—in the past, disdainful of international guarantees—has recently indicated it would now welcome such a guarantee.

To be sure, such an Israeli-American alliance would represent an extension of formal U.S. commitments and would thereby carry some risks. However, the truly vital nature of U.S. national and moral interests in an Arab-Israeli settlement justifies the risk. Moreover, in the context of a comprehensive peace, it seems clear that most Arab states would not oppose a U.S. alliance with Israel or a military presence in the area. It would provide them with a powerful argument against militants and rejectionists for not continuing a dangerous and futile struggle against Israel. Also, many Arab states would welcome a U.S. military deterrent against potential Soviet expansionism and, perhaps, even against internal uprisings that threaten their own governments.

In summary, the present Middle Eastern situation is inherently unstable; vital American interests are jeopardized by a continuation of the Arab-Israeli conflict and by Israeli intransigence in that conflict. A combination of U.S. pressures and inducements to Israel to reach a comprehensive settlement, which inevitably must include nearly total Israeli withdrawal to its pre-1967 boundaries and the establishment of a Palestinian state on the West Bank and Gaza, seems to be the only viable alternative left to the United States.

FOR FURTHER READING

Alroy, Gil Carl. *Behind the Middle East Conflict* (New York, N.Y.: G. P. Putnam's Sons, 1975).

Bell, J. Bowyer. *Terror Out of Zion* (New York, N.Y.: St. Martin's Press, 1977).

Bulloch, John. *The Making of a War* (London, England: Longman Group Ltd., 1974).

Elon, Amos. *The Israelis* (New York, N.Y.: Holt, Rinehart & Winston, 1971).

Evron, Yair. *The Middle East* (New York, N.Y.: Praeger, 1973).

Golan, Galia. *Yom Kippur and After* (New York, N.Y.: Cambridge University Press, 1977).

Khouri, Fred J. *The Arab-Israeli Dilemma* (Syracuse, N.Y.: Syracuse University Press, 1968).

Laqueur, Walter. *The Road to Jerusalem* (New York, N.Y.: Macmillan Press, 1968).

————. *The Struggle for the Middle East* (New York, N.Y.: Macmillan Press, 1969).

Quandt, William. *Decade of Decisions* (Berkeley, Calif.: University of California Press, 1977).

Rustow, Dankwart A. and Mugno, John F. *OPEC: Success and Prospects* (New York, N.Y.: New York University Press, 1976).

Safran, Nadav. *From War to War* (New York, N.Y.: Pegasus Press, 1969).

————. *Israel, The Embattled Ally* (Cambridge, Mass.: Harvard University Press, 1978).

Sykes, Christopher. *Crossroads to Israel* (Bloomington, Ind.: Indiana University Press, 1973).

chapter 5

The United States and the Persian Gulf

CARL LEIDEN

Foreign policy is like the Stealth bomber; you can't see it but it still works.

SECRETARY OF STATE ALEXANDER HAIG
Wall Street Journal, November, 1981.

INTRODUCTION

The Middle East, containing as it does the Arab world (as well as Israel) and the Northern tier of Muslim countries from Turkey through Pakistan, is simply immense. It is difficult to imagine that a single, or simple, American policy would suffice for this area as a whole. In fact, American foreign policy in the past has sometimes been no policy at all, or more often a clumsy collection of ad hoc policies concocted for each portion that compels interest.

The United States has great interest in the following areas: Libya and its leader Qadhafi; the Arab-Israeli dispute; oil and the Gulf, including Iran; and the Russian presence in Afghanistan. It is the third and fourth of these

This chapter has been read by my colleagues, James A. Bill, Robert Stookey, and Karl M. Schmitt. They should not be held responsible for the interpretations contained here. The author is, however, grateful for their comments.

that chiefly concern us here, although events in one part of the Middle East are rarely wholly unconnected with those in other parts or with the larger world environment—for example, the Israeli raid on the Iraqi reactor in 1981 or the Israeli invasion of Lebanon in the summer of 1982.

Although American interests in the Middle East go back many years, it is safe to say that these interests—often missionary and archeological in the early days—did not assume a major importance until after the Second World War. The British and French during this period abandoned the major share of their holdings in the Middle East, and the United States felt compelled to intervene. 1947 was the year of the Truman Doctrine and 1948, that of Israel's birth. Although the *area* that Israel occupies is in itself of little intrinsic importance to the United States, the sentimental and emotional attachment that many Americans have exhibited for the Israelis has become a large "given" in the making of contemporary American foreign policy. In addition, the end of the war made it possible for oil production in the Gulf to accelerate in keeping with the quickly growing needs of world industry. Add to this the early imposition of the cold war on the area and one can quickly discern the major dimensions of American interests: the fate of Israel in the Arab world, the safeguarding of oil for the United States and the West, and the containment of possible Soviet aggression in the area. All other interests fade before these.

The Arab-Israeli dispute is treated elsewhere in this volume. This chapter concerns the Persian Gulf (called the Arabian Gulf by many Arabs) and the nations that make up, so to speak, its political drainage.

The Gulf is a shallow sea extending northwestward from the Gulf of Oman and the Indian Ocean. The entry to the Gulf is narrowed considerably at the Straits of Hormuz—the distance between Iran and Oman at that point is only about 35 miles. Some 1000 miles to the northwest the Gulf ends at the mouth of the Shatt al-Arab (the confluence of the Tigris and Euphrates rivers). The countries actually in or on the Gulf are, beginning at the lower extremity and moving clockwise, Oman, the United Arab Emirates (UAE), Qatar, Saudi Arabia, Bahrain, Kuwait, Iraq, and Iran. Beyond Iran lie Afghanistan and Pakistan.

Without going farther afield than the countries just mentioned, the Gulf exhibits a bewildering array of minorities, of religious complexity and of degrees of development and modernization. Although some Arabs live in Iran (in Khuzistan in the southwest) Iran is not an Arab country, although this is often confused in the United States. All of these countries are Muslim, however, although the great split among Muslims is well represented here— that is between the Sunnis (or more orthodox Muslims) and the Shi'ites (who follow the Imams, beginning with Ali, the son-in-law of the Prophet). This division is more than doctrinal and assumes major political importance in the twentieth century. Iran is largely a Shi'ite country, although more than half of Iraqis are Shi'ite too. Saudi Arabia, except for a pocket near the Northern Gulf Coast, is staunchly Sunni. Iran, of course, has many ethnic minorities including the Azerbaijanis, Turkmen, Baluchis, Qashqais, Lurs and so on.

One such minority, the Kurds, Iran shares with Turkey and Iraq. The Kurds today are a troublesome factor for the Iranian government, as they have been for others for many years. Both Afghanistan and Pakistan to the east are broken into ethnic regions as well; the very survival of Pakistan is threatened by them. Of course no country is strictly homogeneous in its ethnic or religious characteristics, but it is important to note that this area displays in considerable splendor the qualities of heterogeneity.

There has been an American presence in the Gulf for a long time, but the first important American entrepreneurs were oil men and they had a foothold in oil exploitation as far back as the end of the First World War. They were preeminently successful in getting Saudi concession rights; the resulting oil consortium Aramco still exists, although today it is under Saudi control. When in 1953 the marketing consortium for Iranian oil was arranged, American companies became important partners in it.

Because of oil and the backwardness of Saudi Arabia, Aramco and the United States assumed many functions not normally those of an oil company or a foreign government. Thus began the diverse American connection for the Saudis that lingers today, as exemplified in the sale of AWACS planes to the Saudi government in 1981.

Our relationship with Iran was never so clear cut, but it was strong by the time it was shattered in 1979 with the fall of the Shah. The United States had cooperated with the British and Russians in their occupation of Iran in the Second World War, but had strongly supported the young Shah (Mohammed Reza Shah Pahlavi) against the Russians at war's end. Ultimately in the abortive adumbration of the Baghdad Pact—in which Iran and Iraq were members—the United States began its military buildup of Iran. Whether client or surrogate or an independent force, the Shah's Iran was to become, in terms of military forces, the most powerful of the Gulf States.

It has behooved both the United States and the Soviet Union to show the flag in the Gulf. The Soviet Union had a naval presence at Umm Qasr in Iraq (a Soviet client state for a time), and the United States had a naval facility at Bahrain. Deep in the Indian Ocean, some 2500 miles from Oman, a major American base has been built on Diego Garcia, and to the west and below South Yemen the Soviets have a base on Socotra. More recently the United States and Oman have agreed on military cooperation.

This sketch of the Persian Gulf is just that; it lacks many details. Some of these details will be added in the following sections. But a final word here: The Gulf is complex and neither easily understood nor predictable. There are few easy generalizations available to us.

THE NIXON-FORD LEGACY

It should be remembered that Nixon's predecessor, Johnson, was mesmerized with Vietnam. His own interests in policy planning for the Gulf—he was instrumental in policy change for the Arab-Israeli dispute after 1967—do not seem to have been overwhelming. He supported the Shah

and American interests there; he expressed conventional wisdom about the
Saudi-American relationship and the importance of Saudi oil. He was concerned about Russian pressure in the Gulf. Certainly it is fair to say that
governmental Middle East specialists, by the end of 1968, had already
turned their attention to the Gulf as being the potential trouble spot that the
United States would ultimately have to face up to. A lonely foreign service
officer, James Akins, was about to begin the dissemination of his message
about the energy crisis that would overwhelm us; he was later to be American Ambassador to Saudi Arabia. Nevertheless, the Middle East, including
the Gulf region, was not the chief focal point of the Johnson administration.

It is too early for the usual flood of revisionist historians to descend
upon the Nixon years and, brushing aside Watergate, discover in Nixon a
remarkable shaper of foreign policy. He was indeed the last American president whose experience, knowledge, and interests made a competent approach in foreign policy possible. Henry Kissinger was his national security
advisor and later Secretary of State. Unfortunately, Nixon's major interests
were elsewhere than the Middle East. Kissinger recalls with some embarrassment (in *The White House Years*) that Nixon agreed to Secretary of
State William P. Rogers assuming direction of Middle East policy (by which
was meant largely that connected with Arabs and Israelis) so that he could
be kept from interfering in more important things.

For Nixon these more important things meant extracting an "honor-
able" peace in Vietnam, coming to a détente with the Soviet Union, and
beginning an affair with the People's Republic of China. These things took
his time and captured his interest; they were to become his achievements.

A very important fact is that Nixon was under heavy domestic pressure from the time of his reelection until his resignation in 1974. Watergate
began as a "caper"; it ended in the destruction of the Nixon presidency.
Certainly from 1 May, when Haldeman and Erlichmann resigned and John
Dean was fired, Nixon had little time for foreign policy. At the very time of
the 1973 Egyptian-Syrian-Israeli war Vice-President Spiro Agnew was
forced to resign; ten months later it was Nixon's turn.

Gerald Ford was a caretaker and did not initiate any new policy for the
Gulf; there was, however, the continuity of Kissinger as Secretary of State.

Things did happen during the Nixon-Ford period (1969 to 1976) that
must be noted.

1. The death of Nasser and the rise of Sadat in 1970.
2. The Jordanian expulsion of armed Palestinians and the threat of
   widening war (1970).
3. The formal withdrawal of the British from the Gulf.
4. The creation of the United Arab Emirates (UAE) in 1971.
5. The civil war in Pakistan, leading to an Indian-Pakistani war
   (1971).
6. The expulsion of Soviet military advisors from Egypt in 1972.
7. The October war (1973).

   8. Oil and the Embargo (1973 to 1974).
   9. The Kissinger peace diplomacy (1973 to 1975).
   10. Reopening of the Suez Canal (1974).
   11. Beginning of a civil war in Lebanon (1975).
   12. The death of King Faisal of Saudi Arabia (1975).

At first glance most of these will seem to have been connected with the Arab-Israeli conflict rather than with countries and events farther east. And although this is correct, they still need to be emphasized. For example, in the death of Nasser, the ruler of the most important and most populous Arab state and *the* Arab nationalist leader in his own right, there were to be ripples all over the Middle East. The Shah had at one time used as an excuse for a military buildup his fear of Nasser. The Saudis had tried to have him assassinated. As his life had interested and affected almost all Middle Easteners, so his death introduced a note of uncertainty and disorder. President Nixon was visiting President Tito when Nasser's death occurred, but he did not make an attempt to visit Cairo for the funeral. (It is true that we did not then have diplomatic relations with Egypt.)

Space does not permit a detailed discussion of American attitudes and policies on all these or other events. The Jordanian battle with the Palestinians in 1970 certainly affected the entire alignment of forces in the area. It also made Lebanon a likelier target for civil conflict than it already was (this jelled in 1975). The United States was interested in this and very much involved as were the Israelis, of course. The expulsion of Soviet military advisors from Egypt in 1972 was a signal to the United States that was not picked up very readily; it was also a signal about Sadat's independence, boldness, and, if necessary, aggressive behavior toward Israel. It forced the Soviet Union to reevaluate its commitments everywhere in the Middle East including the Gulf area. Little over a year after the Russian exodus from Egypt, Sadat (and Syria) launched an attack upon the Israelis. It was a strategic success beyond all expectations. The long war—about three weeks—compelled the renewed support of patron states, the United States and the Soviet Union, both of whom found it politically convenient to go on military alerts and to act as if the peace of the world depended on occupancy of the sands of Sinai and the hills of the Golan. The United States was very much involved in this war and in its aftermath. Two things should be noted here: (1) the war demonstrated that the United States would stand up to the Russians (and from the perspective of Moscow that the Russians would stand up to the Americans); and (2) the war brought on the oil crisis.

The Egyptian costs of the war were partly financed by the Saudis, and the war gave all producer nations a chance to raise the price of oil. World consumption had finally approximated world production; price gouging was now possible. The immediate result was a fourfold price increase (still most modest by 1982 pricing). Also, Arab producers declared an oil boycott on the United States. The Saudis cooperated in this and also threatened to cut oil production by five percent a month until some satisfactory resolution of the Arab-Israeli conflict had been made. Interestingly, it was the Soviet client state, Iraq, that although theoretically supporting the boycott, continued to sell oil to the West. This scramble for oil, the boycott, and the instability of prices brought home to the United States how fragile our oil relationship in the Gulf was and how important some attention to this problem was to become.

The assassination of King Faisal in 1975 was not connected with these political events—he was killed by a fanatical nephew—but it meant the loss of an able, shrewd, and experienced figure as leader of the Saudis. His successor was Khalid, whom most observers quickly labeled as weak or ill or both; in a de facto sense the crown prince and later king, Prince Fahd soon shared considerable power. But any event like this can be an indicator of domestic difficulty and if politically contagious, a harbinger of regional difficulty.

One other event for this period: Pakistan (divided into eastern and western portions since 1947) blew apart in 1971. The East Bengalis (East Pakistanis) had grown disenchanted with their union with the West Pakistanis and were agitating for independence. Putting down riots in Dacca became putting down insurgency in East Pakistan, which was essentially civil war. The Indians intervened almost inevitably, and the result was that Bangladesh was born, but also the fear in the White House that West Pakistan might well disappear under an Indian juggernaut. Kissinger and Nixon took the credit for restraining the Indians, who were friendly with the Soviet Union. Saving Pakistan from Indian (or worse) clutches was considered a major success by the United States.

Nixon left the White House in August 1974, Ford, in January 1977. What was their policy legacy in the Gulf? What was their background of achievement or failure?

Both presidents emphasized the importance of the Gulf to American interests. The Shah was increasingly referred to as the "linchpin" of regional security there. There was no longer any meaningful restraint on the sale of weapons to Iran or on the American expectations of Iran's support and cooperation. We were less certain of Saudi Arabia because it was much weaker, or so it seemed. But preservation of its oil fields was imperative to the United States. Both Kissinger and his chief Ford made vague blustering statements that the United States would not hesitate to use force to preserve those oil fields. Force against whom? Saudis? Russians? Iraqis? It was never made clear.

Both presidents reiterated the Soviet threat and continued in what appears today to have been a less-than-effective effort to build up American force in the area. A succession of American admirals in Manama, Bahrain spoke to visiting Congressmen and others of their confidence that the Gulf could be held. No doubt Soviet admirals said much the same thing to their constituents. But both sides were largely waving the flag. Each had but one meaningful client. The Soviet Union had Iraq (but we should not forget the People's Democratic Republic of Yemen [=South Yemen]); the United

States had Iran. The subsequent Iraq-Iran war may not be wholly a fair measure of what each could have done, but somehow few of us should be reassured.

During the Nixon-Ford years the British finally left the Gulf, and the old treaty relationships were abandoned. Many were quick to label this a "power vacuum" and wanted it filled by Iran and the United States. Perhaps it was. Apropos of this Iran, in 1971, took over Abu Musa and the Greater and Lesser Tunbs, small islands at the Straits of Hormuz, producing Arab discomfort at least as far away as Libya. It also finally abandoned its claim to Bahrain, a positive step welcomed by the United States. Most important of all, in 1975 Iran and Iraq "settled" their old dispute over where the border was between their two countries in the Shatt al-Arab. Iraq conceded to Iran in this; as a quid pro quo Iran stopped supporting insurgent Iraqi Kurds in the north. This was done with American approval.

There has been insurgency in Oman, along the southern coast in Dhofar province, aided and abetted by the People's Republic to the southwest. The Shah offered troops to the Omani government to help quell it, with some success.

In 1977 there was a jerry-built stability in the Persian Gulf for which the United States could claim credit. (One had to overlook the darkening clouds in Pakistan and the unsettled conditions in Afghanistan.) Iraq was not threatening Iran nor even Kuwait as much as it had on occasion. Indeed, Iraq was making strange signals that could be interpreted as dissatisfaction with the Soviet Union. Our relations with Iran were good and warm—at least they were with the Shah. The Shah was strong—never mind the never-ending raucousness of Persian students in the United States—and in him we thought that we had the ideal defender of regional interests. The minor states on the Gulf were reasonably stable and very wealthy. Saudi Arabia was awash with money, but it spent much of it in the United States—and the oil continued to flow. It was almost the best of all possible *real* worlds. As Nixon-Ford faded, the United States seemed to have had every normal reason to be confident in the success of its policies in the Gulf area.

OPTIONS FOR THE CARTER ADMINISTRATION

The election of Jimmy Carter was certainly a reaction of sorts to Watergate. He was a southern Democrat, but an enlightened one. He was a successful farmer; he had been an Annapolis graduate and a naval officer. His role model seemed to be a mixture of Martin Luther King (Junior and Senior) and Admiral Hyman Rickover. He was a born-again Christian. He was a man of very little experience in foreign affairs, but it was said of him that he read a lot and that he was easily the most intelligent president to occupy the White House in recent years. His concern about minorities and human rights was well known. He was an outsider, prided himself on it, and argued that Washington needed the cleansing fresh country air. His Secretary of State was Cyrus Vance, an able professional; his United Nations ambassador was

Andrew Young, undoubtedly able, but out of the Georgia milieu (he is now mayor of Atlanta). Walter Mondale was vice-president, but his interest in or knowledge of foreign affairs was not known to be great. He chose as his national security advisor an emigré Pole, Brzezinski, who was almost by the nature of things inclined to find Russians everywhere and their threats, like the manure of predatory animals, ubiquitous. In the National Security Council staff there were some bright spots, notably William Quandt, who knew the Middle East.

How can we describe the "problem" in Gulf foreign affairs that would be faced by any incoming president in January 1977, and in particular by Jimmy Carter? As we have described above, for many there was no unusual problem, for oil was flowing and the Gulf was reasonably stable. We were friendly with the Saudis, the Shah appeared to be secure and was our strong ally, and Iraq seemed to be having second thoughts about the Russians. There was domestic turmoil in Pakistan (Zulficar Ali Bhutto was overthrown in 1977) and in Afghanistan, some murmurings of difficulties (President Daoud fell in a Marxist coup in April 1978), but generally the Gulf was safe and secure.

This was part of the problem: the assumption that things would not change very much, at least not very rapidly. The complacent attitude about the Gulf was sure to be reinforced by some simple facts about another part of the Middle East, that in which Israel is centered. The Israelis had an election in the spring of 1977 and the old Labor bloc was turned out and the Likud bloc put in. Likud's main party was Herut, and Menachem Begin was its leader now become prime minister. He was an old terrorist; now he was a hard liner. By the end of 1977 Sadat had made his trip to Jerusalem, and the rules of this game had changed. By September 1978 Camp David was in progress; by the spring of 1979 the peace treaty between Egypt and Israel had been signed. All this had repercussions in the Gulf, to be sure, but its effects on the United States were immense. This became, until the crisis in Iran occurred, *the* Middle East for Carter. This was where his attention was centered and where his greatest achievement (Camp David) was to occur. There was little time or inclination to concentrate on other events, at least until they compelled attention.

On the Gulf itself there are three important powers, each very different from the others, but all essential ingredients of any American policy that obtained in the area. These are Iraq, Iran, and Saudi Arabia. They are all oil-rich states. Iraq and Iran were the most developed of the three, both economically and politically. They also had the largest populations (about 12 million for Iraq; about 35 million for Iran) and were the most heavily armed. Each of these two countries was the chief enemy of the other, excluding the Soviet Union. It is impossible to imagine either being attacked by Saudi Arabia. In the case of Iraq, a long peace with Turkey was likely to continue, and although Iraq continually quarreled with Syria it was unlikely that Syria could pose a real military threat to Baghdad. Since 1958 at least, Iraq had had a history of considerable instability while the Shah managed a highly controlled regime. Iran hardly feared an attack by Afghanistan or Pakistan, and although Iraq was a dangerous enemy it was unlikely that it could seriously damage Iran. Of the three, then, Iran was the most powerful militarily—more powerful than necessary in fact—and Saudi Arabia was the weakest.

Except for oil, Saudi Arabia was indeed the weakest of these three countries in all ways. A small population of Saudis (perhaps as few as 4.5 million) already suffocating under large numbers of workers from abroad (Yemenis, Pakistanis, Palestinians, Koreans, and Americans)—madly building cities, roads, factories, schools—was still in many ways in an earlier age. More than conventionally religious, they defined the word *conservative* by much of their behavior. The royal family, the real elite, numbered perhaps 5000, but was not itself of one mind about development or of the Saudi place in the Arab world and the Gulf. Saudi Arabia threatened no one militarily, except perhaps what used to be called the Trucial states (the UAE); it did quite legitimately fear Iraq and perhaps Iran. Less likely but conceivably might be pressure from the two Yemens. Saudi Arabia was a basket case in terms of defense; it was part of the problem.

Afghanistan and Pakistan were on the periphery, but this did not make them less important. It became apparent to the United States after the Soviet Union attacked Afghanistan in December 1979 that a crow's flight from southwestern Afghanistan to the Straits of Hormuz was only about 300 miles, not far even for a crow. Pakistan (at least the tip of it) was equally close. Pakistan was a part of old India; Afghanistan was the traditional buffer between India and Russia. Russia had never occupied either of these territories. Russian control or occupation would outflank the Middle East and put an intolerable strain on the defense of the Gulf and its oil. It was unthinkable that these states might fall into the hands of the Soviet Union.

Pakistan was beset by internal difficulties. Mostly these were linguistic and cultural separatist movements, but religious enthusiasm added its spicy tang. Bhutto was strongly pro-American, but worried; he fell in 1977 and was murdered by his successor, General Zia al-Huq, some months later. Afghanistan had had a coup in 1973, and the old king, Zahir Shah, prudently stayed abroad. His relative and long-time advisor, Sirdar Mohammed Daoud, took over but failed to halt the spreading leftist tide—well organized since 1965. He was (in 1977) very weak, and his country led a fragile existence.

It is now time to state the problem for which the preceding paragraphs have been preliminary. Overriding American interests were to safeguard the oil and to prevent the Russians from damaging the area. The basic problem then was to devise a policy to advance these interests. But the problem also consisted of certain barriers to such policy articulation: (1) the uncertain assumption that things would not change very much very rapidly, and (2) an empirical ignorance of the five major states in the region (Saudi Arabia, Iraq, Iran, Afghanistan, and Pakistan) and what the dimensions of their own instabilities might be and what, of course, could be done about it.

A caveat: It is presumptuous and inaccurate to suggest that our high-ranking American policy makers did not know these things. Some did. But policy at the top—as well as procedures and bureaucratic inertia—is not easy to change. Domestic lobbies—the recent AWACS approval in the Senate provides a vivid example—often become impedimenta to change. And it is true that many foreign service officers have resigned over the years because of what they have viewed as irrational policy making in Washington.

Problems are rarely solved in international politics; sometimes, like Coolidge's problems, they go away; sometimes they are swept aside by stronger and more irresistible forces; sometimes they are circumnavigated or ignored and then very much, sometimes with peril.

What were the options? Real options are often few, although in small details there seems to be an infinite variety of each.

1. The most obvious option for Carter and the easiest to implement was to go on as before, assuming that detrimental change, if it occurred, would be gradual. This option assumed that all actors in the Gulf drama would maintain their relative postures. The chief advantages of this option were that it required little alteration in application and it was also cheap. It was thought also that it bought time. The main disadvantage is that any abrupt change could become a crisis, and we were unprepared to deal with the various crisis scenarios effectively.

2. This option assumes change of some major nature over the period of a presidential term (until, in this case, 1981). As a matter of statistical observation this has indeed been the rule since the Second World War. (Of course we write this from hindsight, the optics of which are better understood than those of foresight). This option then requires careful planning and preparation for an *expected* crisis of some kind in this area or its eastern periphery. Where might the crisis come? I know of no one in January 1977 who was very confident that the next four years would find a Soviet invasion of Afghanistan. In fact this happened, but the indicators for it in early 1977 were too dim to be discerned even now. Iraq was making signals that it was unhappy with its Soviet connection, but these signals too were dim at the time and could, it was thought, be safely put on hold. Pakistan was in trouble, though, and there were many signals of a painful crisis ahead.

   There were many in and out of government who viewed the future of Iran and Saudi Arabia very bleakly in spite of the strong pro-American postures of these countries. King Faruk of Egypt was supposed to have said once that the world would shortly have but five kings, those of Spades, Hearts, Diamonds, Clubs, and England. In early 1977 there were four kings in the Middle East plus a sprinkling of shaykhs and sultans in the Gulf itself: Hasan in Morocco, Husain in Jordan, Khalid in Saudi Arabia, and the Shah of Iran. All of the thrones were shaky, but in the academic world, at least, that of the Shah seemed shakiest. This was not a popular view in Washington in 1977. There were those then and now (and I consider myself among them) who considered the Saudi monarchy in trouble, too, but it was and is difficult to tell when the ultimate crisis may come.

The option then was to assume a crisis of major dimensions and to prepare for it. The chief disadvantages of this were that the precise crisis would be unknown, and one could hardly prepare for them all. Yet this was also the advantage: any preparation was better than none. Moreover, the nature of the coming crisis was not that impossible to imagine. A major friend of the United States would fall and be replaced by someone or something much less friendly. For "major friend" substitute "Khalid" or "the Shah" or "Bhutto." And for Afghanistan, although no one could quite foresee what would ultimately happen there, the leftist nature of the Afghan situation was apparent to literally everyone. The question was what to do when Afghanistan fell into the hands of radical leaders; the Russian invasion was beyond prediction.

3. Theoretically, this option has much going for it; practically, it is a nonstarter. The assumption here is that we and the Russians can come to some agreement in the Gulf area, each recognizing the other's political and economic needs there. Simply stated, it would have been politically impossible for Carter to have enunciated support for such an option, let alone to have pursued it. But without the tension between Russia and America various crises in the Middle East assume a much diminished importance. Crudely spoken, who cares whether a shah stayed or went, or whether the Saudi royal family became emigrés, and so on? As long as the oil could flow, and almost certainly it would, all the rest is essentially inconsequential. But the Russians and Americans are the most stubborn beasts; they persist in enjoying mutual enmity. Given this background, this option would never be more than a *pis aller*.

4. This option assumes that we know the nature of a coming crisis and that we go out to meet it head on. We anticipate it. This can be done in two ways: fighting it and taking advantage of it. American policy makers have been overly familiar with the first way; but Prince Talleyrand, that consummate politician of the French Revolution (and later) was very adept at deriving the maximum advantage from what seems to be. On more than one occasion a little Talleyrandism in the White House would have stood us in good stead. But in the making of foreign policy, we have, as a nation, rarely exercized this talent. We continue to prop up all sorts of odd leaders and systems past their time, while around them and us the foundations are crumbling.

In the Middle East in 1977, as is the case today, religious extremism and a xenophobia stemming from it were on the rise. How could this have been taken advantage of? Whatever the answer, it too is an option, but one that was neglected.

And so it came to pass that the first option secured the support of the new administration.

CARTER'S DIPLOMACY

It is indeed tempting and facile to state that incoming President Carter opted for some single policy in the Gulf. It takes some time for any new administration to find its feet and fill newly vacant slots with loyal and capable personnel. (Instructive here about the early days of the Carter administration is Joseph Califano's recent *Governing America*.) These personnel, too, take time to jockey for preeminence and power—Haig, Weinberger, Allen, and others in the early days of Reagan's administration. Policy qua policy is often left to shift somewhat for itself. Almost certainly, Carter did not receive from his advisors an entire policy for the Middle East or for the Gulf. Rather, what came to him and what required solutions came piecemeal and from different sources. Some policy, quite simply, emanates from the White House (although it may be opposed by the State Department or others); some comes from State or Defense, and some, of course, from Congress itself. All policy is modified by pressures from interdepartmental needs and demands, from lobbying groups, and from the bureaucracy ever present for implementation.

Indeed these kinds of conflicting and cross-cutting pressures are *one* of the reasons why the first option was destined to prevail! It was inevitably the easiest to accommodate.

When Carter took office in January 1977 the United States did not have diplomatic relations with Iraq. We did, however, have resident ambassadors in the various Gulf states as well as in Afghanistan and Pakistan. Ambassadors are normally reshuffled with a new administration, and Carter made some changes. What is not always revealed by a bare recital of changes made is the relative importance of the posts at their various "points in time" or the importance of the ambassadors themselves in terms of personalities, backgrounds, or freedom of action. Excluding Baghdad, there were four posts of importance in the late 1970s: Riyadh,[1] Tehran, Kabul, and Islamabad. There were, during the Carter presidency, some extreme examples of turbulence in three of these places; one ambassador was killed, two embassies overrun and sacked (one twice), and hostages seized. Only Riyadh escaped.

But turbulence and violence in themselves do not make a diplomatic post important. Riyadh and Tehran were important for the most obvious reason; they were the foundations for our interests in the Gulf. The security of Pakistan has always seemed important to American presidents for varying reasons that sometimes have been less than convincing. But Bhutto, its chief, was close to the Shah and to us. Pakistan, an old member of the defunct Baghdad Pact, had to be protected.

Afghanistan was less viable. Since late 1973 increasing evidence showed that the country was (or least its government and Kabul participants) slipped leftward. It seemed already to be on the lee shore of Soviet

---

[1]Technically the American embassy is located in Jidda although Riyadh is the capital.

communism. Almost certainly Carter would have to face this debacle, as indeed he did.

The true professional ambassador is sometimes thought to be a faceless personality with that famous passion for anonymity. Possibly the best-known and most-famous ambassador in the period just prior to Carter's presidency was Richard Helms, former director of the CIA and American ambassador to Iran from early 1973 until 1977. Possibly Iran was the only country in the world that would have welcomed a former CIA chief; in fact Helms and the Shah were old friends, schoolfriends indeed, in Switzerland, going back to the late 1930s. Helms was a powerful personality in his own right, a thorough professional, able, tough and adept at bureaucratic infighting. He had instant *access* to the Shah and whatever ceremony there was between them was bound to be minimal. His importance in the twilight of the Shah's rule was enormous; was he the *fossoyeur* of that rule as some of his detractors have alleged, or did he shore up a collapsing regime past its time?

Carter's major ambassadorial appointment was that of Helms's successor, William Sullivan. A professional, he had earned his reputation in Southeast Asia and in negotiations with the Vietnamese; he was part of the old Henry Kissinger crowd. He was thought of as tough and seemed to appreciate this appellation. He possessed a keen mind and did his "homework," but his knowledge of the Middle East and Iran was not noteworthy. His finest hour was standing his ground in early 1979 when his embassy was overrun by the ubiquitous enthusiasts of the Tehran streets, but by then American fat had long been in the fire.

Perhaps Ambassador Sullivan epitomizes part of the problem we face in international affairs. Personally able, energetic, intelligent, and dedicated, he was put in the wrong post at the wrong time. He was drenched in all the political clichés that had sustained, if that is the right word, the American crusade in Vietnam. He had, so far as I can tell, little understanding of the Middle East or of the Muslim World. He worked well with generals and CIA officials. He comprehended little of what was going on under the surface of Iranian politics. His recently published memoirs notwithstanding, Sullivan had too little background in the Middle East and too little time in Iran to be effective. Yet he was the single most important ambassadorial appointment made by Carter in the Gulf.[2]

There is insufficient space for the many details of issue and policy in this area. As pointed out previously, Carter was swept into the Arab-Israeli dispute early in his administration; less attention could be given elsewhere. With Saudi Arabia we were continually pressed to moderate our pro-Israeli

---

[2]In his *Mission to Iran* he stated that "the reckless manner in which the Carter Administration conducted its affairs continued, the erratic ambitions of Brzezinski were unabated, and the failure to understand Iran was compounded." He ultimately left his post in April 1979 in anger and frustration.

stance. In particular, the Saudis were concerned about Jerusalem. There was little that we could do here. When the Sadat trip to Jerusalem was followed by Camp David the Saudis had perforce to lessen their support for Sadat. But it was not, perhaps surprisingly, a big issue in Saudi-American relations. The Saudis were very active in OPEC politics during this period and, being the biggest oil producer, had a disproportionate influence on pricing. American policy was to curb Saudi pricing enthusiasms and to encourage high production. The charm of Oil Minister Yamani disguised the fact that we did not have altogether that much influence over what the Saudis did; nevertheless, it was a fact that the Saudis continued high production. The Saudis were also security conscious, and, like good hardware salesmen, we quickly produced our catalogs of assorted military equipment. The argument about arming the Saudis rages unabated into 1981 and 1982; but Carter was not unwilling, in spite of Israeli annoyance, to sell the Saudis a modest amount of military equipment, including stripped-down F-15s. (It must be remembered that the 1981 AWACS package contained conformable fuel tanks for the F-15s and a large collection of Sidewinder missiles.) We thus began the process in Saudi Arabia that had grown so out of hand in Iran, the arming of yet another Middle Eastern nation, whose government was at best insecure.

In Pakistan our friend Zulficar Ali Bhutto was in trouble from the day that Carter was inaugurated. Politics were often an unseemly affair in Pakistan. Riots and worse were commonplace, usually spurred by linguistic or religious quarrels. A strong hand was needed, usually a general's hand. Bhutto was not a general, but he was a popular, energetic, westernized leader who tried to function within some modicum of "democracy." Punjabis, Sindis, Baluchis, and Pathans might riot over language preference, but Pakistan was also a Muslim country in which different forms of Islam compete and in which zealots have from the earliest days (1947) tried to make Pakistan into what the Ayatollah Khomeini would like to make Iran.

In 1977, in spite of great efforts to placate his religious foes, Bhutto lost their support and fell in a coup led by General Zia al-Huq. At first Bhutto was imprisoned, then he was "tried"; finally, in 1979 he was killed by Zia. The "Bhutto" problem was the first great crisis for Carter in this area. We had to decide how to deal with Zia; Carter was also determined to save Bhutto's life if possible.

There was actually little that could be done. It was indeed a fait accompli. Neither the Shah nor the United States was willing to really intervene in Pakistani affairs nor was there any easy vehicle for doing so. The sword is not always a useful weapon in politics. Zia had to be stomached. But, in accepting him we pleaded for Bhutto's life. By 1979—after the Shah had fallen—Zia felt strong enough to eliminate his opponent, and the United States could only express its sorrow. So much then for American support for Bhutto. But to carry Pakistan out to its bloody end: In late November 1979 the great mosque in Mecca in Saudi Arabia was seized for a time by politico-religious insurgents; the news reached Islamabad in a form that alleged American implication. The result was that many thousands of rioters stormed the American Embassy in Islamabad and burned much of it; two American marines were killed. Zia apologized, but it was not a friendly moment between the two countries. But a month later the Soviet Union invaded Afghanistan in a move that was either very shrewd or very dumb. This move changed the whole picture in American-Pakistan relations. Afghan "rebels" and guerillas began, along with many refugees, to move into the Northwest Frontier Province of Pakistan and use it as a safe-haven. Pakistan, certainly anti-Russian in this episode, supported the Afghans and supplied arms to their fighters. Some of these arms were supplied in turn by the United States.

The Carter administration had to reevaluate the question of whether to aid Pakistan itself with military weapons. The United States has not been very successful in persuading Pakistan to eschew nuclear arms. Now, in an effort to shore up Pakistan's conventional defense we hastily offered $400 million in aid. It was turned down by Zia as being "peanuts." Later, in the Reagan administration the offer was upped to several billion, which seemed to be more acceptable to the Pakistanis.

In the 1950s Afghanistan was still a sleepy, backward, landlocked Central Asian monarchy with little effort being made toward either economic or political modernization. A few Americans and Russians were there, but essentially it was a backwater. A decade later found a century of change with both the United States and the Soviet Union competing in economic assistance. Modernization did occur in the cities (Kabul, Kandahar, Herat), although the countryside remained somewhat unresponsive. In modernizing it seemed natural to some educated Afghans to create socialist and Marxist movements; they were rich enough in enthusiasm to create several. By the late 1960s agitation was in full swing. The king, Zahir Shah, had been on the throne since 1933, and on a small scale he faced the same problem that all modernizing monarchs face: The monarchies themselves become anachronisms. In late 1973 the king's relative Dirdar Mohammed Daoud attempted to solve this by keeping the king in exile. Daoud lasted but five years more, years that were spent partly in combating the rising agitation of leftist political groups. In April 1978 Daoud was killed in a coup, and Mohammed Taraki, long-time communist leader, took over. By now events were moving fast. Taraki was, in turn, ousted and killed in late 1979 by leftist rival Hafizullah Amin who, in turn, was executed weeks later when the Russians arrived. The Russians invaded to support some sort of client government. They put in, as Afghan leader, Babrak Karmal. In the meantime, some months before (February 1979), in the chaos that purported to be order, the American ambassador, Adolph Dubs, was killed under circumstances that are still clouded.

By December 1979 the United States was, of course, heavily involved with revolutionary Iran, but the events in Afghanistan were viewed very seriously. Until the Russian invasion, policy was to temporize and to attempt to work with the Afghan Marxist government. All this was moot after December 1979.

Once again the sterility of foreign policy based primarily on military conceptions was revealed in the response to the Russian invasion. What were the viable options? Rain missiles on Moscow, drop paratroopers in Jalalabad, or do some other tough stunt? Obviously few presidents could have considered such things; Carter did not. What is left? Strong diplomatic protests, couched in tough diplomatic language can only go so far, and in this case they were wasted telex messages. Carter warned the Soviet Union about SALT II, but it was dead anyway. He embargoed grain and some other things; American farmers and businessmen discovered that they had little concern for Afghan freedoms. Carter's biggest effort, it turns out, was athletic. The Olympic summer games were going to be held in Moscow. Boycotting these games and encouraging other nations to do likewise would be a real slap at the Soviet Union. Such is the unreality of the political world. Not all American athletes were enthusiastic about their being pinpointed for ritual suicide; few foreign athletes were. A half-hearted response followed. Over the months Europe demonstrated quite clearly to the United States that although not "long ago," the Afghans were certainly "far away"; besides, apparently "the wench was dead." Afghanistan simply didn't matter that much. Moreover, Poland was already in the news, and many Europeans felt that Russians in Afghanistan might mean no Russians in Poland, and it didn't seem such a bad tradeoff. It is indeed possible that some American policy makers felt the same way, but they could hardly articulate this openly.

Although subsequent months found the Russians bogged down in Afghanistan—Vietnam is not a wild parallel—they have weathered the political storm from Europe, from the Muslim nations, and from the United States. Most of the practical efforts to embarrass the Russians had eroded by the time Carter relinquished office, and in spite of Reagan's raucous rhetoric he has done little more. The United States has, through various clandestine channels, continued to supply the Afghan rebels with arms and money.

But whatever the outcome, there is no doubt that the United States suffered a serious blow by the Russian act. Many things are weakened by the Russian presence in Afghanistan, a presence that may well be there to stay. Both Iran and Pakistan are now flanked by a nasty foe with plenty of military wallop. We now have a problem that the planners in Washington had always wanted to avoid.

Of course it was the events in Iran that captured American public attention. If Camp David was perceived as Carter's great foreign policy victory in the Middle East, the hostages in Iran would become his greatest debacle.

In January 1977 the truth of our first option seemed most evident in Iran. If there were a strong, stable, loyal, and dependable ally in the world it would have to be the Shah. He had been on the throne for more than 35 years. He now seemed to have money for all the development projects that might come to mind (actually he was already financially strapped); he understood his people; all signals were go. The last moment when this view of Iran and the Shah could be spoken even halfway convincingly turned out to be a year later, in Tehran on New Year's Eve, when Carter, in a champagne toast, praised the Shah's love for his people and his efforts to democratize his regime. Nine days later major demonstrations in Iranian cities touched off a violent confrontation between the Shah and his beloved people. Although few knew it at the time, it was the beginning of the end for the Shah and his government (and probably for his dynasty as well).

How did it all come about? Without a thousand pages to detail it all, let us note a few key factors. To begin with Iran was a very complex nation of ethnic, religious, and linguistic minorities; it was difficult to glue all this together for very long, at least without stresses and strains. Secondly, in spite of infusions of capital and economic growth, the gap between those who had a very great deal and those who had little widened in the 1970s. It was not that poor peasants made a revolution; it was the simple fact that no economy that must drag a baggage of poor, uneducated, unskilled, and inefficient workers in its wake can become productively modern. Inefficient and unproductive masses of workers impede growth and stability.

A third point was that the Shah had created large numbers of an educated middle class that was not co-opted sufficiently well into the ruling elite. Political participation for the bottom wasn't even cleverly fraudulent; for the rising cadres of wealthy and educated Iranians it wasn't enough. The Shah simply wanted to run it all.

In order to run it all, he had to run it increasingly by force. This is a fourth point. Repression, tough police crackdowns, torture, and murder began to characterize the Iranian political process. This was aggravated by Carter's constant insistence that human rights were important and that things should be opened up and pressures eased. But even the Iranians couldn't imagine a gentle and loving SAVAK.

Without painting in all of the detail, Iran was increasingly under pressure from the radical left. After all, there was enough industrialization to produce a proletariat and enough education to create leaders. A communist movement had been in Iran since the Second World War and had had a big moment in the early 1950s. By the late 1970s their numbers had become significantly large. They were hardly monarchists. They were a dangerous element in the already flammable mix. And the most dangerous of the leftists were the Marxist guerrilla groups, not the old remnants of the Tudeh party. The new guerrilla groups expected violence and were prepared for it.

Last (although there are many other points to make) there was religion. Iran is predominently Shi'ite Muslim. Iranians are sometimes called Twelvers, in the sense that they believe in the existence and guidance of twelve Imams (beginning with Ali), the last of whom disappeared or went into occultation in the tenth century. It is believed that this last Imam will someday return. In the meantime, ordinary Muslims accept guidance from *mul-*

lahs on the village level and then from increasingly pure and inspirational leaders, possessed of religious knowledge. The latter are called *mujtahids,* but they sort out into practical hierarchical levels of which the top is the ayatollah (literally meaning the manifestation of God). There are a number of ayatollahs in Iran, perhaps as many as 150 today. Each has a following, students, protégés and devotees. Some are more successful than others; some, more able. Although a few years ago the Ayatollah Ruhollah Khomeini would not have been thought Iran's leading religious figure, the last few years of the Shah's rule elevated him to a predominant position. In exile in France he carried out a well-financed and well-organized attempt to overthrow the Shah. He turned out to be the single most important opposition leader.

Shahs and ayatollahs normally need each other. Both are traditional objects, and the authority of one can be used to bolster the authority of the other. The history of Iran, certainly during the Qajar and Pahlavi dynasties, can be written in terms of the interplay of religious and political leadership. Mohammed Reza Shah Pahlavi was not unaware of the need for religious backing, yet by 1970 he perceived the religious leaders as the last pocket of an opposition that could be destroyed. His attempts to do this were catastrophic. At the same time, the structure of modern Iran that he was building was increasingly an anathema to religious leaders; it is difficult to challenge the logic of their position. More and more they opposed the Shah and his policies. By 1978 the point of no return had been reached.

The American Embassy compound in Tehran is a huge and imposing edifice. The embassy was the center of normal diplomatic activity, but it also was involved with senior military advisors and various intelligence operatives. In terms of quantity of observations and quality of observers, the United States should have been well informed as to conditions in Iran. But somehow whatever information there was did not move rapidly and accurately to those who had to assess the situation in Washington. But let us also state the obvious. Embassies are like any other bureaucratic animals. They will generally report what they perceive their superiors want to hear; Washington always wanted an optimistic appraisal of the Shah's chances.

At any rate, we misjudged the situation terribly. Whatever individual-serving officials knew or guessed about Iran, collectively we did not have an effective mechanism for judging events there. The failure of course had to rest with the president, but he had been badly served by the CIA and other intelligence agenices, by the State Department and by the Joint Chiefs and their subordinates. We had sent too many foreign service and intelligence personnel to Iran who were ignorant of language and culture. Too many of these cultivated the old contacts who told them what they wanted to hear. Supportive messages were sent to Washington. And when occasional cables of dissent were received in Washington, they seemed immediately to be discounted and their messages smothered. Official Washington at least believed that the Shah could not fall.

As 1978 dragged through its weary course, considerable doubts arose in the United States as to the wisdom of the traditional judgment. Carter tried at least to be exposed to new ideas. George Ball, that foreign policy gadfly of recent years, was consulted. He consulted others in turn, including the doubting academics. But by late 1978, it was too late for policy changes to be effective. The situation in Iran would have to run its course.

By mid-1978 the Shah was indeed in trouble. Upper-class and upper-middle-class Iranians were already in flight. Along with them went capital. A point of this kind, indicating the domestic loss of confidence in the likelihood of a government's survival, makes its downfall even more likely. Public order had broken down. The Shah had no new ideas. He began shuffling ministers; in late 1978 he installed an all-military government; finally he turned to an old opposition leader, Shapour Bakhtiar, to form a government. He also threw some of his old supporters to the wolves, including his old hard-line SAVAK chief, General Nassire, and his devoted prime minister of many years, Amir Abbas Hoveyda. He released some political prisoners. He insisted that he was investigating corruption; he promised a new order. His police and soldiers still hassled people on the streets, however, and many were killed. In the meantime, the never-ending cry for the Shah's end came from Paris, and at last it was heeded.

The United States faced several immediate problems when the Shah fled Iran. If a stable successor government could be formed, the United States wanted to salvage something from the mess. If not, we would need to evacuate military men and some of the sophisticated military equipment that we had sold to the Shah; it ought not to fall into unfriendly hands. There was the shadow of a possible military coup; American General Robert Huyser's hurried trip to Iran in January 1979 is still not fully explained, but possibly he was there to discourage the Iranian generals from intervening; probably his job was to assess the situation and, if possible, to keep the Iranian military forces intact. In the long run we had to devise—as we must today—some policy to deal with an unfriendly successor government. It was already apparent that the United States was to become the scapegoat for all that was wrong in Iran. Carter soon became a born-again Satan for Iran.

We soon displayed an unwillingness to accept the Shah as a political refugee. We had accepted a motley collection of tennis players, ballet dancers and others, and large numbers of Russian Jews as political refugees, but our old friend the Shah, on whom we had lavished so much praise and help, was turned aside. The Carter administration was also eager—perhaps this is too strong a word—to prevent the Iranian military from mounting a coup. How close Iran came then to a coup is not known, but could a coup *without* the Shah have succeeded? General Huyser was indeed sent to Iran to do something: Check on the safety of F-14s or urge the generals to play it cool. Whatever, the generals played it cool; moreover they could hardly count on the rank and file. Those later shot by the revolutionary government perhaps had regrets.

The United States Embassy, with Ambassador Sullivan on hand, was overrun in February 1979. Those storming it were said to be leftists. They smashed and looted the embassy for some hours before surrendering it to the police. The United States, of course, protested this unseemly behavior, but accepted the assurances of the government (that of Bazargan now, but always in the shadow of Khomeini) that the embassy would not be molested again. So the embassy remained and an American patchwork policy of working with the new government continued.

In Iran itself, many things deteriorated in the months to come. There were hurried trials of the many henchmen of the Shah, at least those who could be found. Some of the trials were rather summary, and there seemed to be few rights for the accused. Daily life began to change in many ways. Also, divisions quickly appeared among those who, together, had brought down the Shah. The Kurds arose and demanded independence. In the meantime, the Shah shuttled from Egypt to Morocco to the Bahamas to Mexico, and a price was put on his head. But he was already a dying man.

The decision by the United States to allow the Shah to come to the United States for medical treatment was an example of the unfortunate lack of consistency in policy making. We had refused the Shah asylum. Now we let him in, ostensibly for a brief time. The Carter administration claimed that we had informed Iran of this humanitarian gesture and was genuinely shocked at the reaction that it produced. But it was an attempt to have and eat cake—and it didn't work.

Perhaps the embassy would ultimately have been overrun anyway. There is no way to know. But now, using the Shah's trip to the United States as an excuse, "students"—the kind that rarely attend classes—stormed the embassy in early November and subjected it and its occupants to the usual indignities. The hostages—there were 72 of them—were for the most part to be held in Iran for over a year, being released on Reagan's inaugural day.

This was to be Carter's nightmare. Carter himself, it seemed, became emotionally involved in the personal fate of the hostages who were, we should all recall, professionals who were voluntarily in a dangerous and troubled place. It does not lessen their courage or our concern for their fate when we say simply that in this world hostages at that level are expendable; a whole nation's interests should not be overlooked in the efforts to rescue individuals.

But it is easier to state that here—on a random page of a random book—than it was for Jimmy Carter, whose natural instincts about this were different and whose political future depended upon what he did.

It would not be easy to rescue them in any case. The American Embassy in downtown Tehran was not Entebbe, Uganda. Nor did we act promptly; perhaps we could not have. The rescue mission, when it came in 1980, was a disaster: There are those who felt that if it could have continued it would have succeeded. Perhaps. But it is unlikely. It was almost—perhaps not quite—impossible to rescue the hostages by force and with safety to them and their rescuers. Diplomacy and other techniques would have to be used. The United States literally pulled out all the stops. Iranian assets were frozen, commercial transactions halted, threats of one kind or another made;

the PLO was enlisted, and world leaders pressured Iran to give way. But nothing succeeded. Iran was, in fact, immune to most of our threats because they did not address the real world in which the Iranians lived; an 80-year-old ayatollah who was convinced that Carter was Satan could hardly be moved easily.

Yet the pressure ultimately mounted, and the hostages themselves became an embarrassment to Iran. An agreement was finally put together, but in the time that it took to do this Carter was defeated for the presidency, and another Satan was about to take his place.

If Carter had some control over events relating to the Camp David process, he never had control over anything relating to the fall of the Shah and the chaos that followed. But regardless, it was a failure of American foreign policy.

Iraq remains to be mentioned. At one time Iraq—or at least its leadership—was strongly pro-Western. But after the revolution beginning in 1958, it became anti-Western, unstable, and erratic. but it was an oil state. Ultimately it came to relatively friendly terms with the Soviet Union. Over the years it continued to bicker with Iran. It threatened Kuwait openly and Saudi Arabia, perhaps, by suggestion. Its present ruler (late 1982) Saddam Hussein is an aggressive, ambitious leader. The United States has treated Iraq as an unfriendly state and has not had diplomatic relations with it.

And yet Iraq isn't so simply described. It continued to sell oil to the West during the oil boycott in 1973, and it has made a number of overtures to the United States that have either been misunderstood or disregarded. We have thought of Iraq as part of the problem; perhaps it could have been part of the solution.[3]

For the Carter administration it was the events in Iran that threw the Iraqi part of the world into sharper focus. We could, on the one hand, see Soviet pincers (using Iraq as one prong) snatching up the oil fields of Iran. We could also see an attempt by Iraq to expand its own space and control now that its traditional enemy was prostrate. This it did in September of 1980 when it attacked Iran across the Shatt al-Arab. The war has been undecisive with the disorganized Iranians doing better than anyone expected and the Iraqis suffering embarrassment. Iraqi hegemony in the Persian Gulf is a little less imminent. The war itself had to be dealt with by the United States; we proclaimed our neutrality. There is soft evidence, however, that we did in fact aid Iraq—and perhaps Iran too!—with military supplies (probably through Jordan), while our friend Israel helped Iran with supplies. Wars, as well as politics, make strange bedfellows.

THE CARTER RECORD

Planes crash for reasons other than pilot error; the failure of a policy may not necessarily be attributed in whole or even in part to the incumbent president.

---

[3] It is only fair to add that many specialists on the area dissent from this view.

Much is made of presidential freedom in foreign policy, but even in this area the president is encumbered with many inputs possessing their own constituencies. It is not easy to initiate real change very quickly.

At any rate, with this reminder, we must simply admit that with the partial exception of Camp David; the Carter years were those of sad humiliation in the Middle East. Those things that we wanted most did not come to pass generally; those we did not seemed to be smashing successes.

In the Gulf and east of it there were three major failures. They were, chronologically: (1) the coup overthrowing Bhutto in Pakistan; (2) the collapse of the Shah, with the resulting disappearance of the main support nation in the Middle East; and (3) the Russian invasion and occupation of Afghanistan.

These failures were not of equal importance. It is likely that something has been (and will be) salvaged from the Pakistan situation. The death of Bhutto is regrettable, but Zia or his successors no doubt can be dealt with. Rank ordering the other two is more difficult, but possibly, had the Shah not fallen, the Soviets might not have invaded Afghanistan. This suggests that the "Russians in Afghanistan" is the worst scenario once the Shah had fallen, and conceivably the result of that fall. Over the long run this may require reevaluation, with the most important long-run effect: the Russian occupation of Afghanistan. This would assume some reconstruction of sorts in Iran, with which we could deal. It must be recalled that, given time and wisdom enough to make the necessary adjustments, most things in international politics can be lived with.

But any way they are viewed, these three events mark a failure of American policy. It was primarily a failure to anticipate; it was also a failure to support; and it was a failure to respond. The events in Pakistan were there for everyone to read clearly. Bhutto should have been supported economically and politically in order for him to survive as the only viable nonmilitary national leader, not because he was a possible counter to India or that his military forces might rescue Afghanistan or support Iran. We have always tended to inflate Pakistan's ability to perform international acts; had we wanted a real military partner we should have chosen India. Pakistan is important because of its location; even now the main path of succor to the Afghans is through Pakistan. It was the right flank, and we needed a reliable stable regime there. Perhaps Bhutto would have fallen despite our support, but at the time we did not do enough, and the object of our efforts there collapsed.

The Shah and Iran were of immense importance to us. Literally all of our Gulf plans assumed a friendly and stable Iran. Its neutralization was bad enough; its long-run enmity could conceivably wipe out all viable attempts to deal with the two fundamental phases of our policy there: to secure the oil and to keep out the Russians. There were signals in Iran about the weakness of the Shah for those who could read them, but it is only fair to say that few predicted the speed with which he would leave the Peacock Throne once the trouble began. But whoever or whatever is to blame, we did not really *see* the collapse of the regime in Iran, and we had laid no suitable contingency plans for that event. We acted bewildered; the assumption was that we were. We temporized and contradicted ourselves; it was not the way of a great power. And when the hostages were seized all else seemed subordinate to them. No doubt President Carter was sincerely gratified by their ultimate safe return, but for the whole mess in Iran he could surely derive not a scintilla of satisfaction. Although American policy in regard to Iran was only slightly of his making, he was the one who paid the piper.

The fall of Iran certainly jeopardized the flow of oil. The Iran-Iraq war threatened it seriously. We have survived these crises not so much because of determined policy as because of the inexorable flow of events there. (Nevertheless, Carter had enunciated an energy policy for the nation, and the facts show that we have learned to conserve—a little). The Saudis, Iraqis, and Iranians as well as others have wanted to sell their oil and have found ways to do so. Moreover, a world oil glut has made the Iranian and then the Iraqi shortfalls of little significance to the rest of the world.

The Russians in Afghanistan! The very thought has sent shivers through Pentagon corridors for years. And now they were there. Again Carter can hardly be blamed for a generation or more of policy toward Afghanistan or for the more recent Khalq-Parcham ideological minuets. But it took place with the devil's luck in Carter's administration and there was not much of a way in getting them out. (In late 1982 they are still being denounced for being there.)

The world has learned to live with this, so, no doubt, will the United States. If American policy failure is to blame, it took place a long time ago. It is not unfair to say that Afghanistan had been written off as being under Soviet influence *before* Carter arrived on the presidential scene, but to have the physical presence of Soviet troops there was too much.

Perhaps naively we should ask why the Russians did it. The logic for their actions is not that inescapable. Of course we know that they miscalculated. They could not have counted on the resistance that they found among the Afghans. But even assuming swift success, which they did not get, why did they want to be in Afghanistan? Perhaps it was concern over the contagion of religious fundamentalism among their own Central Asian republics. I do not subscribe to the common Haigistic explanation that the Russians are ever seeking new peoples to mismanage (or misgovern) and new lands on which to implant an unsuccessful agriculture. They were hardly endangered by Pakistan or Afghanistan or Iran for that matter. Afghanistan has no port on the Indian Ocean. It has resources, to be sure, but the Russians could have acquired them without the expense of a 110,000-man occupation army. Of course if they were determined to get on with it, December 1979 was quite a good time. But I remain inclined to believe that it was a Russian mistake, for which they too have paid a price.

Nevertheless, to Carter and to Reagan after him this was no solace. Now there was another state, albeit far away, poor and somewhat inconsequential, over which the hammer and sickle fluttered, if not proudly at least defiantly.

Other than these three major areas of extreme disappointment, we maintained our connection with the Saudis and were now worried about their defense. We established good relations with the Omanis. We did not openly woo the Iraqis, but behind the scenes we gave them some support. Our connection with the Ayatollah continued to be filled with static.

All in all, the Carter years were a failure in the Gulf area. It was a failure compounded by many things and in some ways quite inevitable. But Carter was in the Oval Office, and the buck stopped there.

THE REAGAN ADMINISTRATION AND ITS OPTIONS

Ronald Reagan, like Carter, was an outsider when he came to Washington; like Carter again, there was little evidence that he had any expertise in foreign relations. His own campaign was strongly connected with the domestic front, the economy in particular. But on one thing he was certain: We are faced with a deadly Russian foe who would stop at nothing to defeat us. The corollary to this was that we need to beef up our defense, rattle the saber, and stand up for what we believe. To help him do these things he asked Alexander Haig, Jr., an old Kissinger protégé, to be his Secretary of State. The White House was to be downplayed; someone named Richard Allen was to be there. At Defense would be Caspar Weinberger. The Reagan team had been in existence for nearly two years when Haig was benched in the summer of 1982 in favor of George Schultz. Reagan's foreign policy has been vigorously criticized, and his interest in it and control over it have been strongly challenged during this period.

While the bulk of Reagan's foreign policy lies outside the span of this chapter, we can sum up what seems to be the theme. There are two parts to it. The first is a passionate obsession with the Russians. The second is an equally passionate conviction that there are military solutions to the problems facing the United States, thus proving that we learned nothing from the lessons of the Carter years.[4]

Reagan entered the presidency when the hostages returned from Iran. He had nothing to do with getting them in or out, but he basked in the aura of their return. In the spring of 1981, Haig visited the Israeli part of the Middle East and—like a spring shower forcing desert flowers into bloom—Haig's visit seemed to catalyze Israelis, Syrians, and Palestinians into flexing their muscles. Threats, troop movements, and raids began in a big way, and soon Philip Habib, veteran American diplomat, was shuttling back and forth trying to establish a ceasefire in Lebanon. But there was the Israeli election at the end of June. At first Begin was trailing in the polls, but tough stands,

---

[4]More accurately, one should say that Reagan has talked a good military line; he has yet to act (November 1982).

perhaps, helped to rebuild his party bloc and his chances. He took out some insurance by bombing the Iraqi nuclear facility in May (and ensuring that Iraq would probably never support a Camp David process or a Saudi peace plan). It was grating to Reagan, of course, but there was little he could do except remonstrate and symbolically delay delivery—for a few weeks—of several F-15s to Israel. The Israelis followed this adventure with another, blasting Beirut and killing some 300 or more Lebanese. It was Reagan's introduction to what it meant to be Israel's ally: a trying situation for any American president. But he seemed to take some satisfaction from the cessation of fighting in Lebanon and considered it an accomplishment for his new administration. The Israelis continued to rattle their sabers, however, and in June attacked Lebanon, forcing their way ultimately into Beirut. Their purposes were to destroy the PLO military forces if possible; to expel the Syrians from Lebanon; and to put up, support, and agree to peace with a Lebanese Christian government led by the Phalangists. But something happened on the way to Baalbek. Too many people (perhaps as many as 20,000) were killed: Palestinians, Lebanese, Syrians, both military and civilian. A Lebanese president-elect was assassinated, and a massacre at refugee camps near Beirut by Phalangist Christians produced a grave crisis in Israeli domestic affairs as well as a revulsion against Israel over much of the world. American marines landed, and Reagan finally enunciated a vague plan for solving the Palestinian problem.

Back in 1981 Qadhafi was causing problems, so plans to give the Libyans a whiff of grapeshot in the Gulf of Sirte were carried out in August. That seemed to work well tactically at least. Sadat certainly was our friend (conventional wisdom suggested) and Egypt was the center of our strategic presence in the Middle East. Israel wanted to be a part of this, too, and got some sort of assurance in late November; Saudi Arabia was less certain, but it wanted its AWACs. The proposed sale of five of these electronic surveillance planes to Saudi Arabia (first deliveries in 1986) drew into Washington a fantastic array of domestic and foreign lobbies. Enormous pressure was put on the Senate by Reagan to obtain his 52 to 48 victory in October. When it ended it was difficult to determine a winner, but somehow it was intended to mark a new era of Saudi-American relations.

In October Sadat was killed in Cairo by religious fanatics, and Hosni Mubarak became his successor. Sadat's death was the serious loss of an Arab leader who had taken the time to understand America, yet his departure might open up new avenues of policy. What would be the new role of Egypt? How would this affect Arab unity in general? Would it make room for Saudi leadership?

In the summer, the Saudis proposed an eight-point peace plan for the Arab-Israeli dispute. Shouldered aside then, it resurfaced in November and aroused all sorts of controversy in Israel, among the Arabs, and in the United States. The Saudi plan marks an attempt by the Saudi leadership to assert themselves in other than Gulf problems. (The Reagan plan and, later, the Fez plan were not very different from the Saudi plan.)

In December 1981 Operation Brightstar began. Americans (in their new role as rapid deployment forcemen) landed in Egypt and Oman and illustrated to the Russians, at least, that we could move fast and effectively.

As Reagan entered his third year in the presidency, he faced the following conditions in the Gulf region:

1. For the moment there was no sense of oil urgency. There was a glut of oil with production cutbacks and OPEC price instability.
2. A prosperous Saudi Arabia continued its traditional role and maintained its traditional friendship with the United States. Still, it appeared to be hedging its bets by establishing new foreign contacts and patching up old quarrels (for example, the Iraqi border settlement in December 1980).
3. The Iraq-Iran war was essentially stalemated.
4. The government in Iran, although wildly erratic and unstable, was turned inward and concerned with its domestic problems.
5. The Russian military, although bogged down in establishing complete control over the Afghans, was, nevertheless, present in Afghanistan.
6. The government in Pakistan, led by General Zia, was temporarily stable.

In concocting policy for these conditions, what assumptions must we make over the next two years? (1) Over a two-year period it is unlikely that the world oil situation will deteriorate drastically. In the United States there has also been some success in conservation. Oil will continue to be amply available, although pricing will be uncertain. Oil from the Gulf itself, although not absolutely secure, seems to be safe enough for this period. (2) King Fahd will retain his dominence over a relatively stable government in Saudi Arabia, although in a longer run the stability of that government is highly questionable. The Saudis will continue to be dominant in OPEC. Their relations with the United States will continue to be normal. They will cautiously attempt to play a greater role in Arab politics. (3) It probably will take Mubarak in Egypt close to two years to stabilize his own position domestically. Certainly he did not do anything to jeopardize the return of Sinai in April 1982. Egypt will gradually play a greater role in general Arab affairs. (4) The Iran-Iraq war will come to some negotiated end with the status quo ante largely restored. But this will be perceived to be a loss for Saddam Hussein, whose control in Iraq for the next two years seems very much weakened. At the very least, Saddam will have been damaged domestically. His relations with the Soviet Union and the United States are somewhat up for grabs. (5) In Iran, the next two years may see the end of the Ayatollah Khomeini, if for no other reason than actuarial necessity. Nevertheless, it seems likely that religious extremism will characterize Iran throughout Reagan's administration, whatever happens to Khomeini. Iran itself will ultimately become a major crisis area, with various groups struggling for power. Conventional wisdom says that some parts of the army—buoyed by success in its war with Iraq—will prevail, but the Mujahidin Khalq is very strong in Iran. Part of the assumption relating to Iran is its undoubted continuing importance to the United States. (6) The Russians will continue in one form or another to occupy Afghanistan over the next two or three years. (7) General Zia in Pakistan will probably be under strong pressure sometime over two years, with a good chance that he will be replaced by another general officer. (8) There may well be military probings by South Yemen against the western portion of Oman.

The interests that we profess remain the same, coupled with these assumptions: to contain—admittedly a shopworn word—the Russians, to protect the oil, and, within these perimeters, to support the stability of the region.

What are the options for the remainder of the Reagan term? Let me preface my response to these with some general comments. When we talk of protecting Gulf oil we must always ask "Protect from whom?" At the moment the Gulf states are anxious to sell oil, and they themselves want it protected. It is important to note that after the early destructive raids on each other's oil installations, both Iraq and Iran have been careful to avoid excessive damage. Each is vulnerable. In this example of the Iran-Iraq war, how could the United States intervene to protect the oil fields? It would take some doing. It is not altogether obvious that the Soviet Union wants the oil destroyed either, although it is fairly evident that in the future the Soviet Union may want a greater share of the Gulf output. Certainly unlikely is an overt Soviet attack in the fields. More likely and more plausible would be a subversion of Iran internally in which the control of the Iranian fields would be tipped in a Soviet direction. How do we deal with this? Containing the Russians also brings up some weighty problems. We should recall our geography. Turkey, Iran, and Afghanistan lie along Russia's southern border; with the capture of Afghanistan, Pakistan also becomes a neighbor. Although Russian naval units in the Indian ocean currently have a long way to *sail* home, so do American vessels. A penetration of the Baluchi[5] part of southern Pakistan by the Russians—assuming the pacification of Afghanistan—changes the entire geopolitical position of the United States and Russia so far as the gulf is concerned. How would we respond to this? The above-mentioned subversion in Iran offers the Soviet Union many opportunities, and again immediate and effective American responses are difficult to formulate.

Reagan faces a much more flammable Gulf than did Carter, but what will happen is another matter. We must roll with the punches on oil pricing and oil production, offering at least the appearance of understanding and cooperation. Cheap oil in any event is definitely *not* to our advantage, and we should not expend political resources in trying to keep prices down.

We should continue to support the current Saudi system; it is difficult to discover what or whom to support. But we should have contingencies for

---

[5] It is of interest that the rank and file of the Omani army are largely Baluchis.

a severe crisis in Saudi Arabia, or a collapse of the system. If not immediately probable, it is at least possible. We should make every effort to keep abreast of the events, to understand them, and, above all, not to assume that everything that happens is the result of Russian activity.

We should not arm the Saudis in the way that we armed Iran. There will be severe domestic pressures both ways, of course, but sound policy would indicate going slowly on the militarization of Saudi Arabia.

We should not encourage Saudi leadership roles. They are *not* the natural leaders of the current Arab world. The most logical player of this role is Egypt, and we should attempt to get Mubarak and the Egyptians back in the Arab family. In that family, Egypt will play its part. This does not mean an abandonment of Egypt's peace with Israel, but it probably means the scuttling of the Camp David process for any further implementation of peace negotiations. To underline the theme of this paragraph, imagine the situation in which a highly visible, American-backed Saudi regime, attempting to lead the Arab world, collapses at home. We would have lost a great deal.

We should encourage, in what ways we can, the final ending of the war between Iran and Iraq. We should make overtures to Iraq, but should never forget that Iran is the most important country in the Gulf.

Nations cannot afford to get bogged down in considerations of "blame," "gratitude," "friendship," "honor," and so on when dealing with one another. The United States and Iran have much to gain from a new relationship. The past is not too relevant, and we should not let our memory of hostages cloud our good judgment about the importance of Iran (with or without the ayatollahs). We should speed up the current process of sorting out financial claims against each other; if necessary we should waive many of our own claims. We should help Iran get some sort of a system going rather than attempting to punish it for past transgressions. A rapprochement with Iran is needed, and we should set about getting it. Would we rather have the Russians there?

Somehow we have to "deal" with the Russian presence in Afghanistan. We can hardly get them out by threats. Perhaps they will not leave at all, yet efforts must be continued to effect their departure. The initiative should come from neighboring Muslim states—in late 1981 Iran and Pakistan suggested a joint peace-keeping force in Afghanistan—and we should support what we must. Obviously we would prefer a non-Marxist government in Kabul, but even a Marxist one is preferable to one that includes the Soviets. It is the Russian *presence* that is of immediate concern rather than the nature of the government. Whether we like it or not, we must learn to live with Marxist governments in the world. And by foolish policy, we may increase the number of such governments with which we must learn to live.

Much attention is currently given in the United States to a "rapid deployment force." But a brigade or two of men in berets and boots are good for only certain missions. Regardless of presidential rhetoric and Pentagon assurances, such a force—with or without Egyptians, Omanis, and the on-again-off-again Israelis—can hardly conduct any serious military operations in the backyard of the Soviet Union. There is no way to be tough militarily with the Soviet Union, 10,000 miles away from the United States. Thus, such a force is of little value, although it may possess political value.

General Zia in Pakistan is no Marxist, but we have to learn to live with him, too, in spite of warts and political body odor. But he is unstable in any other but the near-term and any policy with Pakistan should be predicated on a possible upheaval and even break-up of the country. And again, as in the case of Saudi Arabia and Iran, we should know what is happening there. Intelligence collecting should be improved and sharpened. (In fact, the first Reagan year was spent arguing the suitability of the CIA's director and the scope of CIA operations.)

As far as Oman and the other small states in the Gulf, their relations with the United States are bound to be somewhat unpredictable and, at the same time, not very significant. It is too early to assess the potential of the Gulf Cooperation Council. Oman, although it cooperated in the Brightstar operation, has real reasons for worrying about its western border with South Yemen. But times, rulers, and conditions change, and little reliance should be put on these states. Interestingly, in November 1981, Saudi Arabia urged Oman not to become too friendly with the United States, in a military sense.

To sum up, President Reagan has some options for the Gulf area, but all present difficulties. It is not easy to build policy for this area with any confidence that it will necessarily work to sustain our interests. In truth, the task facing Reagan is extremely difficult, and it would not be surprising if his administration fails to achieve much there—much, that is, in turning things around. One last word, too, on another part of the Middle East. An unrestrained Israel—overflying Saudi Arabia, invading Lebanon, bombing Iraq—can severely damage otherwise carefully-developed American policy in the Gulf. Somewhere along the line some American government is going to have to control Israel's military adventurism. Perhaps that president will be Reagan, but until that time Israel will be a complicating factor for the United States in the Persian Gulf.

FOR FURTHER READING

Abrahamian, Ervand. *Iran: Between Two Revolutions* (Princeton, N.J.: Princeton University Press, 1982).

Ghareeb, Edmund. *The Kurdish Question in Iraq* (Syracuse, N.Y.: Syracuse University Press, 1981).

Hoagland, Eric J. *Land and Revolution in Iran, 1960–1980* (Austin, Tex.: University of Texas Press, 1982).

Ismael, Jacqueline S. *Kuwait* (Syracuse, N.Y.: Syracuse University Press, 1982).

Ismael, Tareq. *Iraq and Iran: Roots of Conflict* (Syracuse, N.Y.: Syracuse University Press, 1982).

Keddie, Nikki R. *Roots of Revolution: An Interpretive History of Modern Iran* (New Haven, Conn.: Yale University Press, 1981).

Quandt, William B. *Saudi Arabia in the 1980s* (Washington, D.C.: Brookings Institution, 1981).

Saikal, Amin. *The Rise and Fall of the Shah* (Princeton, N.J.: Princeton University Press, 1980).

chapter 6

The United States and Latin America

KARL M. SCHMITT

INTRODUCTION

The Alliance for Progress died in the last year of the Lyndon Johnson presidency. Not only did the bitter debate over the Vietnam War draw attention away from Latin America, but the alliance itself had clearly failed. By 1969 everyone recognized that the United States could not impose democracy in Latin America, that the drive for social reform had stalled, and that the struggle for economic development had produced uneven results. An Agency for International Development (AID) review of the alliance in February 1969 bluntly said that the achievement of the goals set in 1961 could not be accomplished within ten years as the alliance planners had anticipated.

No succeeding administration to date (1983) has attempted to construct an alternative "large policy." True, every administration since 1968 has paid at least lip service to all four of our past "large policies"; the Monroe Doctrine, the Inter-American System, the Good Neighbor Policy, and the Alliance for Progress. But no administration has tried seriously to promote them. Rather, all of the last four administrations have clearly and explicitly stated that such overarching policies made little sense in view of the enormous disparity in size and of the wide variation in historical and cultural traditions of the several countries of the area. Only President Carter seemed to deviate at all from this position with his human rights policy, but even his administration proposed no grand design. Moreover, he applied the policy selectively and with less than well-defined criteria.

Several themes run through the last fifteen years. Each administration has promised to make the U.S. market more accessible to Latin American products, especially manufactures, but none succeeded to any great extent. In fact, Congress passed a more restrictive trade act in 1974 over the objections of the Ford administration. Latin American leaders vigorously protested these restraints and have continued to pressure the United States for more favorable terms, but without success. Latin Americans also object to U.S. application of political criteria (whether for human rights or against left radicalism) to loan requests before multilateral banking institutions such as the Inter-American Development Bank (IDB) and the World Bank (International Bank for Reconstruction and Development—IBRD). They have also been demanding more influence within these banks, international control over multinational corporations (MNCs), and price supports for a variety of raw materials (commodity agreements) through the establishment of a common fund. The United States has consistently opposed these measures, and they remain a constant source of debate and disagreement.

On the question of the amount of U.S. economic and military assistance to the area, the Latin American countries have not raised serious objections. When Congress began to cut back military credits in the late 1960s, the Latin American countries either found other suppliers or began to manufacture their own materials. Throughout the period military grants steadily deteriorated except for small increases in the early 1970s; credit aid fluctuated substantially. In 1968, for the last time, Congress appropriated over $1 billion for direct economic assistance to Latin America. With some variation, the amount steadily declined until 1977 when it reached a low of $350 million; by 1980 it had climbed again, but to only $500 million. The deterioration has gone far beyond the apparent level, given the high rates of inflation in the United States. In place of direct loans from the United States they have turned in the last decade, first, to the multilateral funding institutions and, secondly, to the private banks in the United States and Europe. The Nixon administration stimulated substantial increases to the international lending agencies from the United States, Europe, and Japan; succeeding administrations continued the policy. Consequently the amount of capital available to Latin America for development purposes did not decline, but increased. But the external public debt grew enormously, from about $20 billion in 1970 to nearly $300 billion by 1983. During 1982 the Mexican economy suffered serious reverses as the price of petroleum dropped on world markets. As the peso plunged and capital fled the country, the government faced the prospect of debt default. Drastic monetary reforms and emergency aid from the United States staved off collapse, but Mexico entered 1983 with serious economic problems.

A variety of political and security themes have also persisted through the era. U.S.-Cuban relations and Soviet activities in Cuba have troubled

U.S. relations with the rest of Latin America and provoked internal political disputes within the United States. Every president has talked of easing tensions with Cuba, but each ran into difficulties. At one point it appeared that President Ford was about to take a major step toward renewing relations, but the intervention of Cuban troops in the Angolan civil war brought talks to a halt. President Carter negotiated the establishment of "interest sections" in each capital, but further steps ceased with reports of Soviet combat troops in the island. The Reagan administration in early 1982 showed alarm over Cuban-based Russian strategic bombers and criticized the Castro regime for giving arms to guerrilla forces in El Salvador. In the late 1970s, civil conflict resulted in the overthrow of the Somoza dictatorship in Nicaragua and the military government in El Salvador. In both countries the United States tried to find a politically centrist solution. Carter failed in Nicaragua to prevent the Sandinistas from taking power, but he—and Reagan so far—prevented the rebels from seizing control of El Salvador. U.S. efforts to intervene in these conflicts have created dissension in Latin America. Mexico has objected vehemently to U.S. policy, but other countries have supported the search for a middle path between radical nationalists and the reactionary old guard. With respect to the Panama Canal, the first three administrations all pushed vigorously to conclude an acceptable treaty. Carter placed great importance on this issue and at one point personally intervened to break a deadlock. His administration saw a successful conclusion to long years of negotiation, and he pushed vigorously for the ratification of the treaty over strenuous opposition. Ronald Reagan, as presidential candidate, severely criticized the treaty, but as president has taken no action to rescind it or in any way impede its implementation.

On the security question, the Reagan administration confronted a situation not faced in living memory: armed conflict between a European and a Western Hemisphere nation. On April 2, 1982 Argentine military forces seized the British colony of the Falkland Islands (called the Malvinas in Latin America) in the south Atlantic. Argentina had long claimed the islands, but negotiations with Great Britain seemed stalemated. "Experts" offered a variety of explanations as to why the Argentine military government chose that particular time to strike, including: to distract national attention from serious economic and political problems at home; to face the British with a fait accompli with the expectation of British compliance; to win at least U.S. neutrality (if not support), given Argentine assistance to U.S. objectives in Central America. Whatever the motivations and calculations of the Argentine regime, the Argentine people initially responded enthusiastically to the seizure. The British, however, dispatched a military force within three days and, when attempts for a peaceful solution failed, undertook military operations on sea and land with material and moral support from the United States. On June 14 all Argentine forces surrendered. Every Latin American country supported (and supports) Argentina's claim to the islands, although many disapproved of its military action. Virtually all Latin American countries were dismayed by U.S. support of Great Britain even though they understood the vital nature of the U.S.-British alliance. By the end of 1982, damage to U.S.-Latin American relations appeared minimal as a consequence of the Falkland Islands war.

Other issues that confronted all four presidents included mass migration of peoples into the United States, the drug traffic from Latin America, nuclear nonproliferation, and disputes over territorial waters and fishing rights. None of these were resolved and continued to be subjects of negotiation. Despite years of study and internal debate, the United States has not been able to adopt a migration policy that will satisfy even minimally the several contending political forces within the United States, much less satisfy the government of Mexico, whose people form the largest single group of migrants. Drug policy, on the other hand, has created few difficulties, but implementation is at best sporadic. The millions of dollars involved in drugs tempt thousands of smugglers in the United States and abroad, including high government officials in Latin America and drug traffic enforcers in the United States. At best, the traffic has been slowed. U.S. attempts to prevent the production of weapons-grade plutonium in nuclear power plants in Latin America have not succeeded very well. Although President Ford took a hard-line approach in stopping the export of U.S. technology, Carter softened U.S. criticism of Brazilian developments, and Reagan has demonstrated little concern with further proliferation in Argentina and Mexico as well as in Brazil. Territorial waters long troubled U.S. relations with many Latin American countries. During the 1970s, however, the United States, out of self protection, established a 200-mile fishing conservation zone and concluded treaties with Mexico, Cuba, and Venezuela over Gulf of Mexico and Pacific Ocean maritime boundaries. Under pressure from tuna fishermen in California, however, every administration has refused to recognize tuna as coming within the 200-mile jurisdiction set up by several Latin American Pacific coast countries. Consequently, U.S. tuna fishers refuse to seek licenses to fish within the zones, violate local laws, and frequently find themselves under arrest and subject to fines. These disputes led to the abrogation of fishing treaties with Mexico in late 1980. Despite these unresolved problems, they have not yet produced serious altercations in U.S.-Latin American relations; migration, drugs, and fishing are all subject to almost continuous talks and negotiations.

In sum, relations between the United States and Latin America during the last decade and a half have been rather amicable. Tensions and differences certainly exist, but most of these are subject to negotiation and compromise. No country, not even Cuba and Nicaragua, wants to break completely with the United States. Castro has given numerous indications of a willingness to restore relations, but at a price, of course. The Sandinistas and the rebels of El Salvador have also made overtures to the U.S. government for negotiations and compromise. Suspicion in the U.S. Congress over the intent and goals of these forces and the hard-line attitude of the Reagan administration make this issue the most serious area of contention in 1983. On the other hand, the successful conclusion of the Panama Canal Treaties;

the availability of capital for development in Latin America; and the willingness of the United States in recent years to listen, to talk, and to negotiate
have prevented the differences from flaring into the kinds of confrontation
that we saw in the 1920s and 1950s. Perhaps in the long run the most serious
problem in inter-American relations consists of the difficulty most Latin
American nations may have in paying off their enormous external debts.
Part of the solution to that problem will be access to the U.S. market for
their exports, the proceeds of which may be used to pay those debts. Undoubtedly these matters will continue to be subjects of hard negotiation.

THE NIXON ADMINISTRATION

When Richard Nixon took office in January 1969, Latin American policy did
not constitute one of the priorities of his administration. The Alliance for
Progress, criticized from all quarters, was by then virtually defunct; Nixon's
experience in the area eleven years before, when he was vice-president in
the Eisenhower administration, had simply confirmed his negative views on
Third World nationalism and state-controlled economies so evident in the region. Early on, he gave lip service to continued U.S. support for economic
development, but seemingly he bought time for himself with two moves
before announcing the main thrust of his policy position. First, he encouraged the leaders of Latin America to meet together to draw up an
agenda and a set of proposals to serve as guidelines for U.S.-Latin American
relations. Second, he commissioned Nelson Rockefeller, with a high-
powered team of some twenty experts and advisers, to visit and report on
conditions in every country in Latin America and the Caribbean. Only after
receiving the recommendations of these two groups did Nixon indicate the
direction that his administration would take toward Latin America.

Quickly picking up on Nixon's suggestion for a common front, Brazil
and Chile invited all Latin American countries except Cuba to send representatives to Viña del Mar, Chile, to draw up a joint economic policy statement. In several sessions they formulated some 35 proposals, the main
thrust of which called on the United States to provide improved conditions
for trade and aid. There was little new in a program that called for commodity agreements to stabilize prices; expansion of Latin American exports into
the U.S. market through trade preferences; greater loan benefits through the
easing of terms, the lifting of purchase restrictions, and the lowering of
shipping costs; and greater access to technology with fewer restraints. The
emphasis on technology transfer was relatively new, but the other proposals
with their implied "special relationship" of hemisphere countries were simply refurbished old issues.

Just a few days before the Latin American gathering at Viña del Mar,
the Rockefeller group set off on the first of four trips. Covering Mexico,
Central America, and Panama in a whirlwind tour of nine days, the team
started off, auspiciously enough, encountering serious student demonstrations only in Honduras and Nicaragua. More serious trouble developed as

the mission moved into other areas. The Peruvian government rejected the planned visit on May 23 when the United States announced the cancellation of arms sales and the withdrawal of the U.S. military mission in response to Peruvian-claimed territorial waters. More damaging, Venezuela canceled the visit on June 1, while the team was on its Andean tour (May 27 to June 2). In addition, strong protest demonstrations appeared in Colombia, Ecuador, and Bolivia, so serious in the last that the interviews had to be cut short. Only in the last stop at Trinidad and Tobago did the group receive a warm welcome. In the Southern Cone violence and threats greeted Rockefeller everywhere except in Paraguay; Chile, like Venezuela, canceled the visit at the last minute because of strikes and other forms of violence. In the last trip through the Caribbean, the reception was mixed. Haiti, Jamaica, and Barbados welcomed the team without incident; Guyana kept order through tight security measures; the Dominican Republic broke out in violent demonstrations.

The hostility encountered proved to be a sobering experience for Rockefeller and his associates, but they emerged from it with a positive, although not particularly innovative, program. In submitting their report, "Quality of Life in the Americas," to President Nixon early in September they portrayed a sense of urgency and crisis in Latin American affairs. Rapid change, rising nationalism, spiraling inflation, injustice, poverty, and violence all presented challenges to the United States, they said, to find new ways to help these societies and to give them an example of how free societies can resolve their own problems. Stressing partnership and cooperation between the United States and Latin America, another variant of the "special relationship," the Rockefeller report paralleled the consensus reached at Viña del Mar in several specifics. It recommended commodity agreements, tariff preferences, rescheduling of debts with lowered interest rates and more lenient repayment terms, and the repeal of various restrictions on aid. The report differed from the consensus, however, in that it recommended increased military assistance and maximum encouragement to private investment.

With these two documents in hand, Richard Nixon made his first general policy statement on Latin America at the end of October in an address at the annual meeting of the Inter-American Press Association. Although it was low key and lacking in details, the statement clearly rejected every one of the main points of the Alliance for Progress. Rather than promote democracy, the president said that the United States would deal with governments as they are; he did not seem to mean, however, that he was willing to accept the Castro regime in Cuba. Rather than encourage and promote social reform, the president said that the United States would not intervene in domestic affairs and that Latin America would advance under its own leadership. And finally, rather than promote economic development under government auspices with comprehensive state planning, the president said that the United States would encourage private enterprise as the proper mode, that U.S. aid programs would support locally owned private business, and that his administration would *not* encourage U.S. investors to risk their capital where it was not wanted. He did, on the other hand, commit his administration to consult with Latin American countries on trade problems, to reduce both tariff and nontariff trade barriers, and to support trade expansion through technological and financial aid. He made one specific promise: to untie aid loans for the Latin American area. This concession was a far cry from the request made at Viña del Mar and from the recommendation of the Rockefeller report, because relatively little development trade was moving within the Latin American area.

In subsequent years, the Nixon administration's general approach to Latin America became further clarified. In presidential statements and in reports by government officials, the terms "low profile," "special relationship," and "mature partnership," repeatedly emerged. In 1971, Assistant Secretary of State Charles Meyer told a House subcommittee that the administration had no general Latin American policy that applied to every country. He called the Alliance for Progress an "unrealistic" program. Moreover, presidential counselor Robert Finch told the American Chamber of Commerce in Buenos Aires that Nixon himself rejected policies such as the Good Neighbor or the Alliance insofar as they lumped all Latin American nations together without differentiation. The administration, therefore, substituted a country-by-country approach and simultaneously began to shift aid funds from direct bilateral relations to the multilateral agencies such as the Inter-American Development Bank and the World Bank. The president himself heralded this latter move as early as February 1970 in his foreign policy speech to Congress. He stressed again, in conjunction with the new approach to loan policy, that the United States should contribute to, but not dominate, development policy in Latin America.

Despite its preoccupation with other areas of the world and its low-profile approach, the Nixon administration had to give continuing attention to day-to-day problems in Latin American relations. Mexico loomed ever more important with thousands, some would say millions, of migrants crossing the border without documents looking for work in the United States; with its enormous petroleum discoveries; and with its growing irritation over maritime boundaries and the salinity of the Colorado River as it crossed into Mexico. Foreign commerce and credit operations affected U.S. relations with virtually every country, U.S. investments and threatened or actual expropriations required attention, the drug traffic constituted a worrisome and worsening problem, military sales provoked debate at home and abroad, and territorial waters and fishing disputes provoked nasty exchanges from time to time with several countries. Negotiations for a new Panama Canal treaty dragged on for months, created a minor crisis in 1973, and were moving toward resolution when Nixon resigned. Finally, perceived security problems focused continued attention on Cuba and its Soviet ties and, from 1971 to 1973, on Chile under the Marxist administration of Salvador Allende. In fact the most critical issue for the Nixon administration in Latin America was relations with Chile.

The Chilean elections of 1970 presented the Nixon administration with a major security question. U.S. interest in Chilean elections dates back at least to the early years of the Alliance for Progress when the Kennedy administration (and later the Johnson administration) saw in the Christian Democrats the kind of moderate reformist party that would cooperate in carrying out social change and economic development under democratic political auspices. In 1964 the Christian Democrats, with money funneled by the CIA into campaign coffers, won an impressive victory. By 1970, however, the Christian Democratic president, Eduardo Frei, and his party had lost much popular support and suffered a defection of the left wing of the party because of the slow pace of reform. As a consequence, the Socialist party candidate Salvador Allende, a well-known Marxist, won the 1970 election on September 4 with a plurality of 36.2 percent of the popular vote in a field of three candidates. Contrary to 1964, the U.S. role in this election was minimal. Rather than $2.6 million as in 1964, the U.S. government spent only $300,000, most of it going for an anti-Allende propaganda campaign rather than directly for party work.

Because Allende won with less than a simple majority of the votes, the election for president was thrown into the Chilean Congress, where a final decision was scheduled for October. At this point U.S. intervention became significant. Officials of International Telephone and Telegraph Corporation (ITT) contacted government officials including Henry Kissinger, then National Security Adviser, and Richard Helms, director of the CIA, to coordinate activities to forestall Allende's election by the Chilean Congress. Nothing came of the ITT initiative, but Central Intelligence prepared a memorandum; it concluded that an Allende victory would in no way alter the strategic balance of power, but would entail economic and psychological costs for the United States. After reviewing a variety of options, the Forty Committee, a subcabinet executive agency responsible for oversight of major covert activities, authorized an economic and propagandistic campaign against Allende and instructed the U.S. ambassador to Chile to approach President Frei and military leaders about means, including a coup, to stop Allende. In late September the ambassador reported that encouragement of a coup by the United States would result in "an unrelieved disaster for the United States and for the president."

In the meantime the White House secretly ordered the CIA to attempt a coup despite the agency's serious doubt about the possibility of success. CIA efforts to promote violence to provoke a coup and to enlist Chilean officers to support it ended in failure. So too did attempts to engage U.S. companies and banks in economic pressures against Chile. Although ITT was willing to cooperate, General Motors, IBM, Anaconda, and Ford as well as major banks in the United States showed no enthusiasm for the project. They could see only severe losses for themselves in a collapse of the Chilean national economy. The Chilean Congress met without further intervention and, despite the minority position of Allende's coalition support, duly elected him president of the republic. He took office November 4.

Before the year was out, the Allende government began to nationalize a number of both foreign and domestic businesses. The two U.S.-owned companies, nationalized in November 1970, received prompt and adequate compensation. Furthermore, the sweeping plans announced by the Minister of the Treasury gave no indication that private banks, land, and the copper industries, also scheduled for nationalization, would be treated differently. Chile's reestablishment of relations with Cuba did provoke Secretary of State Rogers to comment that the action was playing into Cuban and Soviet hands, and President Nixon singled out Chile for discussion in his message to Congress on world affairs in February 1971. Nixon remarked that the United States did not seek confrontation with anyone and that his administration was prepared to have the kind of relationship with Allende that Allende was prepared to have with him.

Conflict broke out between the United States and Chile over the question of compensation for the expropriated copper companies. During 1971 Allende, with overwhelming support, pushed bills through Congress for the expropriation of the remaining foreign assets in the copper industry. Then on December 30, he suspended the payment of $5.8 million, the first installment of a total of $92.9 million due to Kennecott Copper Corporation. Allende justified his action on the grounds that the copper companies had made excess profits and that when these were deducted the companies owed Chile rather than Chile owing them. Kennecott filed suit in a federal district court in New York and appealed in a special copper tribunal in Chile. In mid-February 1972, a federal court blocked all Chilean assets in the United States, at which point Chile agreed to pay $84.6 million rather than the original $92.9 million. The federal court unblocked the assets, and Chile made the first payment at the end of March and the second, in early July. In the meantime, a second U.S. copper corporation, Anaconda, followed the Kennecott script with similar results, except that its second payment in July was withheld, again on grounds of excess profits. Anaconda once more brought suit in federal court and froze Chilean assets. Kennecott, with mixed success, attempted to freeze Chilean copper shipments in Western Europe and eventually came to terms with the Overseas Private Investment Corporation, a U.S. government agency, for an insurance settlement of about $67 million.

While the copper conflict raged, Chile battled with its creditors, including the U.S. government. In November 1971 the Allende government requested a renegotiation of its debts and warned that it might suspend payments during the talks. Then, in February 1972 it reached a tentative agreement with a group of U.S. private banks for refinancing some $300 million in debts. Two months later in a general settlement, Chile and its creditors, including the U.S. government, refinanced $600 million of its debts with easier payment terms, but Chile had to agree to pay for nationalized property. The Allende government, however, reneged on the repayment principle in August; from then on the White House ordered U.S. representatives in the multilateral lending agencies to veto further loans to Chile. Several

U.S. private banks also cut their lines of credit. At the same time, international copper prices fell, and by fall of that year Chilean foreign reserves had plummeted to only $80 million, while $200 million was needed to import food and spare parts. How seriously the credit embargo of the United States damaged Allende is a subject of dispute, because new lines of credit from sympathetic Latin American, West European, and East European states closed the gap. Whatever the answer, President Allende aired all his grievances in a speech at the United Nations on December 4, 1972. He accused the U.S. government and private interests of trying to prevent his accession to office, or promoting "financial strangulation," of cutting off lines of credit, and of interrupting Chilean commerce in copper.

Supporters of Allende have frequently charged that the United States government sought to overthrow him from the day of his inauguration. There is no evidence that U.S. officials assisted or participated in the coup. The CIA did, of course, have knowledge of coup plotting during the summer of 1973, and the Assistant Secretary of State told the Senate that the U.S. government had about 12 hours advance knowledge of the September 11 coup. Furthermore, the Chilean military knew that the United States had attempted to promote a coup in 1970; there is no way, however, of assessing the impact of that effort. At the same time, the Nixon administration, though adopting a "cool but correct" public posture, clearly desired to "destabilize" the Allende government, that is, to prevent the consolidation of its political position and to restrain its efforts to carry out policies that the White House perceived as damaging to U.S. interests. In the three years that Allende occupied the presidency, the U.S. government spent some $7 million to support opposition groups and anti-Allende propaganda. These small efforts obviously contributed something to the overthrow of Allende, but would have been totally inadequate had the regime not seriously alienated large sectors of the population and, most importantly, the military. The Kennedy administration could not stop the coup in Honduras in 1963 (though it tried); the Nixon administration could not have stopped the coup in Chile (but of course it did not try).

During the last seven months of the Nixon administration, the United States and Chile restored their previous good relations. Loans increased sharply after the coup, and settlements were eventually reached about rescheduling the Chilean foreign debt and compensating expropriated companies. Private investors only slowly returned to Chile, despite the new favorable climate. Repressive measures adopted by the military government, including torture and widespread killing, brought few words of protest from the White House. U.S. popular reaction presented a different story. Congressmen received thousands of communications from academics and church groups protesting the coup and suspected U.S. involvement. Senator Kennedy tried to amend the Foreign Assistance Act, when it came up for discussion in October, to deny all but humanitarian aid to Chile until the president could report that Chile was respecting human rights as provided in the Universal Declaration of Human Rights. The Senate defeated the amendment but did request President Nixon to call on the military regime to respect human rights. Nixon's approaches to the military regime, whatever they may have been, had no measurable effect in protecting human rights, but Nixon left office with official relations between Chile and the United States on a harmonious basis.

THE FORD ADMINISTRATION

Controversy, false starts, and steady negotiations marked the abbreviated presidency of Gerald Ford. Within three months of Ford's taking office, Congress passed the Trade Reform Act of 1974 that provoked outcries of protest and dismay from a score of Latin American leaders because of certain discriminatory clauses. On the other hand, the Ford administration, without much fanfare, sought avenues to normalize relations with Cuba, although in the end these efforts came to nought with the Cuban military intervention in Angola. At the same time Ford continued previous efforts to control the drug traffic from Latin American into the United States, to conclude a new treaty with Panama over the canal, to negotiate an international agreement on ocean boundaries and resources through participation in the Third Law of the Sea Conference, and to prevent spread of nuclear weapons in the hemisphere.

Gerald Ford did not favor the Trade Reform Act of 1974, and his Secretary of State, Henry Kissinger, strongly disapproved several of its provisions. Congress, however, responding to constituent cries of alarm and anger over steeply rising petroleum prices, an economic downturn, and competition from a variety of imported products, passed the bill over administration reservations. The section that outraged Latin American leaders was the one that denied preferential trade benefits to members of the Organization of Petroleum Exporting Countries (OPEC); in Latin America that meant Venezuela and Ecuador, the latter being one of the poorest countries in the hemisphere. Other clauses that drew protests from Mexico and Brazil, the two largest and most powerful countries, were those that denied preferential access to the U.S. market for shoes, textiles, steel, and other manufactured products. As an immediate response to the law, the Argentine government "indefinitely" posponed a meeting of Latin American foreign ministers with Kissinger that was scheduled for March 1975 in Buenos Aires. (The meeting of foreign ministers finally convened in San José, Costa Rica in July.) More importantly, the Trade Reform Act promoted the founding of the Latin American Economic System (Sistema Económico Latino-Americano— SELA), which included Cuba but excluded the United States. The idea for such an organization first arose in 1974 with the failure of the Organization of American States to lift sanctions from Cuba. Then in March 1975 with the widespread anger in Latin America over the new U.S. trade law, Presidents Luis Echeverría of Mexico and Carlos Andrés Pérez of Venezuela formally invited the heads of 24 Caribbean and Latin American states to send representatives to meet in Panama City first in July and then in October to sign the charter. SELA's impact has not produced basic changes in U.S.-Latin American relations. It has, however, strongly symbolized the growing awareness throughout the hemisphere that in many economic areas that relationship is conflictive rather than harmonious, as presumed by such other instruments as the Organization of American States and the Rio Treaty of Reciprocal Assistance.

With respect to Cuba, President Ford supported Secretary of State Henry Kissinger's moves, begun under Richard Nixon, to improve relations with that country. Premier Castro indicated a willingness to begin conversations, and Foreign Minister Raúl Roa reportedly met secretly with U.S. officials in Switzerland in late August. Although Roa quickly denied the report, the U.S. representatives to the OAS stated that the United States was willing to reexamine the policy of economic and political sanctions against the island. By late September it appeared that the stage was set for the revocation of the sanctions at the meeting of foreign ministers scheduled for early November in Quito. Two-thirds, or fourteen, members signatory to the Rio Treaty were needed to approve lifting the embargo, but at the last minute two countries, Bolivia and Guatemala, switched their votes and abstained. Three countries voted against the resolution, and four others, including the United States abstained. Several of the delegates severely castigated the United States for the debacle, but it appears that the measure lost in large part because of inadequate planning and attention rather than because of ill-will or opposition on the part of the State Department. From all accounts, the United States delegation expected the measure to pass.

The next effort to normalize relations with Cuba was prepared more carefully. First the foreign ministers met in late July 1975 in San José, Costa Rica and amended the Rio Treaty to permit the removal of sanctions by a simple majority vote. They also voted to include in the treaty endorsements of "ideological pluralism" and "collective economic security," the last of which the United States opposed. The delegates then reconvened and voted 15 to 3 with two abstentions to remove all OAS-imposed sanctions and permit each state to conduct its relations with Cuba as it deemed best. The United States voted with the majority, and the chief U.S. delegate noted that conversations might soon begin that might lead to normalization of relations between Cuba and the United States. Three weeks later the administration announced that it would permit foreign-based subsidiaries of U.S. corporations to sell their products to Cuba and that it would cease imposition of penalties on nations that traded with Cuba.

These auspicious beginnings for a new era in U.S.-Cuban relations came to an abrupt halt with the Cuban intervention in the civil war in Angola. By the end of November the State Department was reporting that 5,000 Cuban troops had landed, with other contingents in at least nine other African countries. President Ford severely criticized these military movements and noted that they were eroding any possibility for improving Cuban-U.S. relations. There the matter rested until the end of the administration.

The Ford years, then, produced no new departures, no grand policies, and no major controversies. Rather, Ford and Secretary of State Kissinger pursued the basic aims of the Nixon administration of reducing the U.S. role in economic and social development, in asking few questions about the nature of political systems unless they were perceived to threaten the United States in a cold war context, and in pursuing specific goals such as settling the Panama Canal issue and improving relations with Cuba. In summary, the Ford years were not "bad" years in terms of U.S. relations with Latin America, but neither were they particularly good. Certainly they were unimaginative. Drug problems, the canal treaty, the sea conference, and the nuclear nonproliferation problems were pursued with quiet but steady diplomacy and with little rancor. With the Trade Reform Act of 1974, Ford could probably do little to stem congressional desires. The one area in which he might have demonstrated statesmanship was Cuban relations, but he obviously felt constrained by popular and congressional repugnance at Cuba's Angolan adventure.

THE CARTER ADMINISTRATION

In foreign policy as well as in domestic policy, President Carter tried to distance himself from his Nixon-Ford predecessors. Primarily he wanted to convey the impression that Latin America played a larger role in U.S. global policies and that the United States was abandoning the "low profile" and "benign neglect" of the previous eight years. Although the president never commissioned a high-powered team to conduct a study tour of the area (as Nixon did with Nelson Rockefeller), Carter early on dispatched Assistant Secretary of State Terence Todman on a get-acquainted tour to four countries. Then in June, Rosalyn Carter, the president's wife, visited seven countries over a two-week period. Two months later U.S. Ambassador to the United Nations, Andrew Young, covered ten countries in a whirlwind tour, and in mid-November Secretary of State Cyrus Vance visited Argentina, Brazil, and Venezuela. Carter himself planned a trip to Brazil and Venezuela for later in that same month, but crises elsewhere forced a postponement until the spring of 1978.

Discussions with foreign leaders during these tours, official speeches, and public statements by the president and leading figures of his administration during 1977 rather clearly laid out his general approach to Latin America. First and foremost, Carter insisted that the United States would become a spokesman for the protection of human rights and would protest their violation wherever in the world they might occur. Second, he promised that the United States would no longer treat Latin American economic problems on a regional basis, but rather in global terms because economic problems transcended the hemisphere. In effect, he seemed to be abandoning the concept of the "Western Hemisphere Idea" and the "special relationship." Finally, Assistant Secretary Todman told a press conference in Caracas that the United States rejected the Nixon-Ford policy of treating Brazil as the leading country in Latin America and of regarding its economic development plan as the model for the area. On his next stop in Brasilia, however, Todman mollified the Brazilians by noting that Carter would honor the Ford administration memorandum that gave Brazil "special consultant status."

Despite these policy statements, Carter did not attempt to construct a general broad-scale Latin American program. U.S. officials presented no models to instruct Latin Americans on how to achieve economic growth and development, and the Treasury funneled more U.S. aid funds into multilateral institutions than to individual countries or projects. Carter also refrained from making social reform or the establishment of democratic government prerequisites for U.S. recognition or support. Rather, the administration, except for the human rights issue, approached Latin America on a country-by-country basis in attempts to solve (or perhaps just to manage) problems large and small as they arose: the Panama Canal; the Cuban embargo; the drug traffic from a variety of countries; migrants from Mexico, Cuba, and Haiti; nuclear nonproliferation; and revolutions in Nicaragua and El Salvador. Only on the human rights issue did Carter depart from post-Alliance trends and adopt a policy that was to be applied universally.

The Panama Canal   Carter gave a high priority to the settlement of the Panama Canal issue. In his first major address on Latin American affairs in April 1977, he pledged to the assembled diplomats to negotiate a new treaty satisfactory to both countries. True to his word the talks proceeded, and in June at the OAS General Assembly both the U.S. and Panamanian delegations reported substantial progress. When the talks seemed to be foundering over the scheduling of the return to Panamanian jurisdiction of various sections of the canal zone and the size of U.S. payments to Panama until final U.S. evacuation, Carter personally intervened. By mid-August the negotiators reached an agreement in principle, and drafting by the legal specialists got underway. In the meantime, as the final settlement approached, political forces in the United States, opposed to "giving away" the canal, began to organize to defeat the agreements. A group of canal-zone residents filed suit to stop the negotiations, and several congressmen and senators, mostly Republicans, attacked Sol Linowitz, the chief U.S. negotiator, on grounds of conflict of interest. Linowitz had been a board member of a bank with business in Panama and had long proposed generous terms for Panama in any new treaty. These protests in no way impeded the final arrangements, and President Carter and General Omar Torrijos signed two treaties in Washington, D.C. on September 7, 1977.

The first treaty, called the Panama Canal Treaty, provided for immediate assumption of Panamanian jurisdiction over the so-called *canal zone,* and a new agency consisting of five U.S. and four Panamanian citizens to oversee operation of the canal. The treaty also provided that the United States would manage and defend the canal until the end of the twentieth century. For this purpose the treaty placed certain land, water, and installations (including military bases) under U.S. control. Other articles of the treaty established a formula for economic payments to Panama, guaranteed jobs to all U.S. employees, and provided for the passage of all ships including warships through the canal. By the second treaty, the Neutrality Treaty, Panama guaranteed the perpetual neutrality of the canal. At the expiration of the Panama Canal Treaty, Panama not only assumes the operation of the canal, but also its military defense. The United States, however, will continue to have the right to defend the neutrality of the canal. Another article guaranteed U.S. warships "expeditious transit," that is priority in passage.

By their nature treaties involve compromises of positions and interests, and they seldom, if ever, satisfy everyone. These treaties proved no exception. As the terms of the agreements became public, opposition intensified in both countries. Despite this opposition the ratification process proceeded. General Torrijos asked for a 90 percent approval of the treaties in a popular referendum and placed his personal prestige at stake in supporting the treaties despite intense opposition. After a 40-day national debate, Panamanians went to the polls on October 23 and approved the agreements 66 percent to 34 percent. Torrijos was somewhat disappointed, but publicly announced his pleasure with the result. Pressure then shifted to the United States. When Congress reconvened in January 1978, treaty consideration ranked high on the Senate's agenda. Late in the month the Senate Foreign Relations Committee endorsed the treaties, but recommended strengthening the language insuring U.S. defense rights and transit privileges after 2000. General Torrijos said the treaties, which were already ratified in Panama, could not be amended, but the new language was added as an addendum to the Neutrality Treaty. On February 1 President Carter addressed the nation by television in support of the treaties, and for the next two months debate raged on in the Senate and among important sectors of the public. State Department teams roamed the country and argued the merits of the treaties. Opposition in the Senate peaked, and the protreaty forces gathered strength. The Senate ratified the Neutrality Treaty on March 16 and the Panama Canal Treaty on April 18. Over the next several years, some die-hard opponents in Congress tried to impede implementation of the treaties by withholding appropriations. These moves provoked some vehement protests from Panama and caused embarrassment for the Carter administration, but proved ineffective in sabotaging the treaties.

Improving Relations with Cuba   Just as the Carter administration moved early to settle the Panama Canal issue, so too did it announce the hope of normalizing relations with Cuba. Secretary of State Vance raised the question just after his appointment to office in January, and Castro shortly thereafter said he would like to talk with Carter, "a man of morals." In mid-February 1977 Carter said he would like to see Cubans withdraw their troops from Angola, "remove their aggravating influence in this hemisphere," and respect human rights at home. Castro responded that he was very interested in improving relations, especially in resuming trade, but he angrily rejected linking normalization to human rights questions in Cuba. Following these early exchanges both countries moved cautiously throughout the remainder of the year to encourage exchanges, to reduce hostility, and to move toward more formal relationships. The first breakthrough in concrete terms came in March. It did not consist of renewal of the hijacking agreement that the United States had suggested, but rather of the inauguration of "friendly" athletic competition. Castro had suggested that a U.S. team visit Cuba; the State Department approved, and President Carter went further and ended travel restrictions to the island and eased currency restrictions for U.S. tourists to Cuba. A U.S. basketball team, assembled from two South Dakota universities, traveled to Cuba the first week of April with a 90-member delegation including members of Congress. The legislators talked to Cuban officials about renewing relations, but Raúl Castro, Fidel's brother and Chief of the Armed Forces, insisted that the United States must first lift the trade embargo. This stipulation remained a Cuban precondition for negotiations and remained a stumbling block to normalization throughout the Carter years.

Despite difficulties, quiet talks continued through the summer between U.S. and Cuban officials. Finally, on September 1 the two countries set up "interest sections" in each other's capitals. The sections began functioning virtually as embassies in Washington and Havana. Technically, however, the Cuban section operated as an office of the Czech Embassy and the U.S. section as an office of the Swiss Embassy. A week later the U.S. Maritime Administration announced the lifting of the 14-year policy that backlisted third-country ships calling at Cuban ports, forbidding them to haul U.S. government cargo or to refuel in U.S. ports.

The establishment of the "interest sections" proved a high-water mark in U.S.-Cuban relations during the Carter regime. Both countries stated publicly that certain issues had to be settled before full diplomatic relations could be reestablished. Castro insisted that relations could not improve until the United States removed the trade embargo and evacuated Guantánamo. On various occasions U.S. officials raised the question of Cuban troops in Africa, political prisoners and human rights violations in Cuba, and Cuban revolutionary activities in other parts of Latin America. Nonetheless, relations remained relatively friendly for about two years. Although Castro refused to renew the hijacking agreement or the regular exile flights, he offered in 1978 to release about 1500 persons for emigration to the United States. The two countries reached an agreement for U.S. screening of the emigrants, and by the end of the year over 500 left the island. During the process Castro invited some exile leaders in the United States to visit Cuba to help reunite families. Some responded to the invitation and met with him during November and December. Castro promised that he would free all political prisoners in Cuba (he said there were about 3600) and would permit some 7000 former political prisoners to leave if the United States would accept them. The exile community in Havana split over the issue of negotiating with Castro, but the U.S. government kept channels of communication open.

Despite these auspicious developments, Carter's Cuban policy ended on a sour note. Two events served to reinforce old suspicions and distrust and to freeze U.S.-Cuban relations indefinitely. The first event occurred in the late summer of 1979 when a U.S. intelligence report revealed that some 2000 to 3000 Soviet combat troops were stationed in Cuba. A Soviet presence in Cuba offered nothing new; advisers had arrived in the mid-1960s, but combat troops presented a new situation. Repercussions in the United States were out of proportion to the report's importance. Despite a State Department evaluation that said the troops posed no security threat and a call for calm and restraint by President Carter, the media had a field day with banner headlines. With national elections approaching in 1980, many congressmen felt moved to respond. Unfortunately, Senator Frank Church, Chairman of the Senate Foreign Relations Committee and a leading proponent of normalization with Cuba, came out with a sharp denunciation of the Soviet action. More seriously, Senator Church postponed the scheduled SALT discussions, noting that the Senate would not likely ratify any SALT agreement until the troops withdrew. Carter said that the troop withdrawal should not be linked with SALT, but talks with the Soviet Ambassador produced no results, and *Pravda* even denied their presence. The whole affair ended in a mild disaster. Carter feebly insisted that the situation had to change but proved powerless to do anything. The Russians were annoyed because the troops had arrived in Cuba several years before without incident. And Castro again faced being the subject of debate between the two superpowers with virtually no ability to affect the outcome. A sullen mood settled over U.S.-Cuban-Soviet relations.

The second event that increased U.S.-Cuban tensions began with a dispute between Peru and Cuba over refugees in the Peruvian Embassy in Havana in April 1980. The controversy escalated when the Cuban government withdrew its police guard. Within a week over 10,000 Cubans sought refuge in the embassy. In this chaotic situation, the Cuban government promised them safe passage out of the country. By mid-April only about 800 had flown to Costa Rica, but on April 21 some 50 small boats set out from Florida for the port of Mariel to pick up refugees. In the next few days a mass exodus began. About 120,000 Cubans were brought out until Castro finally stopped the flight in September. Early in the exodus Carter pledged an "open arms" policy to the refugees, and efforts were made to process them and settle them quickly in American life. Their numbers, however, soon overwhelmed regular procedures, and the government began sending them to military camps that were little better than prisons. Unrest grew about the refugees; the Cuban exile population, particularly in Florida, became critical of official handling of the problem; and many Americans began to question the policy of "open arms." Complicating the settlement question was the fact that the Castro government used the opportunity of the exodus to rid itself not only of the politically disaffected but of the socially maladjusted, in some cases common criminals.

At the very end of the Carter administration, Castro made a few conciliatory gestures such as releasing a few remaining Americans in Cuban jails, returning two refugees from a hijacking, and promising not to punish 400 people who occupied the U.S. interest section in Havana. In sum, Carter made some net gains in normalizing Cuban relations, but when he left office in January the trade embargo still held, U.S. forces still occupied Guantánamo, Cuban troops were still in Angola, and some U.S. officials began to criticize Cuba for its encouragement of revolution in Central America.

Migration Policy   Carter also inherited the growing problem of irregular migration—largely from Mexico—from his predecessors, neither of whom had developed a coherent policy. A variety of political forces in the United States offered different and even contradictory suggestions. Organized labor wanted the borders virtually closed, some agribusiness groups wanted them virtually open, and Mexican-American groups divided among themselves about a proper approach. Facing these contrary pressures, President Carter commissioned a study of the situation and, in August 1977, announced a policy on which he asked Congress to move quickly. The policy called for the following:

1. Permanent resident alien status to be granted to all who entered the United States before January 1, 1970 and resided here continuously;
2. Temporary five-year resident alien status with no rights to federal social services to those who entered the United States between 1970 and 1977;
3. Aliens who entered after January 1, 1977 to be deported;
4. Employers who knowingly hired illegal aliens to be fined up to $1000 per worker, and brokers who supplied illegal aliens to be subject to criminal penalties;
5. The border patrol to be strengthened;
6. An identification system for alien workers to be instituted.

Congress did not move quickly, as opposition to the plan surfaced almost immediately. Mexican-American groups, fearing that its implementation would lead to job discrimination against them, vehemently opposed the identification system. Mexican government officials complained privately to U.S. Ambassador Andrew Young when he stopped off in Mexico on his Latin American tour. They pressed upon him their unhappiness with the general approach, arguing that the ultimate solution lay in an expanded Mexican economy. They once more urged the United States to grant trade concessions for Mexico's exports to help the economy, which in turn would create jobs, reduce unemployment, and relieve the pressures to migrate. No Mexican official publicly criticized the Carter policy, but Jorge Bustamante, a consultant to President López-Portillo on migration and Mexico's leading expert on the subject, denounced the plan as "unfriendly" and "unilateral." He said that it showed a lack of sensitivity to Mexico's economic situation and that a forced return of migrants would cause social disruption along the border. Similar denunciations greeted a plan by the Immigration and Naturalization Service during 1978 and 1979 to build a 12-foot steel fence for some miles at both El Paso and San Diego to restrain migrant workers. As the outrage grew both in the United States and in Mexico against this Berlin Wall and Tortilla Curtain, the INS delayed construction; in April 1979 the Justice Department announced its cancellation. In the meantime, President Carter appointed a distinguished commission under the chairmanship of the Reverend Theodore Hesburgh, president of Notre Dame University, to conduct still another study. The commission completed its work at the very end of the Carter administration and made its report to President Reagan early in 1981.

Caribbean migration, although not nearly of such magnitude or steadiness of flow, created more severe problems for the Carter administration than did the Mexican influx. In addition to the entry of Cubans since 1959, Haitian refugees have been entering the United States in makeshift craft for many years. The huge Cuban migration in 1980 further encouraged them, and while their numbers in no way matched their neighbors, they came in sufficient numbers to command attention. Black, and on the whole poorer, less educated, and less skilled than the Cubans, the Haitians found little welcome. The U.S. government declared them "economic" refugees rather than "political" refugees and on that ground sought to deport them. U.S. blacks and other American groups denounced U.S. policy as racist and sought relief in the courts. In June 1980, President Carter gave some 15,000 Haitian boat-people a six-month reprieve from deportation proceedings. It was estimated that another 10,000 to 15,000 Haitians, most of them also in Florida, also would be subject to deportation if they came to the attention of the authorities. The case dragged on through the courts with the result that few, if any, Haitians were deported.

Central American Policy The four countries lying between Mexico and Costa Rica have been troubled with internal disorders since the 1960s. Assassinations, murders, and shoot-outs reached alarming proportions in Guatemala in the early 1960s; civil war broke out in Nicaragua during 1978 after several years of violence and turmoil; sporadic violence has troubled Honduras; and increasing violence and civil war finally overtook El Salvador during 1980. For many years the U.S. government took little note of these events except to shore up existing regimes and plead for elections and the establishment of moderate reformist civilian government. Economic and military aid were willingly accepted, but the accompanying pleas were largely ignored. Then in the spring of 1979 it appeared that the Somoza regime, contrary to all expectations in the United States, could not overcome its armed opponents. The U.S. government finally had to pay serious attention to Central American developments. In mid-June Washington called a special meeting of the OAS and laid before the delegates a proposal calling for the resignation of the dictator Anastasio Somoza, and the sending of an OAS team to Managua to assist in setting up a government with broad representation of national forces. The assembly overwhelmingly defeated the proposal as the military regimes, out of concern that they might suffer a similar fate at some later time, joined the traditional opponents of intervention. The OAS then called for the resignation of Somoza and condemned intervention. The United States joined in the latter resolution; in Managua, new ambassador Lawrence Pezzulo bluntly told Somoza it was time to go. Finally, on July 17 he resigned and fled the country.

The revolutionary forces, calling themselves Sandinistas after former guerrilla fighter Augusto Sandino, quickly mopped up remaining resistance and set about establishing a new government. Carter recognized the regime on July 23, but members of his administration harbored deep fears that the revolutionaries would opt for the Cuban route. Washington's plans for a moderate successor government lay in ruins, and its approach to the Sandinistas betrayed great uncertainty. On the one hand the Defense Department recommended increased military aid for Guatemala and El Salvador, while the State Department called for concessions to democracy in those countries. At first President Carter took a somewhat hostile line toward the new regime in Nicaragua, but in August he seemed to believe that the best interests of the United States would be served by establishing good relations. Given the destruction of the civil war, the Sandinistas sought economic assistance from all quarters. The Cubans, responding with alacrity, sent medical and educational teams and modest amounts of monetary aid. The United States moved more slowly, but late in 1979 Carter recommended to Congress an emergency aid program of $75 million. Strong opposition to the measure centered around both Cuban-Nicaraguan relations and Sandinista hostility to the United States. The U.S. Senate passed the bill in late January 1980, but the House delayed any action for over a month. Final passage took several months longer, and release of the funds did not begin until September. By the end of the Carter administration $60 million had been sent to Nicaragua; the Reagan administration inherited the remainder. The hesitation with which the bill passed the U.S. Congress, the nature of the debate, and the substance of several amendments only intensified Nicaraguan distrust of U.S. intentions and made normal relations more difficult.

The development of U.S. policy toward El Salvador in the wake of its civil war has proven just as difficult and uncertain. The response of the Carter administration was to seek a middle way between military dictatorship and Marxist revolutionaries. As the violence of the military government and its opponents intensified, with neither seeming able to control events during 1979, about 20 European and Latin American countries closed their embassies, but not the United States. Following the fall of Somoza in neighboring Nicaragua, Washington stepped up its pressure on the military regime to restore order, respect human rights, and continue preparations for elections scheduled for February 1980.

In October 1979, a junta of moderate military and civilians overthrew the military government and attempted to initiate some modest changes, including land reform. From the beginning, the junta split over bringing violators of human rights to justice, and hard-line military officers simply defied junta orders. The U.S. response to this situation was to recognize the government as moderate reformist, to support it with military and economic assistance, to pressure the right wing to give ground, and to hope for military victory over the left. The policy created opposition in both the United States and El Salvador. Oscar Romero, the reformist Archbishop of El Salvador, asked Carter not to send military aid; moreover, liberals in the United States argued that the uncontrolled military in El Salvador represented the most oppressive and retrograde forces in the country. Violence continued to mount in El Salvador. In March, unknown assailants assassinated the archbishop himself; university authorities estimated 2000 died between January and March.

Although the government clearly lost control of events and forces, Carter saw no option except continued support for what he perceived as the middle course. The revolutionaries, despite peaceful overtures to Washington in August, remained tainted by Cuban support, although it was merely verbal. The extreme right also had little government backing; the army, ostensibly subordinate to the junta, seemed to be a law unto itself. Neither efforts by Mexico and West Germany nor the unpunished killing of four U.S. nuns could sway the Carter administration from its course. True, Carter temporarily suspended the aid program, but he authorized renewed military and economic assistance as he prepared to leave office in January.

Human Rights Policy   Support for human rights constituted President Carter's only major Latin American policy applicable, at least in theory, to the whole area. Jimmy Carter came to the presidency with a deep and abiding faith in the Christian religion, and that faith provided the ground for his human rights policy. Fortunately the president found support for his position from powerful sections within Congress and among the populace at large. Stung by criticisms growing from the Vietnam War and from support of oppressive regimes in Latin American that the United States was playing the roles of "arms merchant" and "policeman of the world," Congress began passing legislation in the late 1960s restricting aid, particularly military assistance to regimes that engaged in brutal repression or ignored severe social dislocations in their own countries. Then, in the last year of the Ford administration, Congress included in the Foreign Military Assistance Act of 1976 a provision that states committing "gross violations" of human rights would be denied credits for military sales unless the president believed that extraordinary circumstances warranted another course of action. The legislation also stipulated that the State Department report on human rights conditions in all states receiving military aid.

Although Gerald Ford had interpreted the restrictive clause as damaging to U.S. interests, the Carter administration gave early indications that it would pursue a different course. Secretary of State Cyrus Vance, in testifying before the Senate in February 1977, said that the United States planned to reduce aid to Argentina and Uruguay because of human rights violations in those countries. He also reported that the administration would conduct a country-by-country review and that human rights concerns would be weighed "against economic and security goals." In mid-March the State Department made its first report on human rights, as required by the 1976 legislation, and singled out Brazil, Argentina, and Uruguay as serious violators in the Western Hemisphere. The report noted arbitrary arrests, the use of torture, terrorist killings, and lack of fair trials in the three countries. When Carter made his first major address on Latin America a month later, he gave predominant attention to the human rights issue. He promised to support those countries that respect individual liberties; to seek Senate ratification of the 1969 American Convention on Human Rights;[1] and to urge Senate approval of the 1967 Treaty of Tlatelolca, which would ban atomic weapons in Latin America, including areas under U.S. jurisdiction such as Puerto Rico and the Virgin Islands.

At the General Assembly of the OAS in June, the U.S. delegation again pushed the human rights issue. The United States sponsored the first resolution against torture, summary executions, and prolonged detention without trial. It also supported two others: one against political terrorism and the other for economic assistance from advanced countries to help alleviate social tensions in poorer countries. In some of the strongest language to date from members of the Carter team, Secretary Vance said that "gross violations of human rights" make a mockery of "cooperation in economic development" and that one best defeats terror by promoting justice. As an earnest of good intentions Vance offered, for the first time, access of the Inter-American Human Rights Commission to the United States.

Human rights continued to hold a prominent position through the remainder of Carter's first year in office and, in fact, retained salience throughout his four-year term. Ambassador Young lashed out at violations in Haiti on his trip there; Treasury Secretary Blumenthal insisted at an IDB meeting that economic and human rights are closely linked; Congress, in an authorization bill for $5 billion for multilateral banks, required that U.S. delegates oppose loans to human rights violators unless the aid could be directed specifically to poor people. Carter himself held up weapons sales to several Latin American countries on a number of occasions, pushed (unsuccessfully) for ratification of the American Convention on Human Rights, and spoke frequently on behalf of his policy. At the annual General Assembly of the OAS either Carter himself raised the issue, or the U.S. delegation led debate and supported resolutions in behalf of human freedom. Some of Carter's actions in the waning days of his administration were to defend his human rights policies against growing criticism from the ascendent conservatives. He made that defense the keynote of his last address to the OAS General Assembly in mid-November, and he defended the policy again on

---

[1] Carter officials later pointed out that certain clauses of the convention, such as the right to life from the moment of conception, would not apply in the United States.

January 16, 1981 in his last State of the Union address. Without question he considered it the most important Latin American policy of his administration.

How did Latin America react to the Carter human rights policy? Obviously the regimes of the area reacted according to their own characteristics and orientations. Early in 1977, Venezuelan president Carlos Pérez called it the "best message the President of the United States could give Latin America." The governments of Brazil, Argentina, and Uruguay, however, responded angrily to the State Department report on human rights violators. All three rejected the accusations and refused to accept aid linked to human rights issues, calling the policy intervention in internal affairs. In addition, Brazil canceled its 25-year-old military aid treaty with the United States. At the OAS General Assembly in June the resolution against torture and summary executions passed unanimously, but eight countries abstained and three others absented themselves. Uruguay complained that the Inter-American Human Rights Commission attributed all violence to government activity and ignored other sources of aggression. Argentina and Chile argued that suppression of human rights comes not from poverty, but from subversion and terrorism sponsored by the Soviet Union. Even some of the democratic countries in Latin American had difficulty with the Carter policy. Colombia, for example, abstained on the General Assembly resolution, and most Latin American countries insisted that within the Inter-American Development Bank loans be judged strictly on economic, not political criteria.

Critics have labeled the Carter human rights policy a failure; even before he left office the president felt constrained to defend himself. How accurate is the criticism? Measuring the results of Carter's human rights policy is difficult, because something as nebulous as the protection of human rights presents almost insurmountable problems for evaluators. What was the meaning of human rights in Carter's terms? What were the goals and benchmarks? What would constitute "success"? None of these can be answered with any precision. Certainly, Carter revived the Inter-American Human Rights Commission and widened its jurisdiction with an increased budget and access to the United States. Undoubtedly, too, his emphasis on human rights led to the adoption of the American Convention on Human Rights when a sufficient number of countries ratified it. Unfortunately for Carter, he was unable to persuade the Senate to ratify it for the United States. Beyond this, it is difficult to judge. Carter supporters claim that the president's firm support of his policy led to an amelioration of brutality in several countries, but it is almost impossible to point to specific releases of people or to specific policy changes that took place in response to the human rights policy. In some countries conditions improved clearly because of political realignments. Perhaps the most important result of Carter's human rights policy was the changed image of the United States, both in our eyes and in the eyes of our neighbors. Although Carter could be faulted for some inconsistency in his policy, few accused the United States of being an arms merchant or a supporter of oppression in Latin America during Carter's four years in office. Fidel Castro in Cuba, the Sandinistas in Nicaragua, and even the rebels in El Salvador all regarded James Carter as a moral person with whom they could reach an accommodation despite differences in political and social values. That he could not reach peaceful accords lay in forces beyond his control.

THE REAGAN ADMINISTRATION

Even before taking office, Ronald Reagan and his advisers indicated that the new administration would substantially alter a number of Carter's policies toward Latin America. They harshly criticized Carter's concern for human rights and his alleged neglect of security interest in Central America and the Caribbean. Reagan's advisers called for large increases in military assistance for El Salvador, a decrease in the importance of human rights considerations, and a go-slow policy with respect to support for the revolutionary government in Nicaragua. Both Ambassador Robert White in El Salvador and Ambassador Lawrence Pezzullo in Nicaragua deplored these "leaks" from the Reagan team that undermined Carter's policy in the area, thus weakening the influence of the ambassadors and contributing to political unrest in those countires. Pezzullo bluntly declared that to seek solutions by supporting right-wing extremists was "lunacy." Neither ambassador found favor with the Reagan administration and they were eventually removed.

The incoming Reagan administration faced a series of other issues in Latin America: trade and aid, military sales, drug traffic, nuclear proliferation, migrant workers, and petroleum purchases. The president himself placed the highest immediate priority on establishing good personal relations with the president of Mexico, José López-Portillo. He perceived Carter's relations with Mexico, the country in Latin America most vital to U.S. concerns, as nearly disastrous. Consequently, on January 5, 1981 President-elect Reagan and President López-Portillo conferred for about an hour in Ciudad Juárez, just across from El Paso, Texas. They discussed no specific issues, but they pledged to establish close personal relations to ease tensions.

Despite Reagan's desire to establish harmonious relations with Mexico, the civil war in El Salvador and revolutionary conditions in Nicaragua preoccupied the administration in its first weeks. Reagan had hardly taken office when Secretary of State Alexander Haig opened a major diplomatic attack on Cuba, Vietnam, and the Soviet Union for intervention in El Salvador. Furthermore, Haig accused neighboring Nicaragua of providing the conduit for arms to the guerrillas. In February the State Department published a report entitled *Communist Interference in El Salvador* that supported these charges. Critics questioned the authenticity of the documents upon which the report was based, and Soviet spokesmen denied that the Soviet Union was supplying arms to El Salvador. Nonetheless, Secretary

Haig, insisting upon the validity of the documents, said that the United States would continue to send aid to the government and to its military forces.

With the escalating Salvadoran question occupying the attention of the media and the public, Reagan's White House advisers counseled a cooling-off of that issue, which was drawing attention away from the president's domestic programs: taxation, welfare, and budgeting. Secretary of State Haig bowed to White House directives and lowered the level of public attacks on Nicaragua, Cuba, and the Salvadoran guerrillas. However, on April 1 the U.S. government cancelled the aid program to Nicaragua, originally approved by Congress under Carter—all but $15 million of a total of $75 million had already been disbursed—and quietly increased economic and military aid to the Salvadoran regime.

In the fall of 1981 Secretary Haig reopened his campaign against Nicaragua and the Salvadoran guerrillas. Both he and Edwin Meese, White House Counselor, refused to rule out the possibility of blockading or mining the harbors of Nicaragua. At the December OAS meeting in St. Lucia, Haig accused Nicaragua of becoming potentially "the platform for terror and war in the region," and spoke of organizing some kind of collective action. He also asserted that the United States would increase both military and economic assistance to El Salvador. Finally, in an effort to retain the support of other nations in the area for his hard-line approach to leftist regimes and insurgent movements, Secretary Haig proposed what he called the Caribbean Basin Initiative. This new project envisioned a three-part assistance program for the area: trade preference in the U.S. market; special incentives for private investment; and increased support for balance-of-payment difficulties (as were experienced by Costa Rica in late 1981). Several delegations reacted cautiously to this proposal for fear that U.S. assistance might be tied to political orthodoxy. Others expressed doubts about the emphasis placed on private investment because the poorest countries needed to build infrastructure (roads, electric power, water systems), which only government can provide, to attract private investment in the first place. The Reagan administration laid its plans for Caribbean development before the U.S. Congress, but by the spring of 1983 only an emergency aid package of $350 million had been enacted into law.

In the meantime the administration supplied El Salvador with $140 million in aid during 1981, one-third of which was military. During 1982 the United States raised this amount to over $200 million with 40 percent being military and requested an additional $163 million. For fiscal 1983 the administration proposed about $226 million, of which 27% is military. Moreover, during 1981 U.S. military personnel were dispatched to El Salvador to train the Salvadoran armed forces; in 1982, 1500 Salvadoran officers and men came to the United States for training as special forces. The administration was strengthened in its conviction that its Salvadoran policy was correct by the massive turnout for constituent assembly elections in March 1982. To the present, then, the administration's hard line on radical governments and leftist movements in Central America and the Caribbean has remained basically unchanged. Implacable enmity marked the U.S. attitude toward Cuba, Nicaragua, Grenada, and the Salvadoran rebels. Friendship and support marked the U.S. attitude toward conservative and rightist regimes in Jamaica, Guatemala, Honduras, and—of course—El Salvador, where the goal remained military victory.

Next to the crisis in Central America, the Reagan administration paid closest attention to its relations with Mexico. Following their pre-inaugural meeting, the two leaders met again in June in Washington, D.C. Despite an auspicious start, relations between the two governments were not entirely harmonious. López-Portillo refused to receive the documents that allegedly proved Cuban intervention in El Salvador. Moreover, just a few days later, López-Portillo, in signing a new sugar agreement with the Castro government, called Cuba the Latin American country "most dear" to Mexico. With respect to El Salvador, the Mexican president warned against U.S. intervention, insisted that a military solution was not possible, and called for a political settlement. One should not exaggerate these differences, however. At the very time that Mexico was criticizing U.S. policy in El Salvador, the State Department approved the sale of about a dozen F-5 aircraft to Mexico. In addition the June meeting came off smoothly, and in late summer the two countries reached a new agreement on special petroleum purchases.

Following the June conference, Central American problems once more interrupted the smooth flow of Mexican-U.S. relations; in late August, Mexico, together with France, recognized the guerrilla forces in El Salvador as a "representative political force" and called for a negotiated settlement to end the conflict. The two powers also argued that the armed forces had to be thoroughly restructured before "authentically free" elections could be held. The Reagan administration was unmoved and seemingly mustered its Latin American support when nine countries not only criticized the Mexican-French initiative, but also accused the two powers of interfering in the internal affairs of another country. The latter charge, striking at the basic principle of Mexican foreign policy (nonintervention), provoked an angry denial from Mexico. Again, one should not overstate the seriousness of the dispute. In mid-September López-Portillo attended the dedication of the Gerald Ford Presidential Museum in Michigan and met in conference with Ronald Reagan and Pierre Trudeau of Canada. Then Reagan attended the Cancún summit in October as he had promised López-Portillo in June. It too went smoothly, although little was accomplished.

Early in his administration, Reagan had to confront the problem of illegal migrants, primarily from Mexico. The Select Commission on Immigration and Refugee Policy under the chairmanship of Father Theodore Hesburgh, the president of the University of Notre Dame, made its final report. It called for a one-time amnesty for most illegals already in the country, an increase in the basic immigration quota, and stricter enforcement of immigration laws. Its most controversial proposal was its call for civil and criminal sanctions against employers who knowingly hired illegals.

Reagan rejected the report and appointed his own President's Task Force on Immigration and Refugee Policy, chaired by the Attorney General. Reporting in late May, the task force basically followed the Hesburgh Commission recommendations, although it suggested a more limited amnesty. It did call for employer sanctions and the issuance of counterfeit proof Social Security cards. Its most innovative feature proposed an experimental "guest worker" program on the European model. The task force recommended that 50,000 workers with spouses and children be admitted during each of the next two years. They would be eligible for schools and health care, but not for welfare, food stamps, or unemployment insurance. Two months later the administration announced its policy, a much-watered-down version not only of the Hesburgh, but also of its own task force reports. It called for modest civil sanctions only against employers and for documentation, but no special identification cards for workers. It would grant temporary residence to illegal workers already in the country since January 1, 1980, but they would be ineligible for a wide variety of benefits. The policy finally called for an increase in the quotas for Mexico and Canada, a tightening of border and boat patrolling, and a two-year pilot project of 50,000 guest workers per year for two years, but without families. To the present no immigration policy has been implemented, and Congress continues to struggle with a series of proposals for a new immigration law.

Perhaps the critical issue of the petroleum trade between Mexico and the United States best exemplifies their relations, a relation of bargaining and compromise based upon mutual self-interest. With the oil glut on the world scene in the spring of 1981, the Mexican government came under pressure to cut prices in line with international markets. During the summer several of Mexico's customers began to cancel their contracts. As sales remained sluggish, the U.S. government began negotiations with Mexico for purchases for its strategic reserve, and the two quickly reached an agreement. Petróleos Mexicanos (PEMEX) agreed to sell a total of about 110 million barrels between September 1, 1981 and August 31, 1986 at $31.80 per barrel, a reasonably good price. The benefits were obvious. Mexico's enormous foreign debt and continued balance-of-payment problems made exports indispensable. For the United States the benefits were also obvious. The planned goal of a 750-million-barrel strategic reserve was slow in filling because of Arab opposition. Mexico had the surplus oil, we needed it, and a satisfactory price was negotiated. Moreover, when Mexico experienced more severe economic problems during 1982, the Reagan administration increased its oil purchases, made advance payments, and assisted Mexico in obtaining additional financial assistance.

A third area of concern for the Reagan administration was the human rights issue. While the Reagan team did not totally repudiate Carter's preoccupation with human rights violations, the Reagan White House indicated that such violations would not elicit the same threats and reprisals, especially against friendly regimes, as they had during the previous administration. Following the State Department's release of its annual world survey of human rights in early February, Secretary of State Haig said that he disliked issuing "report cards," and that he preferred to deal with violations "through diplomatic channels." U.S. Ambassador to the United Nations Jeane Kirkpatrick spoke of "quiet diplomacy" as the proper way to handle human rights issues.

The administration soon indicated what direction it would take to support these general statements of policy. Just a few weeks after inauguration, Reagan nominated Ernest Lefever as Assistant Secretary of State for Human Rights and Humanitarian Affairs. Human rights advocates in and out of Congress expressed outrage and the process of Lefever's nomination provoked a major political battle. In the hearings before Congress, Lefever's ultraconservative positions became public, particularly his long and vehement opposition to Carter's human rights policy. Lefever maintained that there was a substantial difference between human rights violations in totalitarian countries (Communist regimes) and in authoritarian countries (military and civilian dictatorship as in Latin America), and that U.S. human rights policies should acknowledge that difference. After prolonged and heated debate, the Senate refused to confirm his nomination.

In the meantime, Secretary Haig announced the easing of some sanctions against Chile that had been imposed by the Ford administration for the assassination of Orlando Letelier, a Chilean opponent of the junta, in Washington, D.C. Haig said that the U.S. government was ending the ban on export-import bank loans and was inviting Chile to join the annual joint naval exercises in 1981. The secretary explained that priorities were changing and that a more important goal of this administration was to stop international terrorism. Next, the administration moved to repeal the ban on arms sales to regimes violating human rights. The State Department targeted Argentina as the first recipient, but Congress continued to block such sales not only to Argentina, but to Guatemala and Chile as well. Despite this congressional rebuff the administration issued export licenses for military trucks and jeeps for Guatemala simply by reclassifying the equipment. Then in October the Senate agreed to lift the restrictions on arms sales to Chile if the president could certify that "significant progress has been made" in the protection of human rights. Within hours, the State Department reported that, in fact, Chile had made such progress. Finally, the Reagan administration removed U.S. opposition within international lending agencies to loans for Argentina, Chile, Paraguay, and Uruguay. A government spokesman said that the administration had reviewed the human rights situations in these countries and that it had found no justification for continued opposition. Critics in Congress found themselves in a minority position to resist these changes and could only protest weakly when Secretary Haig insisted that there had been "dramatic reductions in abuses." In late 1981 the Inter-American Development Bank, with U.S. support, approved a $27.5 million loan for Paraguay. Secretary Haig claimed that the Stroessner regime had made "impressive changes," but the Paraguayan Human Rights Commission reported deterioration in some areas and "ominous stability" in others. Despite continued violations of human rights in Argentina, Guatemala, El Salvador, Chile, Haiti, and Honduras, U.S. assistance in varying amounts continued to flow to these countries. Congressional critics slowed the aid projects, but seemed powerless to stop them.

One final issue needs comment: Reagan's move away from previous U.S. policy on the prohibition of the sale of nuclear fuels to countries that refuse to accept comprehensive safeguards on all nuclear facilities and fuels. Brazil was threatening to buy its fuels in Europe if the United States cut off these materials. In mid-October, Vice President George Bush announced in Brasilia that the administration would pose no obstacle to Brazil's purchase of fuels for its U.S.-built reactor. Brazil has steadfastly refused to accept the principle of comprehensive inspections to prevent the diversion of nuclear fuels to weapons purposes. Bush explained that Brazil was a "special case exemption," but indicated that the administration would probably move toward a further easing of restrictions. It is impossible to know whether the Reagan administration was moved by a desire to placate Brazil and win its support for the U.S. Caribbean policy, or whether it simply judged that it could not in reality prevent Brazil from buying from a consortium of West European companies. Whatever the explanation, this constituted the first such exemption in Latin America and may set an ominous precedent.

CONCLUSIONS

The Meaning of the Era   Policies pursued between 1969 and 1983, constituting a sharp break with the immediate past of the Alliance for Progress, imply that U.S. leaders have learned a number of lessons from failures of earlier policies. First of all, they came to recognize that Latin America exhibited great, if not extreme, diversity and that Brazil and Mexico could not be treated like Bolivia and Guatemala. In fact, throughout the period the two largest countries of the area attracted major attention. If this chapter has devoted more attention to Mexico than to Brazil, the explanation lies in the fact that the United States had more intense contacts and more serious differences and problems with Mexico.

Second, our leaders apparently learned that the United States cannot direct or control the future of Latin America. The failures of the alliance taught us that we do not sufficiently understand the process of economic modernization and development to promote that process successfully in another environment. We have learned that throwing money, technology, and management at problems produces no automatic solutions. We have learned that we can be of some assistance, but that the developing country must make the basic decisions to promote growth and social redistribution. The United States can help or retard that process to some extent, but both U.S. developmentalists and dependency critics of U.S. policy have exaggerated U.S. ability to affect the outcome. We have also learned that we can do little to stop military coups, promote democratic elections, or even restrain brutal repression and violence in Latin America. Except in small countries in the Caribbean area, U.S. armed intervention has ceased to be a thinkable response, and even there most Americans believe "sending in the Marines" is inappropriate today.

We have also learned that contributions to multilateral funding agencies serve our interests better than bilateral lending. This concession to Latin American requests has removed some of their criticism of U.S. lending practices that have tied aid to a variety of stipulations. Although the United States carries much influence within institutions such as the IDB, it cannot place the same kind of demands on loans as it can in bilateral arrangements. Naturally some aid funds have been retained for bilateral negotiations, but during the past 15 years a dramatic reversal of roles between the two types of aid to Latin America has occurred.

In sum, we have learned that we cannot create Utopia: that economic development, social reform, and democracy do not come in a single package as the Alliance for Progress promoters believed. The lessons of Latin America have demonstrated that a country might attain one of these, perhaps two, but never all three at once. We have not yet bitten the bullet in deciding which one we want to support. We lean to economic development, but object to the repression it brings in countries like Brazil; we lean to democracy, but deplore the lack of growth in Costa Rica; we lean to social reform, but recoil from the political consequences in Cuba.

Finally, we have come to accept that changes in strategic weapons have altered our military situation in the Caribbean. Coaling stations and ports of call lost their importance long ago, but until the 1970s certain military leaders insisted upon the need to own and control the Panama Canal for defense purposes. When that doctrine became seriously challenged even within military circles, the way opened for the return of the canal zone and the control of the canal itself to Panama. In the signing and ratification of the treaties, common sense, decency, and enlightened self-interest won out over traditionalism and chauvinism.

What We Failed to Learn   The post-alliance era was marked by a groping for a new perspective in U.S.-Latin American relations. Both U.S. and Latin American leaders occasionally spoke of North-South dialogue, common world problems, and industrial versus Third World interests, but none of this ever developed into a coherent approach. Despite some lip service to these new concepts, the old "special relationship" or Western Hemisphere Idea proved to have considerable life. Venezuela and Ecuador may have joined OPEC, but they desire trade preferences within a hemisphere framework. Mexico may promote the New International Economic Order, a global concept, but it is reluctant to surrender its special agreements with the United States. The United States, for its part, has acted petulantly, at one time threatening to withdraw from the Organization of American States (OAS), but each administration except Ford's sent fact-finding teams around Latin America. Despite language and behavior that disavowed treating the area in a unified manner, each administration has conceived of Latin America as a separate entity in terms of U.S. policy. Latin American issues may be treated separately, but they are still treated within a hemispheric—not a global—context.

We have not yet learned to promise no more than we can deliver. Every administration has made general promises of increased economic assistance. Both the Carter and Nixon administrations repeated such promises on several occasions. None of these were fulfilled, with the result that the credibility of the United States suffered. Only Ambassador Andrew Young in his Caribbean tour bluntly told his hosts not to expect much economic aid despite the fact that the Carter administration sympathized with their problems.

Finally, we have failed to learn to live with divergent politico-social systems. Every administration except Reagan's has attempted to improve relations with Cuba. Carter made some progress, but in the end all attempts foundered in part because of domestic political restraints. No administration has had the understanding or the courage to educate the U.S. populace (and to challenge opponents) on the point that Cuba, Nicaragua, and El Salvador pose no strategic threat to the United States; that establishing relations with Communist, Socialist, or radical nationalist regimes may in fact reduce and undercut Soviet influence in the hemisphere by giving these regimes options in economic and political affairs; and that verbal attacks on the United States do us no damage and serve as safety outlets for political pressures in those countries. We have not learned that taking this chance, this risk, will not cause a further deterioration in our relations with revolutionary regimes and might well improve them. We have not learned that anti-Communism is not enough for U.S. support, although President Carter tried to teach that lesson. We have not learned, despite the lesson of Nicaragua, that oppressive right-wing anti-Communism leads to unrest, revolt, and violent anti-U.S. sentiments, and that this sequence of events does not serve our national interest.

Some Mistakes We Have Made   Our governments since 1968 have mishandled migration policy, human rights policy, trade policy, Latin American expropriations of private U.S. property, and fishing disputes. The two latter issues involve direct protection of private interests and can be treated summarily. It seems patently ridiculous that the U.S. government permits the tuna industry to dictate fishing policy to the damage of wider relationships with several countries. The argument that tuna are "migratory" and therefore do not fall within the regulations of 200-mile economic zones establishes a general principle with a single application. No other nation accepts this rule; it should be abandoned. On expropriations, one can understand the difficulty of changing a hallowed policy of such age. Political leaders have long identified private interests abroad with the public national interest. Slowly we have recognized that some private interests are totally unrelated to any public interest. It is time that we understand clearly the distinction between public and private interests; that private investments involve risk as well as profit; and that the expropriation of private property even without compensation may involve legitimate national interests in Latin America. We cannot expect rapid change in U.S. policy on this issue but it is time to face the issue squarely and to open public debate in the United States. Never again should our government attempt to "destabilize" a regime, as it attempted in Chile, over property expropriations and political orientation.

Carter's human rights policy was well conceived but poorly implemented. It was time that we gave consideration to what kind of people we wanted to be and how we wanted other people to see us. We did not want to be, or to be seen as, the policeman or the arms merchant to the world. We did not want to be known as supporters of dictators, torturers, and oppressors. We wanted to be known as supporters of democracy, human rights, and social reform. Unfortunately, as we knew, we could do little to promote these actively. Unfortunately, too, President Carter deviated from a policy of words to a policy of action. In most areas where he applied punitive measures to oppressors of human rights, his actions seemed futile and ineffective, and because he could not apply his policy consistently he also appeared hypocritical. We need to return to the human rights policy, but it must be largely a policy of words, a condemnation of behavior, and only selectively a policy of public action. Where public action is taken, the case must be notorious for particularly heinous behavior and susceptible to pressure for ameliorating the unacceptable condition.

Trade policy has particularly aroused the wrath of Latin American political leaders and economists. Twenty-five years ago when Latin America was asking for an aid program similar to the European Marshall Plan, the Eisenhower administration responded that one part of the solution of Latin America's economic problems was increased trade, not aid. Over the next quarter century Latin America experienced rather substantial and sustained economic growth and industrial diversification. In some areas, production and quality have combined to make a variety of goods competitive in the American market. Today many Latin American countries request trade rather than aid, but find the U.S. market closed or partially closed for their manufactured products. Again private interests in the United States feel threatened by unrestrained imports, but if Latin America is to pay off its enormous debts, owed largely to American banks, it must export its products or eventually default. Trade policy needs to be reconsidered in this broader context of both U.S. and Latin American interests.

Finally, the United States urgently needs to develop a coherent migration policy rather than to continue to handle migrants and refugees on an ad hoc basis. We have a constant flow of immigrants, many without papers, from all over Latin America, but three countries in particular present us with acute but different problems. Most important in terms of numbers are Mexicans who cross the border, with relative ease, in search of jobs. Their exact numbers remain unknown, but estimates run to several million. Proposals to treat this problem range from an open border to a Berlin Wall. Currently we have no policy that the border patrol can consistently enforce. The Mexican government must cooperate in any effective program, but thus far neither the United States nor Mexico has shown much enthusiasm for such cooperation. Internal domestic factors influence both governments and impede negotiations and settlement. Our government needs to be alive to Mexican sensitivities, to the feeling of Mexican Americans, and to the needs of the migrants themselves. No one can impose a policy; it can only emerge with understanding, compromise, and cooperation of all parties involved. But we must have a policy for the border. Next we need to resolve the question of political versus economic refugees. We have welcomed Cuban exiles as refugees from an oppressive (Communist) regime, but we have in general rejected Haitian exiles as refugees from a stagnant economic regime. In fact, the regime in Haiti is perhaps more repressive politically (albeit non-Communist) than the Cuban. Moreover Haitians are black, while Cubans are mostly white. A suspicious element of racial discrimination consequently creeps into the official discussion of the problem. Again for our image at home and abroad we need to resolve this question and avoid the slightest taint of racism in the final determination.

Conflicts of interest trouble U.S. relations with most Latin American countries in varying degrees. Despite these tensions and disagreements, U.S.-Latin American relations have proceeded along rather smooth lines. No issues have escalated to a nonnegotiable stage; all are subject to negotiation and compromise. No issues are locked in concrete, and although many countries have adopted firm positions on some issues, all are willing to give some ground. The most immediate problems involve U.S. relations with Cuba, Nicaragua, and El Salvador. But even here, the revolutionary groups have indicated an interest in talking and negotiating with the United States. In the long run the most serious problems may revolve around debt burdens, trade, and Latin American access to the U.S. market. What needs to be done is to keep negotiating, remain fluid, and be willing to compromise.

FOR FURTHER READING

Books

Fagen, Richard R., ed. *Capitalism and the State in U.S.-Latin American Relations* (Stanford, Calif.: Stanford University Press, 1979).

Ferris, Elizabeth G. and Lincoln, Jennie, eds. *Latin American Foreign Policies: Global and Regional Dimensions* (Boulder, Colo.: Westview Press, 1981).

Martz, John D. and Schoultz, Lars, eds. *Latin America, the United States, and the Inter-American System* (Boulder, Colo.: Westview Press, 1980).

Sigmund, Paul E. *Multinationals in Latin America: The Politics of Nationalization* (Madison, Wis.: The University of Wisconsin Press, 1980).

Articles

Bath, C. Richard and James, Dilmus O. "Dependency Analysis of Latin America: Some Criticisms, Some Suggestions," *Latin American Research Review* XI (1976), 3–54.

Lowenthal, Abraham F. "The Caribbean," *The Wilson Quarterly* VI (Spring 1982), 113–145.

Schoultz, Lars. "U.S. Foreign Policy and Human Rights Violations in Latin America: A Comparative Analysis of Foreign Aid Distributions," *Comparative Politics* XIII (January 1981), 149–170.

chapter 7

The United States and Sub-Saharan Africa

LEON GORDENKER

American policy towards Africa south of the Sahara has rarely been highly active. Yet this area of the world has obviously begun to loom larger in the deliberations of the foreign policy apparatus in Washington. Congressmen make impassioned speeches about the example of Zimbabwe. Carter was the first American president to have visited Nigeria and Liberia. New interest groups, some representing American blacks, issue demands about American policy in South Africa. Politicians, frightened of Soviet expansion or incensed by what they think of as Cuban effrontery, point to Africa as an example of their concerns.

Even an occasional television documentary treats African affairs as little more than quaint doings beside a tribal campfire. Clearly, African affairs have impinged on the consciousness of both political leaders and broader publics. Was American policy towards Africa significantly redefined during the Carter administration? Has the Reagan administration set out on a new course?

THE CYCLICAL PAST

The record of American policy toward sub-Saharan Africa can be characterized as a cycle in which brief, close attention to specific situations alternates with lengthy periods of quiescence and even indifference.

148

In general, African affairs have rarely had much influence on the structure of international politics. At the end of World War II, only three governments in sub-Saharan Africa—Ethiopia, Liberia, and South Africa—operated internationally. The rest of the continent was considered to be colonial territory, treated as exclusive preserves of the European metropoles. These territories were governed largely as technical addenda to European political systems, and they caused little stir in the metropolitan capitals. There was neither expectation of early independence for the colonies nor wide interest in programs to develop their political and economic capacities.

While the United States usually kept its distance from specific issues of colonial affairs, its government *did* endorse ideological positions that still influence policy. Under President Franklin Roosevelt's guidance, American policy opposed colonialism. This opposition was sometimes gentle, as in its support for the mild but significant provisions of the United Nations Charter for international surveillance of the colonial regimes.

Sometimes it was much more forthright and ideological, as in the strong support given by the United States to the UN Universal Declaration of Human Rights (1948), which contained explicit provisions against racial discrimination and in favor of democratic participation in government.

Furthermore, the United States supported direct economic aid to colonial territories through international agencies. Throughout the postwar period, the United States generally favored decolonization of Africa and unhesitatingly welcomed a stream of new members to the United Nations. By 1982, the decolonization process had operated so thoroughly that the United Nations had nearly 50 members in the African group.

However clearly the United States may have taken a principled position on human rights, against colonialism and for economic development, its main policy concerns usually subordinated African issues. The security of Europe from Soviet domination or pressure took priority over decolonization.

The principal colonial powers, the United Kingdom, France, Belgium, Spain, and Portugal, were either principal contributors to the North Atlantic Treaty Organization or provided it with important services. Consequently, the United States was often reluctant to interfere explicitly with the colonial powers' plans for decolonization. Moreover, such American pressure would have had unpredictable domestic political effects on the colonial powers. As a result, the United States for the most part applauded, rather than managed, the decolonization process.

As for its use of the UN surveillance mechanisms, the United States was inhibited by its own vulnerability to criticism as privileged administrator of the Pacific Trust Territory under special provisions to reduce outside supervision. It could, therefore, scarcely claim objectivity. Furthermore, the United States increasingly feared the expansion of the international surveillance mechanism, when, after 1960, newly independent countries focused attention on such American territories as Puerto Rico and Guam.

American concern with the expansion of Communist influence deflected attention from Africa until recently. Earlier, neither Soviet political influence nor the Communist doctrine, despite occasional forays, made any significant headway in sub-Saharan Africa.

Generally, during the first postcolonial years, the spirit of nascent nationalism had a strong attraction to governing elites. Furthermore, the first independent governments usually modeled themselves on parliamentary systems and sought foreign investment. These regimes were quickly succeeded by military dictatorships with little to hope for from the Soviet Union, which was busy with its own defense; difficulties with East German, Hungarian, and Czech unrest; China; and its allies in the Middle East. Africa, therefore, was hardly a battlefield in the cold war.

The American position on human rights vacillated sharply. After the Truman administration's commitment to creating and protecting an international standard, the Eisenhower government practically abandoned this concern. A brief resumption of interest during the Kennedy administration declined under Johnson and remained submerged in the Nixon-Ford period, only to re-emerge under President Carter. The Reagan administration proclaimed its hostility to a human rights approach along Carter's lines.

Yet, American claims to exemplary status in the human rights field always could be heard, and they have, at least, some effect on its stance towards Africa. The United States made known its repugnance for the institutionalized racial discrimination of South Africa, and it favored advances towards majority government in Rhodesia and the Portuguese colonies. The United States generally criticized arbitrary and brutal behavior by governments—whether they had a leftist flavor like that of Guinea, or a lethally arbitrary tone like that of Uganda under Amin.

Jutting out from this rather low plateau of interests were two peaks of American involvement during the two decades before the Nixon-Ford administration. The first of these was occasioned by the breakdown of the new government of the Congo (now Zaire) in 1960, followed by UN intervention and the beginning of a four-year effort to hold the country together.

The United States strongly supported this venture. President Kennedy's political supporter from Michigan, Governor G. Mennen Williams, as Assistant Secretary of State for African Affairs, made flamboyant speeches. He irritated the colonial regimes and South Africa, and he drew backing from American interest groups. He offered American economic aid and suggested that Africa held extraordinary possibilities for development. The Kennedy administration proclaimed its abhorrence of the repression of the South African majority, and favored rapid independence of the remaining colonial territories. But the United States made few commitments outside of the economic field, and even these were narrowly limited.

Partly because of the deepening conflict in Indochina, Africa had a lower priority at the end of the Johnson administration than at the beginning. This declining concern was followed by reduced economic assistance and a defensive stance when African states demanded heavy pressure on Rhodesia after the Smith government declared independence from Britain in 1966. Here the United States generally followed the British lead, including support and execution of the UN program of economic sanctions against the Smith government. As for South Africa and the Portuguese colonies, the United States resisted efforts by the UN majority to apply coercive pressure.

Although the Nixon-Ford administrations entered office without special commitments to Africa, many of the governments on the continent sensed that a subtle change could be expected. During the first term of the Nixon government, a shift of emphasis in American policy was ordered by the president and Henry Kissinger. Based on the assumptions that the white-ruled governments of southern Africa would neither quickly nor easily be replaced, the United States showed less zeal on the Rhodesian case.

The administration's unenthusiastic opposition to the Byrd amendment, which ordered the government to violate its treaty commitment to carry out the sanctioning orders of the UN Security Council, was a symptom of change that many African governments noticed. Business "as usual" with South Africa was another symptom.

Continued sympathy for Portugal, whose colonies of Mozambique, Angola, and Guinea-Bissau were in various stages of revolt, also was made clear. Policies towards Nigeria—the largest of the African countries—during the insurrection of the Ibo population in Biafra resulted in sour relations.

American activity in Africa during most of the Nixon administration remained subdued and low-key, frequently reflecting an indifference to the problems there. This changed sharply, however, in the Ford administration. Secretary of State Kissinger influenced dealings in reaction to the collapse of the Portuguese colonial system and the fracturing of the government in Lisbon under its impact. The embattled and discontented armed forces pushed aside the disintegrating civilian government in Lisbon and moved at once to give independence to the colonies. By the last year of the Ford administration, Mozambique and Angola were free, and the American policy once more reached a peak of involvement.

This new involvement centered on Rhodesia. Kissinger himself flew to Africa to seek a peaceful transfer of authority from the Smith regime to a government based on participation of the black majority of the population. Yet, Rhodesia was hardly the issue. Rather, Africa had slowly gained importance as an arena for Soviet-American competition, sometimes involving the diplomatic front, liberation movements, and less often, rival programs of economic assistance.

This competition exploded in the aftermath of the Portuguese revolution. Mozambique assumed independence under an avowedly Marxist government whose leaders, during their war against Portugal, had received aid from the Soviet Union. In Angola, where the situation was less clear in 1974, an American-backed liberation movement based in Zaire contended with a Soviet-backed group, while a third organization got some aid from the United States and South Africa. The sudden injection of more than 15,000 Cuban troops, with the encouragement and logistical support of the Soviet

Union, settled the matter in the months succeeding independence in 1975. The presence of the Cubans quickly induced a raid by South African troops who failed, however, to get public backing from Washington and withdrew. In addition, Congress flatly rejected pleas by Secretary of State Kissinger for an appropriation to finance additional military aid to the Angolan groups, which had earlier received covert support.

Against this background, the Kissinger initiative in Rhodesia can be understood as an effort to retain an American voice and to restrain Soviet influences among the new black states of southern Africa. In the process, the United States made a practice of consulting and cooperating closely with the states bordering or having a special interest in Rhodesia: Tanzania, Mozambique, Zambia, and Botswana.

CARTER'S ALTERNATIVES IN AFRICA

The Carter administration entered office with less than a free hand on African policy. Inevitably, the programs and decisions of the previous administration influenced the agenda of the new one. Furthermore, with American involvement in Africa at one of its cyclical peaks, any sharp reversals would necessarily create a new domestic outcry. In addition, expectations created by the 1976 presidential campaign would also have some bearing on what was done in Africa.

The strong reaction by the Ford-Kissinger foreign policy team to Cuban involvement in Africa posed a dramatic set of options. The new administration could treat Soviet intentions in Africa as a major test of relations between the United States and the Soviet Union. If it did so, then the cooler, softer approach toward the Soviet Union, which had characterized part of the Nixon administration's dealings, would have to be reversed.

In his presidential campaign, however, Carter had offered high hopes of improving relations with the Soviet Union. His tone thus implied the option of assessing Soviet aims in Africa as limited and negotiable and not requiring a major test of strength.

The Cuban intervention in Angola and reports of its possible extension to other territories could also have been viewed as the deliberate widening of the involvement of Communist countries in Africa. Such a view would have been consistent with treatment of Africa as a major developing area of Soviet-American contention. On the other hand, the presence of Communist forces did not necessarily imply almost unlimited Soviet aims. Alternatively, the Cuban intervention could have been handled as an isolated and limited incident, consequent on fears by the Soviet Union that the United States sought dominance over Angola through clandestine means.

A basic choice on a more regional scale had to do with the new administration's approach to relations with African governments. As a world power, the United States could attempt a policy of general influence, seeking to persuade or press each government to act consistently with American views. Although Africa consisted of many states that participated to some extent in the Organization for African Unity, most of them were weak, small, and poor. Some—perhaps almost all—expected to respond to attention from the United States.

Alternatively, the United States always had an open policy of supporting governments friendly to its outlook. Generally, this had been the approach over the last decade that had produced close cooperation with Zaire, Liberia, and Kenya—and earlier, Ethiopia and Nigeria. Continuing such a course would accord bureaucratic patterns already well established, and it had the virtue of relatively low costs.

Yet another alternative to dealing with Africa lay in the direction of international institutions. The global organizations of the UN system had increasingly begun to represent African grievances against poverty, neocolonialism (which meant special influence of the former colonial masters) and *apartheid*. The UN system also broadcast hopes for economic cooperation and more assistance for development.

In the Sixth Special Session of the UN General Assembly in 1974, African governments prominently joined in demanding a New International Economic Order. Thus African aims could be understood as an integral part of issues that pitted North against South. In such a conceptual framework, organized approaches to Africa offered the advantage of existing machinery for policy formation and execution, multiple forums for negotiations, common standards for all North-South relationships, and consequent tidiness of relationships. In addition, American policy could benefit from the support of other governments of the North.

Bilateral economic relationships with Africa constituted another element of American policy. Generally, any government in Washington would seek to foster smooth, beneficial economic relationships. Yet, American private investment in Africa, while growing, neither ranked high in comparisons with other regions nor received any special emphasis.

The oil trade with Nigeria had a considerable meaning for the future, and minerals from such producers as Zambia and Zaire affected American corporations and markets. Yet, trade and investment in the Republic of South Africa loomed larger than that of any other single African country. Purchases of minerals from that country involved a considerable proportion of American imports.

In the economic field, the United States could choose either to foster trade and investment generally or to try to shape it for certain defined ends. The latter choice would certainly have a bearing on relations with South Africa. The former would perhaps cause local resentment about the imperialistic role of American corporations. Nevertheless, on purely economic grounds, the entire African relationship could hardly claim a primary place in the policy process.

A similar set of choices could be made with regard to official foreign assistance. Africa had never claimed a great share of the now-dwindling American aid to developing countries. During the Nixon administration, what aid there was went mainly to selected "countries of concentration" such as Ethiopia and Kenya. Other segments of foreign aid flowed through international organizations, such as the UN Development Program and the World Bank, where the United States did not direct the allocations but could argue persuasively for its goals.

In addition, the United States usually reacted quickly to natural disasters and to flows of refugees, often furnishing supplies on a humanitarian basis. The beginning of the Carter administration offered a moment to outline new emphases for review of existing programs. Some of these programs would involve bilateral negotiations, while others depended on American influence in international bodies.

Allocations of military assistance had never figured prominently in American treatment of Africa, generally, but they had, in fact, been used in several local contexts. The general question of expanding their use faced the new administration, especially given the fears that the Cuban troops in Angola created in Zaire and Zambia. Furthermore, the United States had furnished military material and training to the Ethiopian armed forces, which had taken over the government in 1974 and, since that time, moved increasingly to the left and toward a close relationship with the Soviet Union. Shortly thereafter, a contingent of Cubans entered Ethiopia.

The government of Zaire also looked to the United States for military equipment. Nigeria, which had built up its armed force to one of the largest in Africa, might have become a customer as well.

In addition, the United States had been involved with clandestine military efforts in Angola and could choose a deeper connection there and in Zaire. Despite these past practices, Carter had promised during his campaign to reduce the international arms traffic, and he had criticized the Central Intelligence Agency for employing methods like those used in Angola.

Finally, the new administration could not avoid difficult policy choices with regard to Rhodesia, South Africa, and Namibia. Although each of these situations had its own peculiarities, all of them posed issues of human rights. In South Africa and Rhodesia, the majority of the population had no voice in government and suffered racial segregation. The same was true in Namibia. As an erstwhile ward of the League of Nations, for which the United Nations now took legal responsibility, Namibia had an especially strong international aspect.

Options open to the new administration were to continue trying to bring the Rhodesian authorities into an international round table discussion that would eventually be executed under UN auspices, to spur the development of an "internal settlement," to abandon the territory to its fate, or to support liberation movements.

As for South Africa and, in general, for South African-occupied Namibia, the options available to the United States were, on the one hand, the treatment of racial injustice as a matter of national jurisdiction or, on the other, as a matter of broad international concern.

The Carter administration's campaign promises effectively eliminated the first option, but still posed difficulties in regard to the second. The United States could continue to try to exert persuasion through a bilateral route, move towards the more radical demands for coercion that the UN General Assembly voiced, attempt to find negotiated solutions through the United Nations, or arrange some other form of coalition. The United States could also attempt to press South Africa into behaving with justice toward its majority of blacks. As for Namibia, South Africa might be induced to allow the territory independence, if some incentives were offered. Or, it might be coerced as the majority of the members of the United Nations demanded.

Dealing with any of these issues could prove hazardous and costly. Adopting a cold war attitude toward Soviet and Cuban involvement in Africa implied that other relationships, such as arms negotiations, might suffer. Furnishing economic or military aid could open an expensive and unpredictable competition, which Congress would be loath to support.

The same was true of greatly expanded foreign aid, the absence of which could suggest to the Third World that the American position on the North-South dialogue, and demands for a new international economic order, was hostile. The reaction could conceivably disrupt the whole world economy, as the oil boycott of 1973 demonstrated.

Assistance to liberation forces could cause a conflict with the Soviet Union, their major military supplier; yet it would not guarantee the successful replacement of minority regimes by those who are friendly to the United States. Failure to act on southern African issues would undermine American friendships elsewhere in Africa. Strong action against Rhodesia and South Africa might fail and would, in any case, require large expenditures.

As for the choice of machinery, dependence on bilateral efforts would cause suspicion that unsavory deals were being arranged by the United States. The "front-line states"—the loose group of countries bordering on or closely involved with Rhodesian and South African affairs—had limited capacity and sometimes could not achieve unity. Use of the United Nations brought uncertainty about the outcomes and complexities in execution, especially because the Soviet Union had an unavoidable omnipresence in the organization.

As for sizable clandestine operations, the Vietnam War and its bitter aftermath induced a redefinition of the role of the American Central Intelligence Agency and an unmistakable limitation on its use. Decision makers in Washington and influential groups in the country were not likely to support its "operations." To cap these difficulties, a growing sense of skepticism about the propriety and usefulness of American efforts to shape events in Africa began to be increasingly visible in Congress.

CARTER'S DIPLOMACY: UNCERTAIN RECORD

Two major principles governed the Carter administration's initial approach to African affairs. The first of these related to competition with the

Soviet Union (and, less urgently, China) and its allies for influence in Africa. The new administration sought to disconnect its behavior in Africa from competitiveness with the Soviet Union.

In fact, the Carter administration expected the blessings of relaxed relationships with the Soviet Union concerning Europe and arms control to frame relationships in Africa. Thus, the Carter administration would cultivate friendships with African governments on the basis of specifically African issues, such as decolonization in southern Africa.

The second principle placed the treatment of African affairs within the broader interest of the Carter administration in promoting higher standards of human rights through American foreign policy decisions. While the emphasis on human rights was global in its design, it was particularly applicable to Africa, where the last governments dominated by a white minority held out against universal disapproval.

Both of these principles proved difficult to apply, partly because a new administration in Washington cannot automatically change the rest of the world. Furthermore, the inattentiveness of American political elites was not suddenly transformed into attentiveness. The Carter administration, therefore, could not assume leadership in African affairs where it wished; it had to react to initiatives of other powers and domestic publics.

The continuing military assistance policies of the Soviet Union and the presence of the Cuban forces in Angola constituted the most important facts to which the Carter administration had to react. Furthermore, the challenge to Washington grew sharply after Somalia invaded Ogaden Province in Ethiopia in 1977. The Soviet Union simply cut its close ties with Somalia, declined to back the latter's claims for the Somali-inhabited parts of Ogaden Province, and supported a transfer of more than 10,000 Cubans to Ethiopia.

This switch in Soviet interests cut across any remaining hopes that the United States may have had for reestablishing the close friendship with Ethiopia that had prevailed during the rule of the deposed Emperor Haile Selassie. It left a choice between neutrality and support for Somali claims on Ethiopia, and it opened the possibility of a sharp conflict with the Soviet Union. Whatever direction the Carter administration chose, the Soviet and Cuban stance in Africa aroused strong sentiments in the United States— above all in Congress—among those who viewed Soviet gains as American losses.

Nevertheless, Washington neither supported Somalian adventuring nor stepped into the breach left by Soviet influence. Rather, it warned the Soviet Union not to provoke broader hostilities in Africa or send Cuban troops against the neighbors of Ethiopia. In fact, the Cubans neither invaded Somalia nor took much part in the struggle that the Ethiopian forces carried on with a nagging insurrection in the province of Eritrea.

There is no question, however, that the presence of the Cubans, along with Soviet advisers and tons of military equipment, heightened Ethiopian military capacities. Consequently, the Somali invaders were driven out, and the Eritrean rebels were severely reduced.

The circumstances of Soviet and Cuban support for an Ethiopian government that explicitly shifted to a Marxist and anti-American posture directly challenged the intention of the Carter government to shun cold war tactics. In fact, National Security Adviser Zbigniew Brzezinski soon spoke of possible damage to the Strategic Arms Limitation Talks.

Even President Carter hinted that his administration's policy of avoiding the cold war was nearing the limit. Secretary of State Cyrus Vance remarked to a congressional committee that the United States was ready to give ". . . sympathetic consideration to military assistance for countries threatened by Soviet arms and Cuban troops. . . ."

Nevertheless, Somalia could not overcome its own past as a Soviet ally to strike up a close friendship with the United States. The Somali government had no visible support in any American public. Moreover, to support it would put the United States into direct competition with the Soviet Union in Ethiopia, where it was conceivable that American influence had not vanished altogether. The Soviet Union, meanwhile, remained firmly ensconced in its new role as principal sponsor of the Ethiopian military dictators.

The rapid tempo of Soviet activity affected American views of the troubles afflicting Zaire, whose government under President Mobutu had received much American support. The ill-starred Zaireian army still suffered from the endemic indiscipline that set off the Belgian invasion of 1960 and the UN involvement. Since then, Zaire, despite help from Belgium, the United States, and other western countries, has had to be rescued repeatedly from its own excesses.

In 1977, the United States poured military material into an effort by Morocco to come to the aid of the Mobutu government in Shaba Province, where guerillas had come over the border from Angola. Again in 1978, the province was invaded. Despite reports about the presence of Cuban troops, the invasions apparently were carried out by fighters who hankered for the days of Moise Tshombe's secesssion, which had been suppressed by the United Nations in 1964.

In 1978, the United States took a more active role and helped to fly in more than 1,000 French and Belgian paratroopers. They turned back the marauding force that had seized the crucial mining areas and killed thousands. The United States continued to furnish supplies to a patchwork African force to replace the incompetent Zaireian troops. President Carter showed much interest in proposals for an African peace-keeping force to handle such incidents, but he later backed away from an idea that was very controversial in Africa.

However seriously the Carter administration sought the exclusion of the cold war from Africa and the peaceful settlement of disputes through local negotiations, the Cuban and Soviet activities demanded a response. In themselves they could perhaps create a certain stability, as Ambassador Andrew Young had untactfully noted. But such Communist-imposed stability would certainly evoke a critical reaction from active American opinion.

Nevertheless, the Carter administration succeeded in dealing with both the Ethiopian and Shaba affairs rather calmly and without direct military involvement. At the same time, the Carter resolve to avoid the transfer of weapons to African states could not be maintained. In 1978, Secretary of State Vance detailed for Congress agreements to sell military aircraft to the Sudan, whose government was disturbed by events in neighboring Ethiopia. Chad was to be allowed to buy arms; Kenya, also made sensitive by events in Ethiopia, would get help with its security requirements. Zaire was already getting basic military materials and training. And in 1979, the United States made American arms accessible to Morocco, which was busy with an Algerian-supported uprising in a desert territory claimed by both.

The Carter administration's emphasis on human rights guided its policies in southern Africa. In that region, it merged with a renewed interest in the use of international organizations as a vehicle for achieving American goals on the basis of broad support among domestic groups and other governments. The most dramatic symbol of this approach was the appointment of Andrew Young as representative to the United Nations.

Ambassador Young brought to his post the optimism and zeal of the American civil rights movement and a growing interest in African affairs. Additional drama was furnished by President Carter when, in his speech in 1978 in Lagos, he emphasized human rights and equitable economic development.

Building on Kissinger's inconclusive efforts in Rhodesia, Young sought a more prominent role both for the United Nations and for the presidents of the front-line states. Although Kissinger, in 1976, had gotten Ian Smith and some members of the liberation movement to attend a conference in Geneva on the future of Rhodesia, the shrewd Smith soon brought it to a stalemate. Young made it clear that Smith need expect no American assistance in dealing with the mounting pressure exerted by the guerrillas of the Patriotic Front, which was made up of two Rhodesian black parties. Furthermore, Carter began a successful quest for repeal of the Byrd amendment.

Young used his UN vantage point to carry out broad negotiations on Rhodesia, cement a working arrangement with the front-line states, and proceed side-by-side, rather than in tandem, with the British in new negotiations. An Anglo-American plan for a countrywide election, and the transition to a majority government involving temporary British and UN observers and peacekeepers, was the central proposition in this active new American diplomacy.

Meanwhile, South Africa markedly withdrew from its slight, but positive, role in cooperating with the United States to secure the end of the Smith government. Both the Vorster and Botha governments in Pretoria resented Carter's human rights policies and pressure regarding Namibia. By late 1979, South Africa admitted that it had a substantial number of troops in Rhodesia, ensuring that its interests could not be taken as merely neutral or benign.

Ambassador Young himself was dismissed in 1979 because of an unfortunate meeting with a representative of the Palestine Liberation Organization. His skillful successor, Donald F. McHenry, had been part of Young's team from the beginning, but as a foreign service officer he had almost none of Young's political capital. Finally, American efforts in Rhodesia had to adapt to the defeat of the Labour government in the United Kingdom and its replacement by the Conservatives under Margaret Thatcher.

The new British prime minister at once pushed into the Rhodesia affair and, in effect, withdrew it from the United Nations arena. Building on the foundations already laid, a British governor had been installed in Salisbury before Christmas 1979 to mark the end of the Rhodesian rebellion and the beginning of the transition to independence via a legal route. In effect, British influence had overshadowed American policy. The momentum built up by Young and his colleagues in Washington had wound down to the point where, at the end of 1979, the United States followed the British lead in ending sanctions in Rhodesia without waiting for authorization by the Security Council.

In dealing with Namibia, the Carter administration's technique of cooperation in the UN Security Council quickly brought promising results.

Soon after taking office, Andrew Young organized the Western powers that were then members of the Security Council—Britain, France, West Germany, and Canada—into a negotiating team to develop alternatives for dealing with South Africa. At one stage in 1978, their foreign ministers personally visited the new South African prime minister, P. W. Botha. South Africa, in fact, moved some distance toward acceptance of a plan endorsed under American leadership by the Security Council. At the same time, however, South Africa continued to encourage a constitutional convention it had sponsored and pleaded a need to mesh the internal Namibian constitutional mechanism with the UN proposals.

A particularly troubling issue involved the status of the South West Africa People's Organization, a liberation movement that the UN General Assembly had treated as the only legal representative of the Namibian people. SWAPO was an anathema to the government in Pretoria. Moreover, South Africa wanted copper-bound assurances that guerrilla activity from Angola would cease.

By mid-1979, South Africa had dampened, but not quite killed, hopes for an orderly process of decolonization in Namibia. It resented the UN role, which would involve some 10,000 officials and soldiers, in administering an election in Namibia. It had by then sponsored its own election and wanted at least some status for the results. Early in 1981, at a conference in Geneva, the South African government brusquely stopped negotiations on a new UN proposal, completing the stalemate. By the end of 1982, the negotiations still had reached no formal conclusion.

Moreover, South African views of the United States turned increasingly sour as the Carter administration refused to abate its promotion of human rights in southern Africa. Pretoria's fears of guerrilla activity in Rhodesia and in Namibia played a strong part in its resistance. And its internal politics, where the governing white elite would brook no political influence from the majority blacks, also helped to toughen South African policy.

It was widely held in South African political circles that the last strong bastion of white government should do nothing to aid a Marxist-inclined SWAPO to take its place beside the "Communists" of Angola and Mozambique. Finally, many South African leaders clearly expected that Margaret Thatcher's Conservative government in London would ease pressure both on Namibia and South Africa.

As for its treatment of South Africa, the Carter administration dropped the Kissinger policy of limited quiet cooperation. The new leaders in Washington were distressed by the evils of a minority regime that rejected majority political and social participation and mishandled such demonstrations as those in Soweto in 1976. Vice President Mondale and Andrew Young openly favored majority rule in South Africa.

In 1977, the United Nations Security Council finally agreed to boycott sales of arms to South Africa and issued a mandatory order to all member governments. This step had little immediate effect, for the main sellers of arms to South Africa had already shut off or greatly restricted the flow.

Rather, it seriously signalled to Pretoria that the United States was prepared to abandon its earlier rhetorical approach to human rights in South Africa. It was willing to move further toward cooperative action through the United Nations. But, in fact, by the end of 1980, little direct action had been undertaken; the United States had given priority to Rhodesia and Namibia.

The resolve to monitor South African armaments was tested late in 1977. The Soviet Union quietly informed the United States that Soviet satellites had proof that a nuclear test explosion was being prepared in the Kalahari Desert. After the United States confirmed the Soviet evidence, President Carter, joined by the French government, insisted that South Africa cancel the exercise. John Vorster, then Prime Minister, insisted that South Africa had no plans to build nuclear weapons and was testing none. Nevertheless, his government cancelled the test after making bitter statements about misunderstandings of South African intentions.

The issues of trade with Rhodesia and the effect of private American investments in South Africa on the *apartheid* system strained economic and financial relations between Africa and the United States. The Carter administration, as the Nixon-Ford administrations, took a rather neutral position on business with South Africa. It did nothing to encourage it, but needed to do little to discourage new investment.

Interest group activity in the United States had induced most of the American corporations doing business in South Africa to adopt the principles suggested by the Reverend Leon Sullivan, a member of the Board of Directors of General Motors Corporation. The Sullivan principles seek fairer and more favorable treatment for the blacks who work for American-owned firms in South Africa. Criticism by American interest groups and the general economic decline of the South African economy, due in part to the riots of 1976, discouraged new American and other foreign investment. Some

American banks even announced that they would no longer make loans to the South African government or to locally owned enterprises, but this restraint soon disappeared.

American trade with South Africa continued at a brisk level. In part, this trade involved minerals, especially those used in making special steels and other raw materials. Some American business interests—a construction company, for example, that had a large share of the work in putting together the new oil-from-coal industry—pressed for a more favorable governmental attitude toward South Africa. They also sought an end to sanctions in Rhodesia.

Nevertheless, the Sullivan principles were quickly applied by many American businesses with operations in South Africa, suggesting that their managers were not particularly wedded to the conditions of work established by rigid *apartheid*. Those firms with large investments, such as the automobile manufacturers who could be expected to have an interest in expanding their sales to blacks, were among the first to accept the principles. At least one opinion survey among American businessmen who knew South African conditions disclosed widespread skepticism about the long-term stability of South Africa as a site for their operations.

In fact, the involvement of American enterprises with the rest of Africa was growing much faster than with South Africa. One recent estimate shows that the United States was selling one-third of its African exports to South Africa and two-thirds to the rest of the continent. Half of the American imports from Africa came from Nigeria, a major oil producer, while South Africa furnished only 10 percent. Furthermore, even though more than 300 South African firms are owned by interests in the United States, only a handful of these had any significant share of their operations and capital in the country. Typically, the great multinationals had approximately one percent or less of their investments, sales, and profits connected with South Africa.

THE CARTER RECORD: AN EVALUATION

The Carter administration's approach to Africa represented both a return to earlier excitement about the continent and a genuinely new approach. This new approach proceeded from two principles: the competitiveness of the cold war should be kept out of Africa, and American policy should promote the advancement of human rights. While both of these principles represented a quite different emphasis from that of the Nixon-Ford administrations, the Carter establishment benefitted from the steps made in the final months of its predecessors.

Yet, despite its head start on southern African problems and its good intentions for the rest of the continent, the Carter policy toward Africa faced many difficulties by the end of 1980. A severe critic might say that the policy had been found wanting in the toughest tests and inconclusive at other times.

Although the United States had built for itself a role in the negotiations about Rhodesia and had reactivated the United Nations with regard to that issue, a new British government made the conclusive moves, apparently largely on its own initiative. The situation in Namibia remained unclear as the South African government neither broke off negotiations nor provided any real help in concluding a settlement. Rather, the U.N. Secretary-General could be found at the end of 1980 still trying to find diplomatic bargains that would allow Namibian independence. Meanwhile, a South African-sponsored government put down some sort of roots in Windhoek.

Furthermore, substantial opposition to deep involvement in Africa had built up in Congress, while publics supporting the new approaches in Africa had lost such spokesmen as Senator Dick Clark, who was not reelected, and Representative Charles Diggs, who gave up his committee chairmanship after conviction on charges of taking kickbacks from his staff. Even Carter's successful effort to repeal the Byrd Amendment came under renewed pressure from conservative elements in Congress.

To protect his adherence to the UN sanction program, the president had to promise to lift the trade embargo as soon as a freely chosen government was installed in Salisbury. Accordingly, the United States acted to do so even before the matter was brought before the Security Council, which had ordered the sanctions in the first place. The African group in the United Nations promptly protested this violation of international law.

Successful shepherding of Rhodesia to a desired new status and Namibia to independence would have had a strongly favorable impact on American prestige in Africa. The United States had managed to create a positive relationship with the front-line states and with distant Nigeria, a strong backer of change in southern Africa. Yet, the administration's commitment, in fact, remained highly limited. It would do everything possible to seek out a diplomatic settlement, but it avoided giving direct support to the liberation movements in Rhodesia and Namibia. As the months went by and resolution of the situation in Namibia grew more doubtful, increasing skepticism about the seriousness of the American intention became evident.

Similar skepticism prevailed in South Africa. The United States under Carter, and earlier, had always avoided an open duel with South Africa. There was every good reason to do so; for, unless the United States and most of the rest of the world were willing to make a broad commitment, including the use of force, probably little could be accomplished in the short term.

Nevertheless, in 1976, many South African political leaders showed apprehension about the new American government, and they might have been willing to accommodate it in some ways. The negotiations on Namibia offered some evidence for such a view. Yet, when South Africa's firm resistance challenged the United States to do the worst, the response from Washington was anything but clear and stirring.

The dubious results of the Carter approach to southern Africa poses

difficulties in the rest of Africa. The Cuban troops still were active in
Ethiopia and Angola, and substantial voices in Washington warned of additional Soviet adventuring.

The president himself cautioned the Soviet Union. If the United States
could neither prevent the reemergence of competition with the Soviet Union
nor resolve the situation in southern Africa, African governments might well
develop doubts about what American policy could accomplish. Such reduced credibility could hardly be resolved by humanitarian aid or contributions to economic development from the United States.

The preference for treating African issues through existing institutions,
especially the United Nations, remained a strong one in the Carter administration. Andrew Young clearly had a leading role in developing policy towards Africa, and he and his staff did much to execute it. He had, in fact,
created obviously warm and trusting contacts with his African opposite
numbers.

Ambassador Donald McHenry, Young's successor, continued to enjoy
the confidence of African representatives. Yet the United Nations had little
capacity to create new politics in Africa in the short term, even with much
American input. It served well during the Carter administration to channel
diplomatic efforts and long-term programs. It helped to legitimize American
efforts and elicit cooperation from the front-line states in order to make
pressure from Washington on South Africa more effective. It also attracted
domestic criticism in an impatient United States where only expert publics
understood the advantages and limitations of dealing with Africa through the
United Nations.

The activity of Carter's African policy dwindled during the last months
of his administration. This reflected the administration's general confusion
about human rights as an issue in international politics and how such issues
should be handled. It also reflected that groups (many comprised of American blacks) who hoped to extend the protection of human rights had a
decreasing influence within the Carter administration. A million Somali
refugees pouring out of Ethiopia generated humanitarian feelings and caused
a momentary surge in the interest level of the American public in Africa, but this spurt did not transfer to other African issues. The Carter
administration ended with good starts on African relationships, but more
questionable results from the application of its policies.

THE 1980 CAMPAIGN AND THE REAGAN ADMINISTRATION:
ISSUES FOR THE 1980s

The 1980 electoral campaign saw heavy attacks on the Carter policy towards
Africa. The most general element in this attack by candidate Reagan had to
do with the human rights approach, the keystone of the Carter program in
Africa. The Reagan attack adroitly took advantage of what could only be a
weakness; the creation of a decent standard of human rights was a task too

difficult, possibly, for even the most brilliant presidential team. Governor Reagan also let it be known that South Africa need not be treated as a pariah and that pressure there, as elsewhere in situations where civil and political rights were denied, failed to serve American interests. Reagan appeared to accept the South African claim that its racial relations were its business or, at least, not that of the United States. In addition, Reagan had little positive to say about the use of international institutions to deal with global political issues. His lack of interest in the United Nations system and his general identification with conservative foes of the world organization left little doubt that the Carter approach would be abandoned. Nevertheless, Africa was no more a major issue in the campaign of 1980 than it had been previously.

As president, Governor Reagan clearly chose to return to a lower level in the cycle of concern that had characterized the pre-Carter treatment of the continent. The new president had little to fear from the reaction of human rights groups and those representing blacks, for he was elected without their help. He endorsed the older pattern of viewing Africa through the lens of relationships with the Soviet Union. He appointed a specialist on southern Africa as Assistant Secretary of State for African Affairs. This suggests that the Reagan administration accepted the notion that what Pretoria did would have great importance on the continent. At the same time, in a spirit of "constructive engagement," the Reagan administration approached South Africa as an anti-Communist friend, a claim the governments in Pretoria never tired of making. President Reagan even asserted in a television interview that South Africa had been a dependable ally in all recent wars, apparently overlooking the fact that the architects of the nationalist government had done their planning during the Second World War in an internment camp for pro-German elements.

As for using the United Nations creatively as a channel for aggregating opinion on Africa and legitimating American positions, the Reagan administration simply began to dismantle the Carter approach. The new ambassador to the United Nations, Jeane Kirkpatrick, showed little interest in the human rights aspects of African politics. Like her superiors in Washington, she saw the world institution as one more battleground against Soviet influence generally in the world and in Africa. If her simple approach became more sophisticated during Reagan's first two years, she nevertheless could not regain lost trust from the UN majority.

In fact, by the middle of 1981, the United Nations served as an indicator of growing African impatience with the approach of the United States in southern Africa. The African governments forced a vote in the Security Council on a resolution condemning the South African government for mounting an attack on Angola. South African troops penetrated deep within the territory in an effort, according to Pretoria, to disarm SWAPO guerillas. The United States vetoed the resolution, thus appearing to stand on the side of South Africa. Whether the United States in fact supported the South

African attack, which it also criticized, its veto was consistent with the Reagan administration's policy of positive engagement in the region. Opponents of this policy in the United Nations noted that it had not prevented another major act of violence.

By late 1982, no conclusive movement had taken place in the glacial negotiations over Namibia. The contact group, inherited from the Carter initiatives, continued the negotiations from a position only vaguely within the Security Council framework. American hopes of extracting the Cuban forces from Angola reinforced South African linkage of that issue with Namibian independence. Consequently, the United States as the senior partner bore the brunt of mounting criticism from the frontline states. Furthermore, the friction over Namibia could be felt in relationships with Zimbabwe, formerly Rhodesia. Contrary to the scare stories that the Western press had featured during the long armed conflict, Zimbabwe turned out to have moderate economic policies and an unslaked thirst for capitalistic investment. But the Reagan administration's doctrine of reliance on the free market allowed little chance to provide official development assistance to the Mugabe government.

Elsewhere in Africa, which appeared to get relatively less attention than the active southern African region, relations with oil-supplying Nigeria continued to move on a reasonably even keel, given the preoccupation with Namibia and *apartheid* in South Africa. The United States took no significant role in turbulence caused in Chad by Libya, still a sworn enemy of the Reagan administration. This unpleasant relationship was only sealed by the downing of two Libyan aircraft by American naval forces in the Mediterranean. Nevertheless, the relationships, with Libya and Egypt as well were largely based on Middle Eastern politics rather than events south of the Sahara. In the Horn of Africa, the United States took an active share in supporting the maintenance of more than a million refugees from Ethiopia in Sudan and Somalia. Especially in the latter, the target of occasional raids from Ethiopia and a standing area of discord, the United States increased its involvement by supplying military equipment as well as relief for refugees from Ethiopian Ogaden Province, but the Somali pleas for what would amount to a formal alliance and base privileges at the Red Sea port of Berbera went unanswered. Finally, the United States tried to demonstrate support and friendship for the governments of such nations as Kenya and the Ivory Coast that pinned their faith on free market economics for economic development.

The strong element of East-West competition in Reagan policy towards Africa was unmistakable. However much the administration insisted that African politics must be subordinated to East-West competition, it still had to face the same choice its predecessors faced: the degree to which Africa can be a testing ground. It will, however, probably end as previous administrations, with primary attention to Soviet activities in the Middle East and the Caribbean areas.

More active anti-Soviet leadership in Africa would probably involve broader American commitments such as support for non-Communist resistance groups, whenever they can be found, and increased levels of development assistance. The first tests of such ideas, including the repeal of the congressional prohibition against covert aid to groups in Angola, attracted little domestic support. In any event, such activities would inevitably stir the deep waters of UN politics, which the Reagan administration regarded with suspicion. The first attempts to ease the pressure on South Africa caused some domestic stir in the United States, enthusiasm in South Africa, and not a whit of movement in Pretoria's effort to cling to control of Namibia. The Reagan administration welcomed the South African foreign minister to the White House and sent the Assistant Secretary of State and his superior, the Undersecretary, to South Africa. However, it was doubtful that the administration would have the political will to put much effort into Africa when Poland and China beckoned as opportunities to thwart the Russians.

The presence of Cubans and East Germans in Angola, Ethiopia, and elsewhere in Africa concerned the Reagan administration even more visibly, perhaps, than its predecessor. Some administration supporters understood the Soviet presence in Africa to be connected with Cuban claims to leadership in the Third World. Fidel Castro's eagerness to represent the views of the Nonaligned Group only strengthened their argument. The continuing Soviet domination of Afghanistan, viewed as evidence of an expansionist policy, added another reason to comprehend Africa as a real, if secondary, theater of East-West competition. Such a view was simply unacceptable to most governments in Africa, however joyous the South African reaction might be.

Furthermore, the Reagan administration, as any American government would, faces parallel categories of difficulties on the continent itself. On the one hand, the continued existence of *apartheid* in South Africa and weak governments in Zimbabwe and Mozambique might encourage armed action by guerrillas and, perhaps, adventuring by outside powers. Such turbulence tends to disturb other relationships and spread from its center. On the other hand, Africa has a share that cannot be overlooked in setting the tone of North-South relationships in the larger sphere of the world economy.

As American connections to the economies of African countries broaden, as they are likely to do despite the relatively modest potential in many places, economic relationships of both specific and general character are likely to require more attention. The stance of African governments on North-South issues will be determined in part by ideological judgments regarding American action to end racism and promote human rights and economic welfare.

Thus, although Africa is unlikely to rival such centers of constant American attention as Western Europe, it, nevertheless, will often figure prominently on the foreign policy agenda.

FOR FURTHER READING

Bienen, Henry. "U.S. Foreign Policy in a Changing Africa," *Political Science Quarterly*, 93 (Fall 1978), 443–464.

Foltz, William J. "United States Policy Toward Southern Africa," *Political Science Quarterly*, 92 (Spring 1977), 47–64.

Gordenker, Leon. "Afrikaner Nationalism and the Plight of South Africa," *The Yale Review* (June 1979), 481–500.

Legum, Colin. "Crisis in Africa," *Foreign Affairs*, 57 (1979), 633–651.

Legum, Colin; Zartman, I. William; Mytelka, Lynn; and Langdon, Steven. *Africa in the 1980s: A Continent in Crisis* (New York, N.Y.: McGraw-Hill, 1979).

Ottaway, David and Marina. *Afrocommunism* (New York, N.Y.: Holmes and Meier, 1981).

Study Commission on U.S. Policy Toward Southern Africa. *South Africa: Time Running Out*. (Berkeley, Ca.: University of California Press, 1981).

chapter 8

The United States and the United Nations

STANLEY J. MICHALAK, JR.

By the mid-1970s, American support for the United Nations reached its nadir in the entire postwar period. In November of 1975, 51 percent of the American public felt that the United Nations was doing a poor job, as opposed to 35 percent who rated the world organization as doing a good or fair job. In the Senate, two sets of hearings were held on American foreign policy toward the United Nations in less than one year, and, by unanimous vote, both houses of Congress voted to prohibit United States participation in The United Nations Decade to Combat Racism and Racial Discrimination.

The basis for all this concern stemmed from a widespread perception that the United Nations had been transformed into a force hostile to American ideals, interests, and policies. Preoccupied with the war in Vietnam, the pursuit of détente, the Strategic Arms Limitation Talks, and the opening of relations with the People's Republic of China, American policy makers directed little attention to the United Nations from the mid-1960s until the mid-1970s.

During this decade, however, the United States increasingly found itself in a minority on a wide range of issues within the world organization. In response to its increasing isolation, the United States adopted a low-profile policy and worked behind the scenes to prevent the appearance of resolutions most distasteful to it. Increasingly, however, American delegates found themselves voting against or abstaining on resolutions in the General Assembly and using the veto in the Security Council.

In 1974 and 1975, the low-profile strategy ran its course as various actions, especially within the General Assembly, presented the United States with a situation of *crisis* proportions in the technical sense of that term—surprise, a high threat to strongly held values and interests, and a perceived necessity to respond with speed.

Immediately after the Arab oil embargo in 1973, the Third World nations hastily called and dominated a Special Session of the General Assembly that rammed through a series of resolutions calling for the establishment of a New International Economic Order (NIEO) over the strenuous objections of the United States and other developing countries.

While many of the proposals contained in these resolutions had been discussed for years, the shrillness and strident anti-Western stance taken by Third World spokesmen was extremely disconcerting to many in the developed countries. Among the proposals themselves, those calling for the formation of more producer cartels along the lines of OPEC, price indexation (the linkage of prices for commodities to the prices of industrial goods), and reparations from the developed to the underdeveloped countries seemed most ominous.

In addition to a vast challenge in the economic sphere, the General Assembly and other international institutions were increasingly taking procedural and substantive actions that challenged American interests and allies. In 1974, Israel was excluded from the regional groupings of UNESCO, and anti-Israeli resolutions were becoming increasingly harsh and common in United Nation forums. In 1975, these anti-Israeli actions reached their climax when Yasir Arafat, leader of the Palestine Liberation Organization (PLO), addressed the General Assembly and the Assembly adopted a resolution equating Zionism with racism.

Impatient with the slow progress in ending the problems of Rhodesia, Namibia (Southwest Africa), and *apartheid* in South Africa, the Third World took new initiatives in these areas as well. In addition to their usual anti-South African resolutions, the Third World majority took the unprecedented action in 1974 of denying South Africa's participation in the work of the General Assembly.

In these same years, American decision makers also feared that a Communist bloc–Third World coalition would terminate the United Nations command in Korea without providing any secure continuation of the armistice arrangements between North and South Korea. More irritating than threatening were efforts by Third World and communist countries to brand American relations with Puerto Rico and Guam as "imperialistic" and "colonial."

On a wide range of fronts, then, the United States and some of its closest allies were the objects of constant invective, attack, and hostile resolutions in the United Nations. Increasingly, in fact, many seemingly non-political institutions or conferences, such as the International Labor Organization or the World Conference of the International Woman's Year, became forums for the consideration and adoption of nongermane political resolutions. The International Women's Conference, for example, included in its final resolution a call for the "elimination of Zionism, *apartheid,* [and] racial discrimination."

Especially irritating to many Americans was a clear double standard in the arguments and actions of the Third World majority. Communist Vietnam was considered acceptable for United Nations membership, but South Korea was not. Israel was condemned and threatened with sanctions for attacking PLO bases in Lebanon, while terrorist activities regularly undertaken by PLO forces were ignored. Human rights failures in Chile and South Africa were regularly denounced, while persistent and more egregious violations in such Third World and communist countries as Uganda and Cambodia were ignored.

At the conclusion of the Twenty-Ninth General Assembly (1974), the American Ambassador to the United Nations, John Scali, spoke out against ". . . the growing tendency of [the United Nations] to adopt one-sided, unrealistic resolutions that cannot be implemented . . . [and] an arbitrary disregard of United Nations rules, even of its own charter."

"This organization," Scali told the assembled delegates, "has become today a clear and present danger. . . ." He concluded by sternly warning that, unless the world organization replaced its current practice of passing resolutions "uncritically endorsing the most far-reaching claims of one side in dangerous international disputes" with efforts at compromise and negotiation, eroding support for the world organization in Congress and among the American people would plummet even further.

THE PROBLEM AND ITS COMPONENTS

The underlying basis for the events related in the preceding paragraphs lay largely in the increased membership of the United Nations and the concerns, interests, and positions of a new majority of developing states. In 1945, the world organization consisted of 51 members, most of which were Western-style democracies or pro-American Latin American dictatorships. At that time, and for at least a decade following, an American-led majority of the United Nations was largely supportive of the territorial, economic, legal, and social status quo; excepting, of course, Soviet territorial gains in Eastern Europe.

Thirty years later, the United Nations was quite a different organization. The membership was approaching 150, of which only about a quarter were democracies. A new majority of Afro-Asian and increasingly independent Latin American states now controlled the General Assembly and all other United Nations institutions where the one nation, one vote principle applied.

Unlike the early majority, however, this new majority sought to change radically the international economic and legal status quo, and to use the world organization not to maintain the territorial status quo, but to change it in the Middle East and southern Africa. Thus, the new majority used its voting power effusively in passing resolutions expressing its own, and often one-sided solutions to the problems it placed on the agenda of international institutions.

In the face of these changes, the United States and other developed countries pursued a policy of "damage limitation" by opposing or abstaining on the increasing number of resolutions it disagreed with. In fact, until the mid-1970s, the United Nations was clearly of minimal importance to American decision makers, and the damage limitation strategy might have been continued indefinitely had it not been for the success of OPEC, the collapse of Portuguese colonialism in Africa, and the intervention of Cuban troops in Angola. The success of OPEC presaged both increased power for the developing countries individually (and perhaps collectively) and exposed serious economic vulnerabilities in the powerful developed countries. The collapse of Portuguese colonialism and the entrance of Cuban troops in Africa meant that the United States could no longer rely on rhetoric to get by in that part of the world.

Clearly, then, continued reliance on damage limitation would be risky. Thus, the United States and its allies were faced with the need for a reassessment and stock taking. The challenges presented by the new majority were, of course, many, but three areas seemed most pressing to Western decision-makers: (1) the economic challenge, (2) the political challenge, and (3) the problem of politicization.

The Economic Challenge

Since the first meeting of the United Nations Conference on Trade and Development (UNCTAD) in 1964, the less-developed countries have been lobbying for major revisions in the existing international economic order, which is based on the principles of free trade, comparative advantage, and most-favored-nation status. Originally operating as a monolithic bloc of 77 countries (thereafter termed the "Group of 77"), the developing countries have adopted, over strong objections from the developed countries, numerous resolutions calling for a new international economic order.

The theoretical basis for the 77's demands stemmed from the work of Raul Prebisch, a Latin American economist and Secretary General of the Economic Commission of Latin America. According to Prebisch, the basic terms of trade under the existing international order have been much to the disadvantage of the largely commodity-exporting developing countries. In a series of papers and reports, Prebisch argued that the prices the developing countries received for their raw material and agricultural exports were consistently declining, relative to the prices of the finished goods and manufactured products that they imported.

In addition to declining terms of trade, Prebisch also pointed out that frequent and unanticipated fluctuations in the prices of primary commodities often presented developing countries with sudden shortfalls in income. These price fluctuations were of such frequency and magnitude, Prebisch argued, that planning for development was extremely difficult.

Moreover, if less-developed countries tried to solve this export problem by processing and finishing the products they exported in order to increase their earnings (say, turning their cacao beans into packaged hot chocolate), this strategy would fail because high tariffs on processed raw materials in developed countries would make the less-developed countries' finished goods uncompetitive with those of domestic producers in developed countries.

If the less-developed countries tried to solve their trade problem by diversifying their economies, they also faced obstacles. If they opened their doors to multinational corporations, they feared the domination and manipulation of their economic and, perhaps, political systems by strong alien forces. If they tried to industrialize on their own, their lack of knowledge about high technology forced them to concentrate on labor-intensive, low-technology industries such as textiles, which faced stiff tariff or nontariff barriers in developed countries because such goods would compete favorably with declining domestic industries.

Even when such barriers did not exist, the lack of technical expertise in less-developed countries often made their manufactured goods less competitive with similar goods produced by exporting developed countries. That is, given the most-favored-nation principle, all countries exporting a manufactured product would face an identical tariff barrier. Because manufactured goods from less-developed countries were often more expensive than the same goods from developed countries, equal tariffs would actually put the less-developed countries' goods at a disadvantage.

Thus, the existing international economic order was seen as "rigged" against the developing countries and as an obstacle to their development. Consequently, a major goal of the developing countries since UNCTAD I (1964) has been to rewrite the rules of the existing international economic order, so that development could proceed through increasing trade instead of reliance on declining amounts of aid from the developed countries.

Of the many proposals that Prebisch made for altering the existing economic order, four were especially sought: (1) commodity agreements to stabilize price fluctuations, (2) the abolition of tariffs in the developed countries on processed and semiprocessed goods from developing countries, (3) tariff preferences for manufactured goods exported by developing countries, and (4) compensatory financing.

Since trade in 12 commodities creates about 80 percent of the export earnings of developing countries, Prebisch advocated agreed-upon prices for these products to stabilize earnings and arrest the declining terms of trade. The abolition of tariffs on processed and semi-processed products would create greater employment and export earnings for the developing countries. Tariff preferences would allow manufactured goods from developing countries to enter the market of developed countries duty free or at a lower tariff than identical goods from developed countries. This would give products from developing countries a competitive edge over exports from developed countries.

A compensatory financing system would provide automatic loans at low interest rates from international institutions to developing countries when prices for commodities unexpectedly dropped and export earning shortfalls occurred. Such a system would ensure greater income certainty in planning programs for development.

Throughout the mid-1960s and early 1970s, the United States and other developed countries balked at these proposals and rejected Prebisch's thesis that the terms of trade between rich and poor countries had been unfavorable to the latter. Commodity agreements were viewed as an interference with the free market and considered unworkable on the basis of past experience.

Tariff preferences might bring back into the international system the trade discrimination of the 1930s and would violate the cardinal principle of equal treatment or "most favored nation" status that had been a fundamental tenet of the liberal postwar trading system. The reduction of tariffs on processed and semiprocessed goods faced serious domestic opposition in most developed countries.

Finally, proposals for compensatory financing and demands that developed countries increase their then-official aid from the existing .3 to .7 of one percent of their GNP, were rejected as implicitly amounting to an obligatory tax that was a violation of sovereignty.

Frustrated with their inability to secure these goals, the demands of the Third World countries became increasingly radical in the 1970s, especially after the success of OPEC in 1974. In addition to commodity agreements, the 77 advocated producer associations or cartels for commodities that would seek not merely to stabilize prices, but to raise them significantly, as the OPEC cartel did in regard to oil. Once such associations were created and prices raised, price indexing schemes would keep the prices of commodities pegged to the prices of industrial goods exported from the developed countries.

Increasingly hostile to multinational corporations, the less-developed countries also began inserting the phrase "permanent sovereignty over natural resources" into their resolutions. This phrase signified that the underdeveloped countries alone would decide what compensation, if any, would be paid to multinational corporations in the event of nationalization and expropriation.

Given this background, the behavior of the Third World countries on economic issues in 1974 and 1975 is easily explainable. In 1974, the struggle for a new international economic system moved from UNCTAD to the General Assembly itself. In the Sixth Special Session of the General Assembly (1974), the Third World majority passed its resolution calling for a New International Economic Order over strong Western objections.

In the regular session of the General Assembly of that year, a Charter of Economic Rights and Duties was also adopted over strong opposition from the developed countries. The United States and the other developed countries, already alarmed over a four-fold increase in the price of oil and one oil embargo, feared facing similar price increases on other commodities. Clearly, the developed countries were facing a major political and economic challenge.

The Political Challenges

The major political challenges that the United States faced in the United Nations during the mid-1970s involved the Middle East and South Africa. While the Nixon administration tried to pursue a "more even-handed" posture between the Arabs and Israelis, the Yom Kippur War, the success of OPEC, and the increasingly pro-Arab actions in the United Nations required a new United States response.

While the greatly increased oil income flowing into the Middle East meant that Arab countries no longer needed to rely on the Soviet Union for arms and other assistance, the need for Arab oil also increased Arab leverage over the developed countries, especially Western Europe and Japan.

In Africa, the collapse of Portuguese colonialism, the entrance of Cuban troops in Angola, and Communist bloc aid in southern Africa generally meant that if the United States did not actively seek to solve the serious political problems on that continent, the African countries might take more forceful initiatives with support from the communist countries. Secretary of State Kissinger's policy of speaking out against the racial situation in southern Africa, but doing nothing of substance to change that system, had become untenable.

The minor political problems facing the United States in the United Nations stemmed from Communist bloc and Third World efforts often led by Cuba, a member of both camps, to isolate the United States on the issues of Korea, Guam, and Puerto Rico. In terms of cold power, withdrawal of the United Nations' command in Korea might make little difference, but the withdrawal of the world organization's imprimatur would weaken the legitimacy of United States forces in that country.

The United Nations clearly had no power to force the United States to grant independence to the territories of Guam and Puerto Rico, the majority of whose populations did not, in fact, favor independence. But, again, continual United Nations pressure and resolutions could further isolate and tarnish America's image.

"Politicization"

Many Third World countries viewed as hypocrisy Western, and especially American, complaints about politicization, "theatrics," and totalitarianism.

Had not the United States used the General Assembly and other United Nations forums to legitimize its positions over the tiny Soviet minority in the first decade of the cold war? Did the United States not engage in bloc building when it led the United Nations majority?

And as to theatrics, did United States Ambassador Warren Austin not jump out from under the Security Council table, brandishing a captured Soviet-made machine gun during a debate on the Korean War? Was not the United States making the same arguments about "automatic paper majorities" that the Soviet Union had made when the latter country was in the position the United States now found itself? The problem facing the United States, Third World delegates argued, stemmed not from voting procedures, but from the fact that American positions on important issues before the world organization were out of step with the vast majority of nations.

While acknowledging that the United States did seek to see its positions prevail in the Assembly during the period when it exercised great influence, American policy makers still saw a qualitative difference in what the new majority was doing. Never had the United States sought to expel a member state, as some members were attempting to do in regard to South Africa and Israel. Never had the United States sought to limit the time allotted to its opponents in General Assembly debates as the Third World majority had done in regard to Israel. Nor did the United States intrude political matters into the agenda and work of the technical and specialized agencies.

For example, while the United States worked to have Soviet intervention in Hungary condemned in the General Assembly, it did not introduce such resolutions in UNESCO or the World Meteorological Organization. In summary, the United States perceived continual and increasing violations of the integrity of the process and charter of the United Nations and its affiliated agencies.

THE FORD-KISSINGER RESPONSE

In the spring of 1975, the Ford administration responded to this situation with a new ambassador to the United Nations and a new strategy of "accommodation and opposition." The new ambassador was Daniel Patrick Moynihan, recent American Ambassador to India and author of a new United Nations strategy for the administration that he outlined in the March 1975 issue of *Commentary* magazine.

Moynihan's basic thesis was that the United Nations was now dominated by a new majority of nations that were heirs of what he termed the "British Revolution." This revolution, Moynihan argued, occurred with the incorporation of key elements of British socialist thought into the ideologies of many recently independent countries in the Third World. Included in this ideology are an emphasis on, if not a preoccupation with, *distribution* over production; a perception of profit as exploitation; a preference for public over private economic ventures; a transfer of the domestic theory of exploitation to the international system whereby the developed countries were perceived as capitalist exploiters and the developing countries as "workers"; and a strong, almost reflexive, anti-Americanism that explained why the United States was so often criticized while the many transgressions of the Soviet Union were ignored.

Moynihan proposed that the United States respond to this situation by "going into opposition." This would entail recognizing that the new majority shared a destructive ideology that was hostile to the developed countries. Furthermore, it was not in the interests of those countries who saw it as a panacea for their economic underdevelopment.

Moynihan proposed that the United States should act in the United Nations as an opposition party would in a domestic parliamentary system, by speaking up against the dominant ideology and offering constructive alternatives to those put forth by the majority. The United States should speak up, Moynihan argued, for the system of liberal capitalism whereby 18 percent of the world's population produced over 64 percent of the world's products.

Economic failures in the Third World, he argued, should be laid to the failures of those nations themselves, while the success stories of those developing countries that adopted market and capitalist models, such as Singapore, South Korea, Brazil, and Taiwan, should be extolled. Thus, the United States would tell the members of the Third World that the answer to their economic problems lay not in a *redistribution* of income from the developed to the developing world, but in greater *production* in the developing countries.

Moynihan also urged that the United States should continuously and vociferously speak out for political and civil liberty. He proposed that one-sided and selective resolutions on civil and political rights should immediately be challenged by pointing out their hypocrisy and the similar, if not identical, transgressions of their proposers. "It is time," Moynihan wrote, "that the American spokesman came to be feared in international forums for the truths he might tell."

Moynihan's essay had a great impact within both the United States and the community of United Nations delegations in New York. Secretary of State Henry Kissinger was deeply impressed by the essay, and he urged President Ford to appoint Moynihan to the post of Ambassador to the United Nations.

Among the United Nations delegations in New York, there was considerable consternation. African delegations were especially wary because of Moynihan's advice to President Nixon some years back—that the former president's posture toward the American black community should be one of "benign neglect."

While Moynihan's tenure as ambassador was a stormy one, significant strides were made toward a greater rapprochement with the new majority.

By the time the Seventh Special Session of the General Assembly met in the late summer of 1975, the American policy-making apparatus had hammered out a comprehensive set of counter-proposals in response to Third World demands for a New International Economic Order.

In a long address read by Moynihan, Secretary of State Kissinger outlined the new American posture. While stating his complete opposition to producer cartels, price indexing, and a common fund to stabilize commodity prices, Kissinger agreed to consider commodity agreements on a case-by-case basis.

He also proposed a new Development Security Facility to compensate for shortfalls in commodity export earnings, a relaxation of nontariff barriers on Third World exports, a reduction of tariffs added to processed raw materials, an international investment trust to increase the production of raw materials in the developing countries, new institutions to transfer and develop technology, a world food reserve system, and a contribution of $200 million on a matching basis toward the recently proposed $1 billion International Fund for Agricultural Development (IFAD).

While Kissinger's speech continually stressed private investment as the most important means for increasing income and development in the Third World, his proposals led to two weeks of serious bargaining at the special session that resulted in a *consensus* document that was adopted without opposition. Although they did not end the tension and conflict between the United States and the Third World over international economic issues, Kissinger's initiatives replaced sterile confrontation with dialogue.

While the accommodation aspect of Moynihan's strategy abated tensions in the General Assembly, the confrontation aspect led to great hostility. By the end of the Thirtieth General Assembly (1975 to 1976), Moynihan's voice was not only feared, but despised by some delegates as well. Throughout the Assembly session, Moynihan did not hesitate to speak out bluntly whenever he perceived other delegates engaging in selective morality, hypocrisy, and lies.

For example, when 33 members tabled a resolution condemning Chile for its violation of human rights, Moynihan pointed out that 16 of these sponsors had political prisoners in jails of their own. When 60 members sponsored a resolution condemning the lack of freedom in South Africa, Moynihan pointed out that 23 of these countries held political prisoners and declared that there was "more press freedom in South Africa than in the rest of Africa put together." While past American spokesmen had criticized selective morality by the Third World majority, never had they been so blunt and biting.

Especially galling to many Third World nations was Moynihan's insistence that the United States tie its bilateral relations with developing countries to the actions taken by these states in multilateral forums. He urged the Bureau of International Organization Affairs to monitor carefully voting patterns of states in international forums and to note instances where states voted and acted hostile to American interests in areas where their own countries' interests were not directly involved, as on such issues as Korea and Puerto Rico.

Moynihan argued that, as long as states bore no consequences for anti-American hostility in international forums, they would continue their behavior. Quick and sharp reactions by American ambassadors in the capitals of nations taking actions hostile to United States interests in international forums would, in Moynihan's opinion, curtail such behavior.

As a result of Moynihan's proposal, aid was suspended to Tanzania and Guyana, while aid to Malawi and the Ivory Coast—two countries more supportive of United States diplomacy—was increased. Moynihan said of these actions: "Let the Tanzanians get their aid from the same capitals from which they get their politics. Let the Ivory Coast know that we value friends."

By the end of the General Assembly session, Moynihan's outspokenness and his personal style were perceived as liabilities by Secretary of State Kissinger. As *New York Times* columnist James Reston put it, while Moynihan had defended United States interests, he also ". . . provoked the Soviets, affronted United States allies, and outraged the Secretary General of the United Nations and the new nations of the Third World."

In February of 1976, Moynihan resigned his position to return to Harvard. To replace him, President Ford nominated William Scranton, a highly respected Republican liberal internationalist with impeccable credentials and diplomatic experience.

While Moynihan's personal style may have left the halls of the United Nations, his major strategic changes remained. Ambassador Scranton spoke out just as firmly and frequently as Moynihan did, albeit with greater tact. Scranton, in fact, was especially forthright in the area of human rights, where he asked why so many delegates restricted their concerns to anti-Israel grievances and racial problems in southern Africa while "consciously ignoring the other obvious and egregious instances of oppression on every continent."

The reason, he replied to his own query, was simple: "Human rights are still treated almost exclusively in a political context, even though positions are cloaked in high moral principles." He then pointed to the following violations of human rights that were ignored by the United Nations: religious persecution in the Baltics, work camps in Indochina, massive detention and torture of political prisoners in Latin America, and mass slaughter in some African countries.

In the Senate hearings on the United States and the United Nations that were held immediately after Moynihan's resignation, Assistant Secretary of State for International Organization Affairs Samuel Lewis told the members of the Senate Foreign Relations Committee that this country would continue to monitor the behavior of other states in the United Nations. They would make it clear that "attacks on the motivation and the good faith of the United States cannot be safely or inexpensively undertaken."

The responsibility for monitoring voting patterns and speeches of other delegations was given to a new Office of Multilateral Affairs, which would then coordinate multilateral issues with bilateral diplomacy. Lewis stated that countries should no longer feel that they could safely attack vital interests of the United States in behalf of some abstract solidarity, when their interests were not involved. If such patterns persisted, Lewis said, the United States would carry out "appropriate," direct bilateral responses.

In his testimony, Lewis also reiterated that the United States would continue to refuse to participate in United Nations activities that this country believed were fundamentally unsound or grossly irresponsible. Thus, the United States would remain a nonparticipant in the Decade for Action to Combat Racism and Racial Discrimination, because of the Assembly's pronouncement in 1975 that Zionism was a form of racism. The United States would also continue with its plans to withdraw from the International Labor Organization because of the increasing politicization of that organization.

The major difference between Moynihan and many of his colleagues and successors lay in their conceptions of the underlying sources of the friction between the United States and the new majority. Many policy makers rejected Moynihan's view that the source of this friction was an ideological, anti-Americanism *per se*. Instead they believed that the differences stemmed from divergent interests and policy positions on fundamental international issues.

In testifying before the Senate Foreign Relations Committee in May 1975, Moynihan's immediate predecessor, John Scali, cited three sources of tension at the United Nations: "The Arab-Israeli dispute, the battle for racial justice in southern Africa, and the growing gap in living standards between developed and developing nations." Noting that the United States differed with the Third World on each of these issues, Scali said that ". . . only sincere negotiations on the problems of critical importance to the Third World can halt the continued deterioration in our relations with these nations."

Scali's views were widely shared by Ambassador Scranton, Assistant Secretary Lewis, and other officials in the Ford administration, including, most importantly, Secretary of State Henry Kissinger. In addition to Kissinger's efforts to be accommodating on economic issues as described above, the Secretary of State made significant *demarches* in the Middle East and especially southern Africa in 1975 and 1976.

On a trip to Africa in the spring of 1976, Kissinger outlined major changes in American policy at Lusaka, Zambia. In his address Kissinger announced that the United States would actively work toward achieving majority rule in Rhodesia within two years and seek an independent Namibia (Southwest Africa) at a fixed early date. He also strongly denounced the South African policy of *apartheid*.

While Kissinger's diplomatic efforts did much to reduce the levels of tension and hostility at the United Nations, the United States still found itself opposing or abstaining on resolutions concerning the Middle East,

Rhodesia, Namibia, South Africa, and various economic issues. In each of these areas, in fact, serious differences remained between the United States and the Third World majority.

In the economic realm, Kissinger's decision to discuss commodities on a case-by-case basis was a long way from the Third World's demand for a $6 billion to $8 billion Common Fund to stabilize the prices of all major commodities, to say nothing of demands for producer cartels and price indexing.

Significant differences also remained on the issues of debt relief for developing countries hurt by sharp increases in the prices of oil and food, aid commitments from the developed countries, technology transfers, and means of regulating multinational corporations. Nevertheless, despite significant differences, negotiations between the North and South were proceeding in the Committee on International Economic Cooperation (CIEC), a 27-nation group that was meeting in Paris.

On issues involving the Middle East, the United States still refused to recognize the PLO and opposed one-sided anti-Israeli/pro-Arab resolutions in the General Assembly. The United States also refused to support arbitrary deadlines for Israel to withdraw from territories gained in 1967, as long as the PLO refused to accept the legitimacy and security of Israel, and the Arab states would not promise to end their state of war with Israel.

On issues pertaining to southern Africa, the failure of Congress to repeal the Byrd Amendment, which allowed Rhodesian chrome to enter the United States in violation of the Security Council's economic embargo, led some delegates to doubt the genuineness of Kissinger's commitment to bring about majority rule.

In regard to Namibia, while the United States favored independence within a constitutional framework drafted by *all* parties, it refused to recognize the Southwest African People's Organization (SWAPO) as the sole representative of the Namibian people. Nor would the United States support "armed struggle" as the road to Namibian independence.

In regard to *apartheid,* the United States opposed Assembly resolutions that called for an "armed uprising" within South Africa, and economic and arms embargoes against the country.

On issues of more direct concern to the United States, the situation remained virtually unchanged. At the August, 1976, summit of nonaligned nations, a resolution adopted on the Korean situation endorsed North Korea's position: the withdrawal of all forces under the United Nations flag, and a dissolution of the UN command. In regard to Puerto Rico, the nonaligned called for a discussion of this matter as a colonial issue. Immediately upon passage of these resolutions, the United States announced that it would ignore any action taken by the United Nations on these issues.

When the Ford administration left office, significant, if not fundamental, differences remained between the United States and the United Nations majority. At the same time, the exit of Moynihan and the pursuit of an accommodationist strategy had significantly decreased the tension level in the world organization.

In his report on the Thirty-First General Assembly (Fall 1977), Ambassador Scranton noted a "lessening of confrontation" over the past session. In fact, Scranton was quite optimistic that a policy of leadership and accommodation would eventually lead to a *rapprochement* between the United States and the Third World.

In January 1977, Scranton wrote to President Carter's newly appointed United States Ambassador Andrew Young as follows:

> If ever the Southern African problem were solved, even the beginnings of it in Rhodesia and Namibia, and further progress were made for peace in the Middle East, the adverse situation of the United States at the United Nations would change around enormously—for us, for freedom, and for an interdependent world.

CARTER AND THE UNITED NATIONS

Jimmy Carter's campaign statements were very encouraging to those who favored an accommodationist policy toward the United Nations. While supporting the initiatives that Ford and Kissinger had taken in the world organization, Carter also criticized them for failing to devote enough attention to what he termed a "new agenda" of foreign policy concerns: "the world economy, freedom of the seas, environmental equality, food scarcity, and the conservation of irreplaceable resources."

While chiding the less-developed countries for "one sided, self-righteousness," "automatic majorities" and "intolerance for the views or the very existence of other nations," Carter often reiterated that North-South tensions were based upon legitimate grievances. His administration, he said, would work to get the less-developed countries "to want to tie their future with ours." In a Carter administration, he said, multilateral diplomacy would become a major part of United States foreign policy.

At the same time, candidate Carter was not a capitulationist. While he favored greater consultation and participation of less-developed countries in shaping economic policies, increased aid and capital transfers, the International Fund for agricultural development, and buffer stocks for commodities, Carter indicated no change from the Ford-Kissinger policy of opposition to price indexing, producers' cartels, automatic response transfers, and expropriation with compensation issues to be decided upon by national courts in the less-developed countries.

In summation, while favoring a more accommodationist and leadership posture, Carter was in no way an economic revisionist. For him, as well as his predecessors, the plight of the developing countries could best be alleviated not through an international redistribution of wealth, but through free trade, private investment, and increased production. Aid, he felt, should focus upon helping developing countries meet the basic needs of the poorest people by helping to increase food production, education, health care, employment, and rural development.

Once elected, Carter filled some crucial foreign policy positions with men whose commitment to using multilateral forums and seeking greater *rapprochement* with the Third World was clear. The appointment of Andrew Young, a black Congressman from Georgia whose youth was spent in the cause of civil rights, indicated that the United States would continue the policies of the Ford administration toward solving the severe racial problems in southern Africa.

As his Assistant Secretary of State for International Organization Affairs, Carter appointed Charles William Maynes, formerly Director of the International Organization Program and Secretary of the Carnegie Endowment for International Peace. In the July 1976 issue of the prestigious journal *Foreign Affairs,* an essay by Maynes had appeared that was entitled, "A UN Policy for the Next Administration." In this essay Maynes chided the Ford-Nixon administrations for largely ignoring the United Nations and regarding it as "marginal to the conduct of international relations."

While arguing that the United States should set limits on the degree to which it would compromise and proposing that the United States should boycott United Nations meetings that were called for political purposes, Maynes called for a major policy of accommodation that would appeal to the large numbers of moderates in the Third World bloc.

He proposed accommodating legitimate Third World demands through constructive proposals, accepting the goal of .7 of GNP for resource transfers to the Third World, a Marshall Plan approach toward development aid, and undertaking initiatives in southern Africa and the Middle East.

Of special significance was Carter's appointment of C. Fred Bergsten, one of the leading academic economists favoring an accommodation of Third World economic demands, to the key post of Assistant Secretary of Treasury for International Economic Affairs. During the Nixon-Ford administration, the Treasury Department under William Simon was the leading ideological opponent of meeting Third World demands. In fact, when President Ford left office, the Treasury was still balking at Kissinger's decision to discuss commodity agreements on a case-by-case basis.

The appointments of Zbigniew Brzezinski as National Security Adviser and Richard Cooper as Assistant Secretary of State for Economic Affairs also indicated an accommodationist tilt. In an essay entitled, "America in a Hostile World," which appeared in the Summer 1976 issue of *Foreign Policy,* Brzezinski called for a new United States policy "that does not ignore [nor reciprocate with doctrinal hostility] the global pressures for reform of existing international arrangements." He urged that the United States respond to the challenges it faced with a set of policies that enabled it "to coalesce around itself the sympathies and support of the majority of mankind."

Cooper, a leading scholar in the area of economic interdependence, undertook a lengthy analysis of Third World demands that appeared after his appointment as an essay, "A New International Economic Order for Mutual Gain," in the Spring 1977 issue of *Foreign Policy.* Clearly delineating the areas upon which an impasse had arisen between North and South, Cooper proposed shifting discussions from those areas likely to generate conflict and concentrating "on those areas where mutual gain to both developed and developing countries is possible through international cooperation." In sum, Carter's campaign rhetoric and his key appointments presaged major changes in America's posture toward the United Nations.

In its four years of office, the Carter administration's policy toward the United Nations was one of significant leadership initiatives, a willingness to negotiate with and accommodate Third World demands, and firmness when acquiescence in such demands would be inimical to significant American interest groups or carry high costs and risks.

Moreover, instead of merely reacting to attacks on the United States and developed countries, the Carter administration took two major initiatives that deflected attention from the United States. In the political area, Carter's strong statements on human rights in his first address to the United Nations put other nations on the defensive, and his administration's persistent emphasis on dealing with the torture of political prisoners added new items to the human rights agenda to which other nations had to respond.

In the economic realm, the administration's insistence upon putting the plight of the "poorest of the poor" at the center of the North-South debate also broadened that agenda and altered the nature of that debate.

On such long-standing political problems before the United Nations as Rhodesia, Southwest Africa, Namibia, the Middle East, and *apartheid,* the Carter administration exercised leadership initiatives that, especially in regard to Africa, relied heavily on the world organization. The following two sections will examine the policies pursued by the Carter administration in regard to African issues and the North-South debate.

African Initiatives Immediately upon entering office, the Carter administration took a series of significant initiatives in Africa. In his first year, Andrew Young made several trips to the African continent to mend political fences and to obtain a greater *rapprochement* with the leaders of such key countries as Nigeria and Tanzania, both of which had been extremely wary of former Secretary of State Henry Kissinger.

In fact, while pursuing a posture of friendship and accommodation with all black African countries, Young established contact with the leaders of Mozambique and Angola, two Marxist countries that had previously been seen as pariahs by American policy makers.

Accompanying Young's extensive personal diplomacy were significant changes in American policy toward the problems of southern Africa. In regard to Rhodesia, the Carter administration replaced the Ford-Kissinger policy of acting as a mediator in that dispute with one of working toward a settlement in concert with the black frontline presidents of Tanzania, Zambia, Botswana, Mozambique, and Angola. Through these actions and the repeal of the Byrd Amendment, considerable lost ground was regained among the black African countries.

Central to the administration's Rhodesian policy was an Anglo-American plan, drafted by Andrew Young and British Foreign Secretary David Owen, that called for a reassertion of British rule in Rhodesia through the presence of a Resident Minister who would preside over an interim period preparatory to one-man one-vote elections leading to a majority rule government. During this period a United Nations peacekeeping force would guarantee order, while rebel and internal political forces would prepare for the election. Although the guerrilla forces of Robert Mugabe and Joshua Nkomo expressed a willingness to negotiate on the basis of this plan, the internal Rhodesian forces refused.

The Anglo-American plan was placed in limbo, however, when in March 1978 the white Rhodesian leader Ian Smith concluded an internal settlement with three black moderate leaders: Bishop Abel Muzorewa, Reverend Ndabaningi Sithole, and tribal chief Jeremiah Chirau. While the black leaders who joined Smith represented about 80 percent of the black Rhodesians, Smith's internal settlement was rejected by the guerrilla forces, the frontline presidents, the British, and the United States.

These parties opposed the internal settlement because it guaranteed the country's tiny white minority 28 percent of the seats in parliament for 10 years—enough to block any constitutional amendments that would end entrenched white power in the military, police, judiciary, and civil service. To most black African leaders the internal settlement was seen as the continuance of white rule under the facade of a black veneer.

At the same time, considerable support for the internal settlement arose in the United States Congress; the Carter administration came under strong pressure to recognize the internal settlement, unilaterally lift the mandated United Nations sanctions, and break with the frontline presidents. After parliamentary elections for a new government were held under the internal settlement in April 1979, pressure in the Senate for recognizing the new Muzorewa government intensified. On May 15, 1979, the Senate adopted by a vote of 79 to 19 a "sense of the Congress" resolution that would end sanctions against Rhodesia within 14 days of the installation of the new Muzorewa government.

The loss of moderate support in the Congress placed Carter's policy of concerting with leading black African states in serious difficulty. The probability of a break with the frontline presidents also increased with the elections of Margaret Thatcher and the Conservative party in Great Britain in May 1979. During the campaign, Thatcher indicated a softening of British opposition to the internal settlement, and some key conservative spokesmen favored outright recognition of the newly-elected government in Rhodesia.

Thus, by the summer of 1979, Carter's Rhodesian policy was in a shambles. Failure to recognize the Muzorewa government might have led to the president's being overridden by a sanctions-lifting Congress, a likely possibility if the Thatcher government lifted sanctions and recognized the moderate settlement.

On the other hand, if Carter had responded to congressional pressures and lifted the sanctions, he would have acknowledged the failure of his own Rhodesian policy and his hopes for a *rapprochement* with the black African states. Had Carter decided to recognize the Muzorewa government, he would have lost the newly gained goodwill of the frontline presidents. He would have destroyed the credibility and authority of Andrew Young among Third World leaders. He would have risked a Nigerian oil boycott. He would have had to face an escalating guerrilla war that might include the entrance of Cuban troops. And, once again, the United States would have found itself isolated in the United Nations.

Luckily, and against all expectations, the Thatcher government saved the Carter administration from having to choose one side or the other in the Rhodesian conflict. At the August 1979 meeting of the Commonwealth, Thatcher hammered out a plan with Presidents Kauanda of Zambia and Nyerere of Tanzania that called for British-supervised elections and a new constitution to be approved at an all-parties conference.

The plan received unanimous support from the Commonwealth ministers, and negotiations got underway one month later in England. The negotiations lasted through December, producing a constitution that contained no white veto power and no entrenched clauses, although whites still had a larger proportion of seats than their numbers would warrant.

On December 14 the members of the Zimbabwe Parliament repealed the Unilateral Declaration of Independence and returned to the authority of the British Crown. At the end of December a cease-fire was signed, the electoral process got underway, and the new state of Zimbabwe was born peacefully.

On the issue of Namibia or Southwest Africa, the Carter administration also saw its significant initiatives run aground. For a year and a half, the five Western members of the Security Council undertook tedious negotiations with South Africa and the Southwest African People's Organization (SWAPO) that led to an agreement upon the basic principles for a peaceful settlement of the conflict.

These principles, embodied in a number of unanimously adopted Security Council resolutions, included (1) free elections under United Nations supervision in which all parties to the conflict would participate; (2) withdrawal of the South African administration and its replacement with a United Nations administration in the interim; (3) the abolition of *apartheid* in Namibia, the release of all political prisoners, and the return of political exiles; (4) the cessation of hostile acts by all parties; and (5) the withdrawal of all but 1500 South African troops. After the United Nations supervised elections, a constitutional assembly would draft a constitution for the new state of Namibia.

As these negotiations took place, however, South Africa was simultaneously pursuing an internal settlement, similar to that pursued by Smith in Rhodesia, that clearly excluded SWAPO forces. In June of 1978, a Turnhalle

Constitution was drawn up in the territory and elections under this constitu-
ion were held in December of 1978. Both of these actions were condemned
by the Security Council and declared illegal.

In a letter dated December 22, 1978, however, the South African government informed the Secretary General that it would cooperate in the expeditious implementation of the Security Council plan and proposed
September 30, 1979 as the latest date at which the United Nations supervised elections would be held. In the winter of 1979 the South Africans
negotiated with United Nations officials responsible for implementing the
Security Council agreement, while simultaneously arresting SWAPO political leaders in Namibia and attacking SWAPO bases in Angola and Zambia.

In May of 1979, the efforts of the Carter administration to secure a
peaceful settlement under United Nations auspices seemed to collapse when
South Africa informed the five Western powers that it would turn its internal
constituent assembly into a legislative authority with extensive executive
authority. With an impending one-week General Assembly session to be
held in late May to consider the Namibian situation, the Western powers
were placed in a difficult situation.

Earlier, President Carter said that if progress were not made on the
United Nations settlement for Namibia, "the United States would be compelled to take strong action in the United Nations." Since the United Nations and the United States had already embargoed arms to South Africa,
some form of economic sanctions, which would be costly to the major Western states, seemed the only logical recourse—unless negotiations resumed
quickly and progress toward an implementation of the agreed-upon plan
were made. But with a deteriorating situation in Rhodesia and eroding support for his African policies in the Senate, Carter's ability to take forceful
action seemed problematical.

When the General Assembly Session on Namibia opened in May, the
UN-Western plan was in limbo. Thus, the South African delegate was denied permission to attend the session, and a resolution was adopted that
condemned South Africa for behaving "deceitfully" in the negotiations and
for pursuing its internal settlement.

Also included in the resolution, which was adopted by a vote of 118-0-
16, was a call for the imposition of sanctions under Chapter VII, the enforcement section of the charter. Among the 16 abstainers were the Western five,
whose spokesman, Andrew Young, called for continued negotiations as the
best means of securing a settlement. Clearly, the administration was not
ready to add to its Rhodesian troubles in the Congress by escalating activities against South Africa.

Throughout the summer and fall of 1979, negotiations and discussions
continued, although little progress was made. In October, the Western five
offered a revised settlement plan that would tighten UN control over
SWAPO bases in the bordering states of Angola and Zambia, in addition to
those within Namibia. One month later, South Africa torpedoed talks on this

plan by insisting that representatives of its internal settlement (the Turnhalle leaders) be included in the proposed Geneva negotiations.

Clearly, South Africa decided to bide its time until the Rhodesian conflict was clarified. If the British-negotiated settlement in Rhodesia succeeded and a stable regime consolidated itself in the country, South African attitudes toward a negotiated settlement in Namibia would probably be forthcoming. If, however, chaos on the order of the Congo crisis of 1960 or a Marxist regime consolidated itself in Rhodesia, South Africa would clearly turn its back on the UN and the Western five and seek a unilateral, internal settlement.

Consequently, the Carter administration had a strong incentive to see that the British-led Rhodesian settlement succeeded; for a success in Rhodesia would most likely mean success in Namibia. A failure in Rhodesia, on the other hand, would also mean the failure of a multilateral and peaceful settlement in Namibia, and this would present agonizing problems and choices for American policy makers.

The North-South Conflict   While leading administration spokesmen such as Cyrus Vance and Andrew Young repeatedly announced their support for a new international economic order, Carter's policies in this area diverged very little from those of Ford and Kissinger.

Like its predecessors, the Carter administration opposed producers' cartels, price indexing, automatic resource transfers, the use of national courts to adjudicate expropriation and nationalization disputes, general moratoria on Third World debts, and the use of funds from the regular budgets of United Nations agencies to finance technical assistance and development projects. Thus, while employing, if not co-opting, the slogans of the Third World, American spokesmen consistently rejected proposals that would entail major changes in the structure of the international economic system.

The Carter administration's major vehicle for economic development was identical to that offered by the Ford administration; increased trade brought about largely through private investment.

As Richard Cooper put it in a speech before the Council of the Americas in the summer of 1977: "We remain firmly convinced that a liberal international economic system, permitting broad flows of private investment across national boundaries according to economic [that is, market] forces, offers the best hope for stable economic growth—in the Third World, in other developed countries, and in our own society."

In his first address before the Economic and Social Council, Andrew Young said that while supporting the "concept of a New International Economic Order, the United States would not endorse or implement the resolutions of the Sixth Special Sessions as a whole."

Within this basic free market framework, however, the Carter administration took a number of accommodative initiatives. It increased significantly United States aid to the World Bank and various regional lending institutions; it supported the International Fund for Agricultural Development, and it worked to create an international grain reserve to help insure against food shortages. In addition to these initiatives, the administration put the Third World on the defensive in the North-South debate by calling for a new development strategy that would concentrate upon meeting basic needs of the poorest people in the developing areas.

In a lengthy and major address to the Economic Commission on Latin America, Andrew Young decried the failure of past aid and economic development to "trickle down" and alleviate the plight of the poor. Of the 70 percent increase in the GNP of Third World nations that took place between 1960 and 1970, Young noted that 70 percent went to the richest 30 percent in the developing countries, while less than 1 percent went to the bottom 20 percent.

Given such results, Young stated that "In the United States, we increasingly have to ask the question, 'Why should the poor of the United States be taxed to help the rich of the poor nations?' " The taxpayers of the United States, he said, would continue to support foreign aid programs only if these programs "are really helping the poor to help themselves."

Shortly after Young's address, United States aid administrator John Gilligan told the United Nations Development Program's Governing Council that the United States wanted United Nations aid programs to be "devised clearly and specifically to meet the basic needs of the poor majority of the world's people."

This meant concentrating on increasing agricultural productivity, insuring equitable income distribution, rural development, health care, basic education, and labor-intensive production projects. In its own bilateral assistance programs, the Carter administration targeted over 80 percent of its funds to poor countries with annual per capita incomes of less than $550. These funds would be allocated to projects designed to meet the basic needs of the poor in developing countries.

On the New International Economic Order, the only difference between the Ford and Carter administrations was the latter's willingness to *discuss* the Third World's proposal for a Common Fund to stabilize commodity prices.

As originally proposed by the UNCTAD Secretariat, consumer and producer countries would establish a common fund of $6 billion that would be used to buy buffer stocks of commodities when prices were falling in order to maintain an agreed-upon level of prices. In times of rising prices, these buffer stocks would be sold in order to dampen price rises. Because many Third World countries viewed the common fund as the heart of their program for a New International Economic Order, Carter's willingness to discuss the creation of a fund was seen as a major conciliatory action.

After two years of hard bargaining, however, the Common Fund that emerged was a far cry from the proposal originally put forth by the UNCTAD Secretariat. Instead of a $6 billion fund of which $2 billion would be contributed directly by the developed countries, the fund that emerged amounted to $400 million of which the developed countries would provide 68 percent or $272 million. This final amount was so small because the negotiated fund would act not as a central regulator of all international commodity trade, but a *contingency* fund that individual commodity agreements could draw upon in emergency situations.

Thus, instead of serving as a central fund that would oversee, control, and hold a wide variety of commodities, the fund would merely help to finance the buffer stocks bought and sold largely by individual commodity associations. This decentralized approach, which places the costs of purchasing buffer stocks on individual producers and consumers of various commodities instead of having all the stocks underwritten by the general international community at large, was a major demand of the United States to which the Third World had to accede in order to get any funds at all.

In addition to the $400 million Common Fund, a second fund of $350 million was agreed upon to finance research and development projects that would aid producer nations in their efforts to increase productivity, process their raw commodities, improve marketing skills, and diversify their economies.

In early negotiations, the United States opposed this facility because it would duplicate the work of the World Bank and create an unnecessary and costly aid-giving bureaucracy. When the Third World agreed that the fund would be financed only by voluntary contributions, the United States dropped its opposition. However, United States representatives made clear that the United States would not contribute to the fund.

On North-South issues, then, the Carter administration strongly withstood the Third World demands for restructuring the international economic system and redistributing wealth from the developed to the developing countries. By focusing on the problems of the poor in the developing countries and speaking out for human rights, the Carter administration succeeded in putting new issues in the forefront of United Nations discussions that diverted attention from the Third World's demands.

Also, the very fact that negotiations were proceeding, however slowly, on such key demands as the Common Fund, a Code of Conduct for the Transfer of Technology, and an international grain reserve made a strident, Third World militancy seem uncalled for.

The strongest bargaining lever that the United States has had in negotiating on most Third World economic demands is a willingness to refuse to compromise, to break off negotiations, and to let the status quo continue. Most Third World economic demands just cannot be fulfilled without the willingness of the United States to accept them.

The Carter administration did not hesitate to use this lever in the Law of the Sea Conference that ran aground in the spring of 1979. Since 1974, the members of the United Nations have been meeting to draft a comprehensive treaty on the law of the sea that would fix territorial limits, develop rules for fishing and conservation, establish rights of military and commercial transit, and establish an international governing body to regulate the high seas lying beyond the 200-mile coastal economic zones.

Designated by the General Assembly as "the common heritage of mankind," the high-seas areas beyond the 200-mile economic zones contain vast quantities of potato-sized nodules on the ocean floor that are rich in manganese, copper, cobalt, and nickel. After years of negotiating and concessions by both sides, the negotiations over the rules to govern the mining of these areas became deadlocked.

By the spring of 1979, both sides had agreed upon a parallel system whereby in any area to be mined, two tracks would be created: one to be mined by a private or national company and the other by the *Enterprise*, an international corporation to be created with funds and technology contributed by the developed countries, but managed by an International Seabed Authority. Each mining operation would then contribute a share of its profits to the international authority, a portion of which would go toward a fund for development assistance.

The remaining split between the developed and developing countries in these negotiations existed largely over the voting arrangements in the Seabed Authority that would set the rules for deep ocean mining. While agreeing that the small council of 36—and not the assembly of 150 nations—should make key managerial and policy decisions, the Third World delegates insisted upon majority control in the council.

The developed countries have adamantly refused to cede on this issue, in part because of a fear that once the private corporations have given the *Enterprise* the expertise and technology to engage in seabed mining, the Third World majority in the council might vote to suspend or prohibit deep sea mining by private or national corporations.

The Carter administration responded to this deadlock by supporting legislation that would set rules for United States corporations to mine the seabeds in the absence of a treaty. While this legislation provides that a portion of the revenues collected be set aside for possible distribution to the developing countries and would lapse when an international treaty comes into force, Third World leaders were furious over the Carter administration's decision to pursue a unilateral course. Despite denunciations of this action as a violation of international law and even threats of force by some Third World leaders, the United States' position did not change.

What this stalemate and unilateral action made clear was that in negotiations with the Third World over North-South issues, the Carter administration was willing to draw firm lines behind which it will not withdraw when vital interests of key American interest groups are at stake. And members of the Carter administration were well aware of the possible costs that such a policy of firmness with unilateralism would entail.

Speaking before the Washington Press Club in March 1979, top seabed negotiator, Ambassador Elliot Richardson, said that failure to reach an agreement would weaken Third World moderates, lead to the emergence of "ideologues and firebrands" in the North-South dialogue, result, perhaps, in political reprisals against the United States when seabed mining begins in the absence of a treaty, and allow "world public opinion" to place primary blame for the failure of the negotiations on the United States.

Despite these possible costs, the United States would not give in to Third World demands and would pursue seabed mining unilaterally until a treaty acceptable to the United States was negotiated. Richardson told the members of the Press Club:

> We should realize that the United Nations itself is on trial at the Law of the Sea Conference. Its effectiveness as an institution is being subjected to a harsh test. It has to prove at this conference that it can successfully mediate the burgeoning problems of global interdependence. Should it fail, those who will have lost the most are the poor, least developed African states who count heavily on the United Nations to help them meet their most urgent economic and political concerns.

The Carter Administration: An Evaluation   There is no question that the Carter administration made a major decision to increase the role of the United Nations and international institutions generally in the pursuit of its international objectives. On North-South issues, human rights, and the problems of southern Africa, the United States took an accommodationist posture coupled with significant leadership objectives. As a result, a great deal of progress was made in reducing the tension and hostility in the United Nations that existed during the Nixon-Ford years. This reduction of hostility, in fact, seemed to pay dividends in a general decrease in anti-U.S. voting and the unanimous vote in favor of the U.S. position during the Iranian hostage issue.

However, while the tension and hostility of the Ford-Kissinger years may have declined, significant differences and obstacles remained between the United States and the developing countries. Support for IFAD, increased funding for international lending institutions, debt relief for the poorest countries, modest trade concessions, the basic needs aid strategy, new programs for technology transfer, and the scaled-down Common Fund did not cause Third World leaders to drop their demands for a radically different international economic order. In fact, the report of the Brandt Commission, which called for further progress in implementing many of the demands for an NIEO, led to a resurgence of activity by the developing states at the close of the Carter administration. In the late summer of 1980, a special session of the General Assembly was called to create an agenda and set of rules for further negotiations on North-South economic issues. After weeks of acrimonious discussion, the session ended in complete deadlock, with neither an agenda nor a set of rules of procedure for the hoped-for future meeting.

While the Carter administration's initiatives in Africa gained the good-will of black nations that had been alienated during the Nixon-Ford years, it was the Conservative Thatcher government in Britain that ended the Rhodesian crisis. As indicated, the United Nations-oriented solution put forth by Andrew Young and David Owen, foreign minister of the Labor government that preceded Thatcher, ran aground. Also, by the end of its term, the Carter administration's effort to end the Namibian crisis through the United Nations had ended in failure. Had Carter been reelected, he would have faced some difficult choices in regard to southern Africa.

At the same time, by the end of the Carter administration's term, voting in the United Nations had increasingly turned against the Soviet Union and its allies. Much to the Soviet Union's surprise, the unaligned nations were almost unanimous in their opposition to the Vietnamese invasion of Cambodia and in their refusal to seat the Vietnamese puppet regime of Heng Samrin. After the invasion of Afghanistan, the General Assembly condemned the Soviet invasion by a vote of 104 to 18, with the 91 nonaligned nations voting 56 to 9 in favor of condemnation (with 26 nations abstaining). Among the nine supporting the Soviets were Afghanistan (the nation invaded), Cuba (head of the nonaligned nations for two years), and the communist states of Laos, Mongolia, and Vietnam. Thus, of the nine, only four were noncommunist countries—Angola, Grenada, Mozambique, and South Yemen—and all of these were heavily indebted to Moscow or ideologically oriented toward the Soviet Union.

In fact, the Soviet invasion was extremely counterproductive in terms of its relations with nonaligned countries. After its vigorous defense of the Soviet invasion, Cuba's credibility as leader of the nonaligned nations almost evaporated. Although at one point winning a seat on the Security Council appeared likely, Cuba withdrew its candidacy. The strong condemnation of the Soviet invasion by the Islamic nations in Islamabad also deflected attention from the United States.

In sum, while the Carter administration succeeded in ending past American isolation in the world organization, serious conflicts remained between the United States and the majority of the organization's members on a whole series of significant issues. Whether Soviet, Cuban, and Vietnamese actions, by adding new issues to the agenda of world politics, would have rendered these conflicts less salient is problematical, since Carter was defeated in the 1980 campaign. Certainly, the Soviet-Vietnamese-Cuban actions would have provided an opportunity for a diplomacy of greater deftness and movement in the world organization. Unfortunately, how successful the Carter administration's moderately accommodative strategy might have been will never be known.

THE REAGAN ADMINISTRATION AND ISSUES OF THE 1980s

The Reagan administration viewed the United Nations from significantly different perspectives than those of the Carter administration. As indicated, the Carter administration perceived the United Nations as a useful institution for three purposes. (1) It saw the United Nations as a viable forum for dealing with a salient new agenda of multilateral issues that required an

American response: North-South economic issues, world poverty, human rights, food, the oceans, world resources, and the environment. (2) the Carter administration sought to use the United Nations to "delink" what it saw as regional issues from the East-West conflict. Thus, for example, the Carter administration sought some *rapprochement* with the leftist regimes in Angola and Mozambique and sought to use the United Nations to deal with the Rhodesian and Namibian issues. (3) the Carter administration saw the United Nations and accommodative positions in that organization as a useful means of gaining the goodwill of the Third World bloc of developing nations.

The Reagan administration shared none of these perceptions. The "world order agenda" and North-South economic issues were hardly given notice by an administration that preoccupied itself with such East-West issues as containing the Soviets globally, strengthening NATO, and increasing American defenses. Moreover, as strong advocates of free-market mechanisms and opponents of government intervention domestically, the Reagan administration was hardly likely to go along with contrary measures at the international level. It would, in fact, be inconsistent and ironic for an administration that was skeptical of the concept of entitlements for poor citizens within its own nation to support anything that smacked of entitlements for poor nations at the international level.

Thus, in one of its earliest actions, the Reagan administration called a halt to the proceedings of the Conference on the Law of the Sea; they were scheduled for March, April, and August 1981 and were to complete the long-awaited treaty that had been in the drafting stage for seven years. Unhappy with some of the provisions of the deep-seabed mining provisions, the administration said it was initiating a "wide-ranging and thorough-going review" of the treaty that would not be completed until early fall 1981. Thus, the administration announced that the United States would be unable to participate in either of the two scheduled 1981 meetings. According to leaks in the press, administration officials opposed such facets of the treaty as the international regime to regulate deep sea mining, the requirement that private companies transfer technology to the international seabed mining organization, the *Enterprise,* which would compete with private mining companies, and the international redistribution of wealth that is central to the seabed mining section of the draft. While many developing countries denounced the administration's action in public, little hostility was expressed in private. Resignation seemed to prevail.

On the wider North-South dialogue, the administration initially stepped more gingerly. It agreed to participate in an October 1981 summit meeting to discuss the Brandt report but only if there were no official agenda and no final communiqué at the end of the conference and only if Cuba were deleted from the list of participants. These demands were accepted at an 11-nation preparatory summit meeting that was held in Vienna in March 1981 (a meeting that the United States declined to attend).

As the October meeting at Cancun approached, the reticence ended as President Reagan announced in two major addresses that on North-South issues his administration would pursue a supply side, free trade, private investment approach. In a speech before the annual meeting of the IMF on September 29, 1981, Reagan highlighted the great success of free-market societies in the postwar period and called upon developing countries to put their financial and economic houses in order and to look to "the magic of the marketplace" as the most sure means of development. Two weeks later the president spoke to the World Affairs Council in Philadelphia and outlined his strategy for Cancun. His message at Cancun, he said, would consist of three parts. First, he would argue that the key to development lay not in "massive transfers of wealth" or "collectivism," but in "free people [building] free markets that ignite dynamic development for everyone." Second, he would defend both the foreign assistance record of the United States and the remarkable records of such major postwar international mechanisms as GATT and the IMF. In short, the United States would not agree to any major changes in the makeup, rules, and policies of these organizations, and it would oppose any efforts to create alternative structures to these institutions. Third, the president would propose a program of action that would consist largely of efforts to increase trade and private investment. And in implementing its program for developing countries, the administration would search for and seek to eliminate overblown public sectors, high tax rates, and policies inhospitable to private investment.

Thus, in his first two addresses on North-South relations, President Reagan failed even to mention, let alone respond to, major specific issues on the South's agenda such as a new global institution to deal with North-South issues, the stabilization of commodity prices, greater funding for food and energy projects, debt relief, and an increase in SDRs allocated to developing countries. Instead of the new international economic order so often promised, but never delivered, by members of the Carter administration, Reagan offered the Third World "freedom . . . still the most exciting, progressive, and successful idea the world has ever known." At Cancun Reagan preached his trade, private investment, and self-help philosophy. He also made it clear that no greater amount of economic aid would come from the United States. The best thing that the United States could do for the poor in the Third World, Reagan asserted, was to reduce taxes on its own citizens, cut federal spending, balance budgets, control inflation, and ultimately lower interest rates. Reagan also rejected Third World demands that all North-South issues be negotiated in a single forum.

In sum, the Reagan administration took American policy back to where it was before Henry Kissinger's conciliatory address to the Seventh Special Session of the General Assembly in 1975. And what was the response of the Third World to this "retrogression"? Quiet resignation. Lopez Portillo, Mexican president and cohost of the conference, noted as the "first achievement" of the conference "the very fact that we gathered here together."

Other actions also indicated the administration's support for the private sector and a "fiscally conservative" approach to the United Nations. In the Spring of 1981, the United States was the only country to vote against a World Health Organization code to regulate the marketing of powdered infant formula. Administration spokesmen argued that this code, which would have banned advertising of infant formula, restrained free trade and restricted free speech. To cite another example, the Reagan administration announced that the United States would not support a $30-billion World Bank energy lending subsidy that would promote increased oil production in the developing countries. The basis for this decision was the belief that "private oil companies can better utilize the world's resources." Finally, the Reagan administration sought to cut the "fat" out of and constrain the growth of the budgets of the United Nations and its affiliated agencies. In an address before the United Nations Association, Assistant Secretary of State for International Organization Elliot Abrams criticized Secretary General Waldheim for not cutting the organization's budget deeply enough. "Here we find no painful cuts, for it is assumed that all budgets are indexed for inflation," Abrams said. He also criticized the budgets of the specialized agencies and chided them for "too much travel, too many conferences, too much misuse of resources, and too little cutting off of dead wood."

The Reagan administration also parted company with the Carter administration's attempt to "delink" regional issues, especially in Africa, from the East-West conflict; in fact, the Reagan administration saw conflicts such as those in El Salvador and Angola as East-West conflicts. Thus, the new administration sought to repeal the Clark amendment which forbids clandestine aid to factions in Angola that oppose the Marxist government there. When further United Nations talks on Namibia collapsed, the administration, along with Britain and France, vetoed an African-backed resolution in the Security Council that called for mandatory economic sanctions against South Africa, and it sought to devise a new plan that would be more acceptable to South Africa. During the controversy, President Reagan referred to South Africa as a friend and ally that had stood with the United States in all its wars. At the same time, given its central focus on East-West issues, the Reagan administration saw the United Nations as a useful device for registering world opinion against Soviet bloc adventurism, as in Afghanistan and Cambodia. How successful the administration will be in this regard is problematical, given its stance on North-South economic issues.

Finally, the Reagan administration spurned the Carter administration's efforts to use the United Nations as a means of gaining the goodwill of the Third World. In his confirmation hearings, Secretary of State Haig referred to the Third World as a "myth." Instead of seeking *rapprochement* with a Third World bloc as a group, the new administration would emphasize bilateral relations, especially in giving aid. In May 1981, an administration spokesman at United Nations headquarters announced that the United States would again return to the Ford administration practice of using United Nations voting patterns as a basis for foreign aid giving. "We will tie rewards and punishments to [UN votes]," the spokesman said. "U.S. policy," he expanded, "will be to illustrate with actions why it is beneficial to

vote with us." Given the minimal amounts of aid that the United States gives
to its nonallies among the developing countries, it is unlikely that this strategy will have much of an impact on voting patterns.

The Reagan administration, then, is approaching the United Nations
with a set of basic attitudes quite different from those of the Carter administration. Much American negativism will confront Third World schemes for
reordering the international economic order and redistributing wealth among
nations. The same fiscal austerity and budget cutting applied domestically
will be demanded of the world organization. Instead of using the United
Nations to insulate regions and conflicts from the East-West conflict, the
Reagan administration will seek to use the world organization as a cold war
forum to be bypassed or ignored when necessary. For security and development, bilateral relations will eclipse international approaches.

Reagan's key appointments have been reflective of these basic
changes. While lacking the hostility and aggressiveness of Moynihan,
United Nations Ambassador Jeane Kirkpatrick made it clear that she would
draw hard and firm lines and would not hesitate to attack what she perceived
to be Third World cant. She said in an interview shortly after her appointment:

> I'm very nonconfrontational. I never seek confrontation with anybody. But if I
> must, I do. It is useful from time to time to affirm that we are not a racist,
> genocidal, imperialist power.

The Assistant Secretary of State for International Organization Affairs
was Elliot Abrams, a 33-year-old international lawyer who had served as an
aid to Senators Moynihan and Jackson. Abrams came into his office sharply
critical of United Nations spending patterns and, as noted above, his early
efforts were targeted at reducing the budget of the organization and its
affiliates.

In sum, the United Nations will play, at best, an auxiliary role in the
diplomacy of the Reagan administration, and plans for creating international
mechanisms to change the international economic system and redistribute
wealth are likely to be vetoed. The organization and its members will also be
under constant attack on budgetary questions and the "politicization of issues." Whenever the organization cannot be used or act in a manner conso-
nant with American interests, it will be ignored.

How well this strategy will work is uncertain. While the United States
differs with the Third World majority on what should be done about such
questions as the Arab-Israeli conflict and economic development, it is not
clear how salient these issues are to the Third World majority. Clearly, on
the major political issues such as the Middle East and Namibia, the great
powers will remain the final arbiters. Namibia is not Angola, and a Cuban-
SWAPO war against South Africa is unlikely. On economic issues, the balance of fear and power may have turned against the Third World. Fears of

little OPECs no longer dance in the heads of Western statesmen. The power of OPEC itself appears to be declining.

The policy makers of the Reagan administration feel neither guilt nor embarrassment about poverty and underdevelopment in the developing countries. Schooled on such works as P.T. Bauer's *Dissent on Development,* "Western Guilt and Third World Poverty," (*Commentary,* January 1978), and other neoconservative writings, they see the causes of poverty as lying in the Third World nations themselves. They point to the success of those countries such as Taiwan, Korea, and Singapore that have integrated themselves into the existing international economic order and have market economies at home.

After treading water in diplomatic forums from 1975 to 1981 and agreeing to only minimal changes in the international economic order, the West may have waited out the Third World. Now split between the rich OPEC countries and the inward-looking non-OPEC countries with staggering oil debts, Third World unity may be only rhetorical, and that shallow unity itself may collapse in the future.

The question for the future is not between an effective or an ineffective United Nations. Rather, the choice is likely to be between a largely ineffective United Nations with serious financial constraints and ever-shifting coalitions in which U.S. interests will vary from issue to issue and an equally financially constrained institution filled with a stable anti-American majority that is largely ignored by the United States.

FOR FURTHER READING

Bhagwat, Jagdish N., ed. *The New International Economic Order* (Cambridge, Mass.: MIT Press, 1977).

Buckley, William. *United Nations Journal* (New York, N.Y.: G. P. Putnam's Sons, 1974).

Cleveland, Harlan. "The United States versus the United Nations," *New York Times Magazine* (May 4, 1975).

Kay, David. *The Changing United Nations* (New York, N.Y.: Academy of Political Science, 1977).

Moynihan, Daniel P. *A Dangerous Place* (Boston, Mass.: Atlantic-Little Brown, 1978).

Rothstein, Robert L. *Global Bargaining* (Princeton, N.J.: Princeton University Press, 1979).

United Nations Association of the United States. *Issues Before the General Assembly of the United Nations* (This annual source is invaluable for learning about the politics of the United Nations.)

chapter *9*

The United States and the World Economy

MILES KAHLER

In the early 1960s, any observer of America's relations with its principal allies would have been struck by the prominent place of security issues in the disagreements and tensions of the time. Problems such as the challenge to American nuclear dominance by Charles de Gaulle, the response with the ill-fated Multi-Lateral Force (MLF), and continuing dissension within Japanese society over the future of its security treaty with the United States dominated much of the public debate. At that time, the economic predominance of the United States seemed unchallenged despite the first nagging worries over the health of the dollar and the expansion of the French challenge into the international monetary arena. The United States was, as one author described it, a "giant among nations," and the major industrial societies were content with America's management of the world economy in an era of low inflation and high growth rates.

From the vantage point of the late 1970s, a revolution occurred in a mere 15 years. Despite concern over the trends in the strategic and conventional military balances (expressed more vocally in the United States than in Europe and Japan), and despite continuing misunderstandings on specific military issues such as the neutron bomb, the great strategic debates of the 1960s have faded.

In the economic sphere, however, the United States seems a faltering giant—and a giant no longer so large in comparison to Japan or Europe. Critics abroad have increasingly complained that the United States was incapable of managing its internal economic affairs and its external economic relations to benefit the other members of the world economy.

That task of management was made even more difficult by the increased sensitivity of the American economy to events outside its borders, whether the oil pricing policy of OPEC or the export drive of Japan. Throughout the 1970s, the foreign economic policies of the Nixon, Ford, and Carter administrations reflected the dilemmas of a time that had seen the erosion of a postwar system based on a dominant American position. With this came the painful acceleration of American economic dependence upon the actions of others.

THE LEGACY OF THE NIXON AND FORD ADMINISTRATIONS: THE FRAYING OF THE POSTWAR ECONOMIC ORDER

The difficult economic landscape that appeared at the end of the 1970s had its sources in the transformations that had occurred in the Nixon and Ford administrations. Most dramatic were the changes in the international monetary system that followed President Nixon's closure of the gold window on August 15, 1971 and successive devaluations of the dollar. Equally significant, and perhaps most painful for the average citizen, were increases in the cost of energy that began during the boom of 1972 and 1973. They were drastically accelerated by the coordinated action of OPEC in 1973 and 1974 and continued in the price increases of 1978 and 1979.

Less noticeable, but linked to the other changes as a source of tension with Europe and Japan, were the growing barriers to world trade that appeared in the late 1960s and threatened to overwhelm earlier achievements in trade liberalization. As a result of these disruptions, industrial countries moved toward closer economic coordination in an effort to stave off even worse economic disorder. Efforts at cooperation symbolized by the economic "summit meetings" of the heads of government began at Rambouillet in November 1975.

Monetary Policy: The End of Bretton Woods

Although the American dollar was to be the linchpin of the international monetary system established at Bretton Woods in 1944, it was not until the late 1950s that this system actually took the shape that its founders had intended. By then the first strains in the system were perceptible.

During the 1960s, efforts at reform centered around the reserve role of the dollar: The fact that central banks used a national currency to build their reserves (and thus expand the world money supply) on the assumption, repeatedly affirmed by the United States government, that the dollar would be converted into gold on demand. As the number of dollars held abroad came to exceed by far the ability of American gold reserves to guarantee them, some people saw not too far ahead the possibility of a "run on the bank" with dire effects on world economic stability.

Yet, if the United States did not continue to supply dollars to fuel the growth in the world economy, it was not clear where the needed increase in liquidity would originate.[1] The solution devised (and instituted in 1969) was the creation of Special Drawing Rights at the International Monetary Fund, an international money based upon a basket of currencies, not just the dollar. Unfortunately, the SDR was only a long-term solution to the dollar's role (and that of gold); today, more than a decade after creation of the first SDRs, the place of this international money still remains secondary.

The central role awarded the dollar in the Bretton Woods system was a politically contentious one in the eyes of Gaullist France, and the terms of the debate set in the 1960s were echoed in the Carter administration. The United States emphasized the burdens of the system upon the dollar and the American economy. That is, while other governments were able to use the exchange rate for economic management by devaluing or revaluing against other currencies, the United States was not able to do this, given the convertibility requirements. The deficits that appeared in the early 1960s and reappeared later in the decade in most massive form were viewed as a necessary provision of liquidity for the world economy.

To Europeans, however, the ability of the United States to run enormous balance-of-payments deficits *was* a privilege that permitted escape from the discipline imposed by the system on other countries that did not "pay their way" intentionally. Those deficits also permitted the easy finance of a large overseas military role (including the Vietnam War), foreign aid, and direct foreign investment by American multinationals—the entire panoply of American power that was challenged by France.

The rising inflation that accompanied the Vietnam War and the divergence in national monetary and fiscal policies (particularly between the United States and Germany) brought the final crisis. In the face of a mushrooming balance-of-payments deficit, President Nixon, on August 15, 1971, announced that the dollar would no longer be converted to gold at the fixed price of $35 per ounce. As an added means of pressure upon other governments, he imposed a temporary import surcharge.

To still domestic criticism of not "defending" the dollar, Nixon implemented wage and price controls that were highly popular. The Nixon administration took these actions because it was convinced that key foreign governments (particularly Japan and Germany) would not revalue their currencies, since this would damage their export competitiveness. Some members of the administration had also concluded that the consequences of changing the rules in such an abrupt way would not be as catastrophic as had been alleged.

Whatever their necessity, the Nixon measures *did* result in a realign-

---

[1]The "Triffin dilemma" was set out by the economist Robert Triffin in *Gold and the Dollar Crisis: The Future of Convertibility* (New Haven: Yale University Press, 1960).

ment of exchange rates in the Smithsonian Agreement of December 1971. But this effort to return to fixed exchange rates was not to last. By early 1973, renewed pressure on the dollar led to a further devaluation and finally to the generalized "float" of currencies that continues at the present.

Efforts at more extensive reform of the international monetary system within the Committee of Twenty of the IMF were shelved after the oil price rises of 1973 through 1974 and the inflation and recession that succeeded them in the industrial economies. Among other changes, the amendments to the Articles of Agreement of the IMF that were agreed to at Jamaica in January 1976 (and entered into force in 1978) legitimized the existing regime of floating exchange rates and sought to further reduce the role of gold in the international monetary system.

The new system (or nonsystem) of floating exchange rates was one legacy of the Republican administration to Jimmy Carter's presidency. Floating exchange rates seemed to possess the final pragmatic value of working during a period of economic turmoil, thereby preventing even worse disruption. But two questions remained unanswered: the degree of intervention desirable to counter "disorderly market conditions" and the level of synchronization among the national economies required for stable exchange rates.[2] The new administration would soon be called upon to provide the answers.

Trade: The Beginning of the Tokyo Round

Reinforcing the belief within the Nixon administration that the dollar was overvalued in the early 1970s was a growing clamor for protection from imports in several key industries. American goods were, in the eyes of many, pricing themselves out of the world market. The most extensive round of postwar tariff cuts, the Kennedy round, had hardly been completed when demands of the American steel industry forced voluntary export restraints upon its Japanese and European competitors.

The textile lobby, particularly important in the Republican "Southern strategy," forced the Nixon administration into a difficult wrangle with the Japanese, a crisis that was much harder to resolve than the reversion of Okinawa to Japanese sovereignty.[3] Most important, however, was the shift of organized labor to an openly protectionist stance, backing the Mills bill in 1970 and the Burke-Hartke legislation in 1971. In the face of the protectionist threat posed by these measures, the 1974 Trade Act offered increased trade adjustment assistance and more avenues for threatened industries to obtain relief from imports, particularly through the International Trade Commission.

[2]Compare the conclusions of Charles Coombs, in *The Arena of International Finance* (New York, N.Y.: John Wiley & Sons, 1976), chapter 12 and those in George P. Schultz and Kenneth W. Dam, *Economic Policy Behind the Headlines* (New York, N.Y.: W. W. Norton & Company, 1977), chapter 6.

[3]I. M. Destler, Haruhiro Fukui, Hideo Sato, *The Textile Wrangle: Conflict in Japanese-American Relations, 1969–1971* (Ithaca, N.Y.: Cornell University Press, 1979).

Despite its protectionist aspects, the 1974 Trade Act also paved the way for new international negotiations to reduce barriers to trade. Thus, the Tokyo round, or Multilateral Trade Negotations (MTN), formally opened in the autumn of 1973. A less auspicious moment for the start of the enterprise could not have been chosen, because it preceded, by a few weeks, the Arab oil embargo that led to giant increases in oil prices and the deepest postwar recession.

The slump multiplied demands for barriers to imports in an effort to save jobs; in fact, only double-digit inflation served to moderate the pressures for trade restrictions. Under these circumstances, the negotiations for trade liberalization and reform staggered on, with little progress to show when the new administration took office in early 1977.

Economic Coordination and Energy: The Limits of Cooperation

By contributing to the combination of deep recession and galloping inflation that struck the industrial economies after 1973, steeply increased energy prices hastened the disintegration of international economic arrangements that were already under strain, in any case. By producing a large balance-of-payments surplus among the oil exporters of OPEC, the energy revolution encouraged reliance upon flexible exchange rates for adjustment and caused serious payment imbalances among the industrial economies.

After the initial shock, Germany and Japan were able to rebuild their surplus position, while first Britain and Italy, and then the United States, slipped into deficit. The need to pay for the increased cost of petroleum also put a strain on trade relations, since Japan, in particular, seemed intent on building a margin of security by exporting to the other industrial countries.

The limited impetus toward cooperation on energy questions that appeared after the first OPEC shock soon dissipated. With the onset of recession and a decline in the demand for more expensive petroleum, the ability of OPEC to set prices temporarily declined, and so did the real price of oil. This respite of the mid-1970s led governments to turn away from long-term cooperation to cope with future energy shortages. The individual industrial states each sought to secure energy supply by national means. Only the relatively toothless International Energy Agency served as a focus for coordinating policies. All told, energy presented the least promising field of joint action left to the Carter administration by its predecessors.

During the Ford administration, efforts to coordinate national economic policies through international organization were supplemented by economic "summit meetings" among the leaders of the major industrial countries.[4] The first, at Rambouillet in November 1975, broke the deadlock between the United States and France on the future international monetary

---

[4]The membership at the economic summits now includes the United States, Japan, the Federal Republic of Germany, France, the United Kingdom, Italy, and Canada.

system; later meetings dealt more generally with the state of the world economy. The increasing importance awarded the summits reflected the declining ability of international organizations to resolve many issues in an era of economic nationalism. The usefulness of these meetings was limited by the unwillingness of governments to submit their domestic economic policies to international scrutiny.

Thus, the postwar arrangements that had so effortlessly regulated international economic relations among the industrial countries were placed under intense strain in the difficult economic conditions of the 1970s. Some disappeared with a bang (energy), others with a whimper (monetary arrangements). By January 1977, although the old order had eroded in many cases, it was unclear what new order, if any, would be born.

THE CARTER ADMINISTRATION: LIMITED OPTIONS

Given the more cooperative attitude that the United States had taken after the "Nixon shocks" of the early 1970s, the new administration seemed to face a few stark choices in foreign economic policy. There was general satisfaction that the world economy had managed, without catastrophe, the strains of inflation, sharply higher energy prices, and disorder in monetary affairs. That there were continuing obstacles to full economic recovery was clear, but from the United States these bars were seldom seen in international terms. The flaws in the new arrangements were largely hidden in early 1977, and even more obscure were their effects upon the economic well-being of the United States.

Among the small number of officials concerned with international monetary policy and in the private financial community, acceptance of floating exchange rates was widespread—a sharp reversal of the attachment to fixed parities of a decade before. But while the new system was believed to have eased adjustment to higher oil prices, officials were worried about the large surpluses amassed by the oil producers and the recycling of surpluses to the consuming countries that needed them.

Thus, the choices in monetary policy seemed to be those of degree: not a return to fixed exchange rates, but how much management of floating rates; not elimination of the central role of the dollar in the system, but retaining that role while asserting America's freedom to attain domestic economic goals.

Choices in trade policy were equally constrained. Protectionist pressures in the United States had eased with the devaluation of the dollar; the American share of total manufactured exports rose from its low point of 19.2 percent in 1972 to 21.3 percent in 1975 before slipping back again. Certain sectors such as textiles and footwear, however, seemed chronically threatened by imports, and their demands could more easily be translated into import-restrictive measures under the 1974 Trade Act.

As the rate of inflation dropped back toward a more normal rate in

1976, another barrier to demands for import curbs was lost. Meanwhile, little had been accomplished at Geneva in the trade negotiations, and the new administration had to decide how forcefully to press those negotiations to a conclusion and on what terms. In the interim, a strategy to stave off a nibbling away of the open trading system had to be devised. Although full-scale protectionism or economic nationalism was not a realistic political alternative, the retaliation of American trading partners against piecemeal protectionism could induce a nationalist backlash.

The Carter administration seemed to face even more stark choices in energy, as the country's oil imports ballooned during the recovery from recession. Like preceding administrations, however, it chose to define energy alternatives in *national* terms. At best, the international implications were perceived to be limited to the Middle East, particularly the reactions of Saudi Arabia to peace initiatives.

The impact of American energy policy upon Europe and Japan was ignored. Although the Carter administration saw energy as a central issue in its economic policy (perhaps *the* central issue), it was seldom seen as part of American relations with the principal economic partners of the United States.

Finally, the international coordination of domestic economy policy (money supply, government spending, growth rates) was so limited that clear alternatives were hard to discern. The economic summits at Rambouillet and Puerto Rico had proven useful, for public relations reasons if no others, and the pattern was likely to be continued under the new president.

After the French-American agreement on new international monetary arrangements, there seemed to be few outstanding sources of disagreement on international economic issues among the rich countries. Their shared concern was a return to the high growth and low inflation setting of the 1960s, but the limited economic consultation that had developed so far promised to do little for good or ill in achieving that goal. America's new leaders did not suspect that Japan and Europe might choose a different economic strategy, based upon a different analysis of the economic givens, than the path chosen by the United States.

Foreign Economic Policy: Liberalism Resuscitated

Thus, few hard choices seemed necessary in foreign economic policy, excepting energy, and even there the choices were defined as domestic ones. Both the economic setting and the predispositions of the new administration pointed to a revival of the American commitment to a liberal world economy: one based on free trade, free movement of capital, and flexible exchange rates reflecting underlying economic conditions.

These tenets were coupled with a belief that such openness could be managed with a minimum of coordination among the principal economic powers and minimum of constraint on the country's freedom of action in economic policy. As economic liberals, the administration held to the assumption that reliance on the market would produce cooperation and not conflict in the world economy.

Such resuscitated liberalism—hardly a partisan point of view—was reinforced by the particular economic givens of early 1977. With the shock of the recession of 1974 to 1975 receding, the United States was in an economic upswing that would prove to be one of the most sustained in its postwar history. This "boomlet" contributed to the American conviction that the worst predictions of economic disaster and nationalist rivalry would not come about.

Such optimism was not shared wholeheartedly by the Europeans, however, whose economies did not show the same vigor in recovery, or by the Japanese who were deeply concerned by their economic dependence. Yet, for America's leaders, economic liberalism in international affairs seemed confirmed by a "return to normalcy" in world economic conditions.

An additional push in the direction of neo-liberalism was given by the president's own background and his personal convictions, which were shared by many of his principal advisers. Carter was a businessman who believed in the virtues of the untrammeled marketplace; a Southerner representing the traditional free-trade sympathies of that agricultural region; a Democrat committed to the postwar system of alliances and economic operation; and, like his National Security Adviser Zbigniew Brzezinski, a member of the Trilateral Commission, who campaigned against the Republican record of neglecting our European and Japanese allies.

It was, then, a return to the "old-time religion" of free-trade liberalism based on American optimism about the economic future that had hardly been dimmed by the bleaker climate of the 1970s. By the beginning of the next presidential campaign in late 1979, though, the old-time religion of economic liberalism had encountered several crises of belief. Reviving the principles that had guided a world based on American predominance proved to be more difficult than had been believed in 1977. To some, the liberal catechism seemed likely to have an even harder time in the 1980s.

Monetary Policy: Floating, Sinking, Intervening

The experiment in floating exchange rates, undertaken of necessity since 1973, seemed to have performed well under conditions of great economic turmoil. The widespread satisfaction with the new monetary system fit neatly with the free-market principles favored by the Carter administration. And despite its recent vintage, the consensus seemed deeply engrained; exchange rates, for the dollar and for other currencies, should be set by underlying economic conditions. Government intervention for stabilization should be kept to a minimum. The requirements of domestic economic management should not be hampered by balance-of-payments considerations.

Autonomy in setting domestic economic policy seemed both desirable and attainable. What the administration neglected was the increasing international sensitivity of the American economy, on this front and on others.

This sensitivity made the management of foreign economic policy more essential and more difficult than it had been in the halcyon days of the 1950s and 1960s.

The first signs of trouble appeared in late 1977, when the dollar's decline in value against the German mark and the Japanese yen became precipitous. The cause seemed evident: in 1976 the industrial economies had recovered in tandem from the recession; in 1977 the United States economy surged ahead. Oil imports, in particular, burgeoned, and the trade deficit grew enormously. The result was too many unwanted dollars.

As supply exceeded demand, the dollar began a slide that continued into 1978. At first, the Carter administration took a relaxed attitude toward the dollar's decline, which it regarded as a reflection of changing economic realities. Eventually, however, its complacency was shaken by the attack. Even using a narrow definition of "disorderly market conditions," the situation seemed to require increased intervention by the government to stabilize the exchange rate. The defense of the dollar came on two fronts: an expansion of the "swap network," in which foreign currencies could be employed to buy dollars and prop up the dollar against other currencies, and a tightening of domestic monetary policy, which would buoy the dollar by attracting capital inflows and, it was hoped, slow the rate of inflation.

The willingness of the Carter administration to countenance a decline in the dollar was sharply criticized by Europeans and by the Germans in particular. They accused Secretary of the Treasury Michael Blumenthal of "talking the dollar down" when his remarks, as reported in the press, led to renewed downward movement in the dollar.

To the Europeans, the cause of the monetary disorder was clear: a gaping United States trade deficit that was attributed to American petroleum gluttony. They perceived the cure in a reduction in American oil imports, with the speediest means lying in allowing American petroleum prices to rise to world levels. For the United States, the blame lay in part on the Germans and the Japanese, who persisted in accumulating large balance-of-payments surpluses.

Thus, the Carter administration argued from the simple fact that every nation could not have such a surplus. With the OPEC countries necessarily in surplus as a group, the counterpart deficits should be borne by the stronger economies of the North and not by the poorer developing countries. In addition, the higher growth rate maintained by the United States, which added to the surge in imports and the dollar's plight, assisted those weaker economies, North and South, that, more than ever, needed the American market in order to meet their oil bills.

The quarrel over who was being greedy, selfish, virtuous, or profligate became heated in early 1978 as the United States pressed Germany and Japan to join it as "locomotives" in lifting the world from lingering recession. The Germans resisted, despite a few concessions to the American point of view at the Bonn summit in July 1978.

In the meantime, however, the dollar seemed to have stabilized only to come under renewed pressure in August 1978. This second autumn descent was marked by a more general decline against the European currencies, not only weakness against the Deutsche mark and the yen. The American consensus on minimal intervention came under even closer scrutiny, since the exchange markets seemed to be overreacting to the "underlying economic trends." In October 1978, some people detected a whisper of panic as the dollar dropped more swiftly on the exchanges. The American government decided, in the words of Anthony Solomon, the Undersecretary of the Treasury for Monetary Affairs, that the point had come "where Adam Smith has to be curbed."

This curbing came on November 1, 1978 with a joint announcement by the Treasury and the Federal Reserve concerning even tougher measures on both the domestic and the international fronts. These measures included the sharpest single increase in the discount rate since the 1920s and large increases in the swap arrangements with the central banks of Switzerland, Germany, and Japan to give the American government additional means to defend the dollar. The measures had been strongly urged upon President Carter by Treasury Secretary Blumenthal and Federal Reserve Chairman Miller, despite the political unpopularity of higher interest rates.

A critical new element that weighed in the president's decision was evidence that the declining dollar *did* have a serious impact on the domestic economy. The Council of Economic Advisers presented evidence that a substantial share of the building inflation could be explained by the depreciation of the dollar, which had increased import costs.[5]

A second concern was the response of OPEC: The continuing decline of the dollar reduced their oil revenues in real terms, and this, it was feared, could touch off another round of oil price increases, thus worsening inflation. The circle had been closed. Not only did the management of the economy (or perceptions of that management) affect the dollar in the international money markets, but also the plight of the dollar, in turn, would affect efforts to achieve the goal of reducing inflation. The insulation of the American economy, declining gradually for many years, was being stripped away.

The November 1978 announcement had a marked effect: The dollar began a recovery that continued through the spring of 1979. Now complaints of a different sort were heard from Europe: The dollar was too strong and imports (such as oil) that were priced in dollars rose to uncomfortable levels. But once again, it was a false spring for the dollar—one which ended with the announcement of sharp OPEC oil price increases in the wake of political upheaval in Iran, and with evidence that the inflation rate in the United States was accelerating.

At the same time, each effort to curb the dollar's decline had included

---

[5] Clyde W. Farnsworth, "Action for the Dollar: Economic, not Political," *The New York Times,* November 13, 1978, D3. The precise estimates of the contribution of the dollar's depreciation to the domestic inflation rate can be found in the *Economic Report of the President* (Washington, D.C.: GPO, 1979), pp. 42–43.

a larger domestic dimension. In the drastic revision of American monetary policy announced by the Federal Reserve on October 6, 1979, no new international support measures were included. Instead, a new consensus was taking shape—one that saw the causes for a weak dollar and a persistent balance-of-payments deficit in an inflationary economy at home.

By November 1979, the Carter administration had moved far along the path of actively managing the level of the dollar against other major currencies. Although that management included substantial intervention in the international money markets, the balance of the measures tilted increasingly toward controlling domestic inflation as a means of strengthening the dollar. No longer was simple reliance on the market to set the dollar's exchange rate regarded as adequate. Nor had domestic economic management secured greater freedom of action. On the contrary, the demands of the dollar seemed to determine more than ever before the balance of internal policy. For better or worse, the United States had begun to feel the "discipline" of its balance of payments like the rest of the world.

Trade Policy: Protectionism at Bay

The commitment of the Carter administration to maintaining an open international trading system was threatened, not by a coherent attack on the theory of free trade, but by the ceaseless search for exceptions on the part of domestic industries complaining of "unfair" competition. The problems facing the American government were not unique. All of the industrial countries during and after the deep recession of 1974 and 1975 faced a similar host of complaints and pleas for help.

But the new administration *did* face circumstances that aggravated the trade position. Although economic recovery alleviated some of the unemployment that could be blamed on foreign competitors, it also drew into the American market products of our trading partners whose economies grew more slowly. Given the administration's bias against direct subsidies and the absence of any policy of industrial adaptation, most political demands centered upon trade restrictions.

The Carter administration fought the trade battle on three fronts. First, it mounted a rear-guard action against demands for import restrictions, offering a concession here, a refusal there, and limited help elsewhere. The principal concessions were made in the negotiation of an orderly marketing agreement on footwear, a similar agreement "voluntarily" restricting imports of color television sets from Japan, and, more importantly, the imposition of a system of trigger prices on steel imports.[6]

The case of the steel industry illustrated the difficulty that the administration had in resisting demands from a key industry. In part, the force of

[6] A summary of recent United States trade measures can be found in IMF Pamphlet No. 24, *The Rise in Protectionism* (Washington, D.C.: International Monetary Fund, 1978), pp. 28–29.

such demands was magnified by the way in which trade policy is made in the United States. Unlike international monetary policy—a streamlined system involving few executive departments, insulated from political pressures—trade policy is often a free-for-all: The executive branch is frequently split between those arguing for the threatened industry and those taking the free trade side (usually the Treasury and State departments). Congress also plays a central role: When relief is sought, Congress usually serves as a mouthpiece for the domestic industry and its workers.

When confronted with a congressman complaining about the loss of 200 jobs due to imports of Danish butter cookies, the president's Special Trade Representative Robert Strauss is reported to have exploded: "I'm not running a butter cookie program, I'm trying to conduct a national trade policy." For better or worse, more congressmen were interested in their own versions of butter cookie policy than trade relations viewed as a whole.

In the autumn of 1977, the steel industry began shutting down plants, while protesting that the closures resulted from excessive imports from Japan and Europe. Since the steel industry is concentrated in the industrial heartland of the country from New York to Illinois, congressmen from that region quickly reflected the industry's arguments by forming a steel caucus that threatened to impose import quotas if the administration failed to act.

The Carter administration had to consider not only the political clout of the steel caucus, but also the need for congressional support on other administration programs, whether energy, SALT II, or the Panama Canal treaties.[7] While a response to the steel industry was required for political reasons, the industry and its congressional supporters were not given exactly what they wanted. This was to be the pattern on other trade issues as well.

The Solomon task force, established by President Carter, recommended the institution of a system of trigger prices, rather than the more restrictive (and inflationary) import quotas. The trigger prices were to be signals to the Treasury department that an investigation of dumping by the exporting country should be instituted.[8] The other parts of the Solomon task force recommendations were directed at the industry's modernization and at easing the adjustment of regions that were likely to lose steel plants.

Thus, the task force also directed attention toward the principal issue: why segments of the American industry were no longer internationally competitive. The trigger price system worked in purely political terms: Despite mutterings about its inadequacy, the industry and its congressional supporters did not immediately push for more restrictive measures. Whether their

---

[7] The power of the sugar producers in obtaining protection, for example, is not unrelated to the representation of sugar-producing states by former Senator Frank Church, who was chairman of the Foreign Relations Committee, and Senator Russell Long, former chairman of the Finance Committee, which deals with trade legislation.

[8] Dumping is usually defined as selling goods in a foreign market below their price on the domestic market. In the case of steel, however, the trigger prices were based upon the cost of production in Japanese steel companies, regarded as the most efficient producers in the world.

acquiescence would continue in a new economic downturn remained to be seen.

The second part of the president's trade strategy, also directed toward the business and congressional audience, was occasional tough talk with our trading partners when they seemed to be engaged in "unfair" trading practices of which simple efficiency was included among them. As the Japanese trade surplus with the United States shot up during the first year of the Carter administration, the American government decided upon confrontation. Mission after mission was sent to Tokyo to tell the Japanese that these imbalances were "simply unacceptable," and to urge the Japanese government to increase its rate of growth, to increase purchases of American imports, and to let the yen appreciate to make Japan's exports more expensive.

The Japanese response was irritation at both the detailed nature of the advice on economic policy and the overbearing manner in which it was offered. By December 1977, when Nobuhiko Ushiba, Japan's Minister of State for External Economic Affairs, took the Japanese government's latest concessions to Washington, relations had reached a low point, and a full-fledged trade war was feared by some.

Although the December measures were labeled "insufficient" by Robert Strauss, the United States chose not to push its case further. In January 1978, during a visit to Tokyo by Strauss, the two governments managed to resolve their differences, at least temporarily. Japan committed itself to reduce its trade surplus and, in particular, made additional concessions on the sensitive question of American agricultural imports. The Japanese had managed to stave off the worst retaliation by the United States with limited concessions; the Geneva round of trade negotiations was also spared, and relations between the two countries improved.

Those trade negotiations, the Tokyo round, were the third dimension in the Carter trade policy—the liberal face that America presented to the world. While earlier rounds of trade negotiations, and particularly the Kennedy round in the 1960s, had concentrated on tariff cuts, the United States was principally concerned with nontariff barriers to trade in the Tokyo round. Nontariff obstacles had become as diverse as the imaginations of civil servants and politicians could make them: setting standards that foreign importers could not meet, devising complex import licensing procedures, limiting purchases by the government to national suppliers, and offering direct subsidies that lowered the prices of exports. Removal of these barriers was particularly difficult to negotiate; they were deeply embedded in the political realities of each country, and their trade effects were hard to predict.

However, when the "final substantive results" of the Multilateral Trade Negotiations were agreed upon on April 12, 1979, considerable progress had been made—at least on paper—toward regulating and reducing these barriers. Codes of conduct were negotiated for subsidies and countervailing duties, government procurement, standards, import licensing, and customs valuation. In addition, industrial tariffs were to be cut modestly (by past standards) over 8 to 10 years. On agricultural trade, the results, from the American point of view, were more meager.[9]

The complete trade agreement promised the insurance against a slide into protectionism that the Carter administration had aimed for, but the measures had to survive the legislative tangle that surrounds any trade question in Congress. Approval of the agreement was simplified by stipulating that it had to be considered as a package on the floor of Congress and could not be amended, only voted up or down. As a result, intense bargaining took place behind closed doors in the congressional committees to ensure that the compromises necessary for passage were made. Robert Strauss, a master politician, had predicted that the battle in Congress would be one of the most difficult that the administration had faced. The old coalition of free-trade forces had been unravelling—agriculture disgruntled at continuing protection of the European market and many industries believing themselves threatened by international competition.

The worst predictions of congressional obstruction proved unfounded. After the hard bargaining in committee, the trade legislation experienced little trouble in Congress. The package was temporarily stalled in the Senate by demands by Senator Abraham Ribicoff that the administration present its long-promised proposals to reorganize the government's trade machinery.

The trade legislation finally passed the Senate on July 23, 1979, a major legislative victory for the president. The implications of the trade reorganization for the future course of American commercial policy were still obscure. The administration had benefited from an economic recovery that had made it easier to stave off protectionist demands. Whether this "Indian summer" of liberal trade, and with it, the new agreement, would survive in the harsher economic climate that seemed to lie ahead appeared problematical.

Economic Coordination and Energy: One Step Forward

The trilateralist enthusiasm of the Carter administration ensured that the economic summits, instituted among heads of government, would be continued and awarded even more attention. The concrete results of the meetings held at London in May 1977 and Bonn in July 1978 resulted in little more than anodyne agreement that the industrial countries should not move in protectionist directions and that certain growth targets (usually those already decided by the national governments) should be adhered to.

The appearance of cooperation at the summits *did* offer the leaders some reinforcement against economic nationalism at home, but each government was determined to keep economic management firmly in its control.

[9]The provisions of the trade agreements negotiated in the Tokyo Round can be found in GATT, *The Tokyo Round of Multilateral Trade Negotiations* (Geneva: GATT, 1979).

Given the importance of economic management to the political future of any elected leader and the divergence in national economic goals, such reluctance to accept international supervision was not surprising.

Although the economic targets set at each summit became more specific, renewed concern over energy gave the proceedings at the Tokyo summit in June 1979 a more urgent quality. Before the Tokyo meeting, and despite pledges to reduce oil imports, the Carter administration seemed to set its energy policy without regard for the wishes of Europe and Japan, despite their greater dependence upon imported energy. In part, the apparent American nationalism could be blamed upon the balkiness of Congress and its dismantling of the president's energy program; in part, the complacency resulted from a comfortable world petroleum supply in 1976 through 1978 and the lingering hold of America's long-vanished energy self-sufficiency. The unwillingness of the United States to accept the different positions of Europe and Japan was apparent in the conflict over development of the fast breeder reactor, which the Carter administration opposed on the grounds that it would encourage nuclear proliferation.

The turmoil in Iran and the increase in oil prices announced in 1979 brought home the need for greater cooperation to avoid competition for a shrinking supply that would only harm the oil consumers. In the final communiqué of the Tokyo summit, the leaders of the industrial countries asserted: "We are agreed on a common strategy to attack these problems. The most urgent tasks are to reduce oil consumption and to hasten the development of other energy sources." To back up this expression of concern, each country agreed to specific targets for oil imports in the years to come. Of course, such targets depended upon the ability of national governments to implement them. Given the fate of President Carter's first energy program, and the uncertain future of the second (announced in July 1979 to meet the Tokyo targets), the pledge given by the United States at Tokyo had to be viewed with a certain degree of skepticism.

Although the resurgent energy crisis in 1979 had pushed the national governments toward additional commitments to each other in the energy field, the obstacles to far-reaching coordination of economic policies remained clear. In energy in particular, it is outsiders (OPEC) who largely set the terms; the policies of the industrial countries respond to OPEC measures. Coordination is not costless: The hard bargaining at Tokyo demonstrated that no national government wants to bear the burden of adjustment, whether in monetary, trade, or energy questions. And even when a cooperative approach is agreed upon, the national leaders must convert their constituencies at home to its implementation.

THE CARTER RECORD: AN EVALUATION

The "old-time religion" of economic liberalism adopted by the Carter administration suffered some rude shocks on the way to 1980, but the faith was not lost. In monetary policy, willingness to accept the verdict of the markets on the dollar was tempered by greater intervention to manage the exchange rate and tougher internal measures to control inflation. In trade, the effort to stave off the worst was successful, but hostages to protectionism had been given along the way. Domestic autonomy in economic management was preserved, but the sensitivity of our own economy to international economic conditions and the impact upon others of American choices had become clearer. Energy took on an international dimension as the consuming nations recognized their common interest, not only in increasing and diversifying supply, but also in reducing consumption. Domestically, however, the United States had not faced up to that commitment.

Despite these shifts in the consensus, the preconceptions of the Carter administration and its short-term political horizon may have obscured some of the choices that are likely to confront decision makers in the years ahead.

International Monetary Policy

The new consensus in favor of more forceful management of the dollar had been born out of an awareness that the dollar's decline could significantly affect the domestic economy. In a public address given before his appointment as Chairman of the Federal Reserve Board, Paul Volcker described the lessons that had been learned and defended the new approach.[10] His arguments and the administration's international monetary policy left important questions unanswered, however.

Volcker disclaimed any attempt to keep the dollar or any other currency at an "equilibrium rate"; he argued instead for "quiet mutual contingency planning." But can such planning take place without some notion of acceptable bands for the key currencies? And what if there is disagreement on those levels, as there was between the United States and Germany in early 1978? The process of mutual adjustment, in Volcker's view, would be more likely to take place through trilateral consultation (as symbolized by the economic summits), rather than within an international organization such as the International Monetary Fund.

But without an international umpire, the domestic pressures on either side may prevent the necessary compromises in determining who should bear the burden of adjustment. In the early 1970s it was feared that countries would engage in competitive devaluations of their currencies to gain trade advantages; in late 1979, a different sort of competition threatened: progressive increases in interest rates to *support* exchange rates in order to lower inflation and keep down import costs.

Without coordination, the risk is a deeper world recession in the short term, and slower recovery in the long term. By ignoring these gaps in existing policies, the new gospel of intervention and international consultation relied upon a liberal faith in international cooperation that was as naive as the previous belief in the total efficacy of the market.

The domestic side of the new international monetary policy also left

---

[10] Paul Volcker, "The Political Economy of the Dollar," *The Banker,* 129 (January, 1979), pp. 41–51.

questions unanswered. Previously, the exchange rate was regarded as the tail that could not be permitted to wag the dog of the domestic economy. After November 1978, the demands of the balance of payments played an ever-larger role in the setting of domestic economic policy. Proponents of higher interest rates would argue that the remedy for strengthening the dollar also curbs inflation domestically, certainly a desirable goal. Yet, the latest dose of monetary medicine administered by the Federal Reserve came when a recession seemed in view. This certainly was an unorthodox policy, if orthodoxy is determined by domestic economic needs.

Finally, like preceding administrations, the Carter administration sidestepped the question of what the role of the dollar should be in the future international monetary system. From the vantage point of Europe or Japan, the so-called "dollar overhang," the surplus of dollars abroad that can be converted into other currencies, is a major source of instability in international monetary affairs. As central banks and private holders of dollars diversified into other currencies in 1977 through 1979, they induced some of the precipitous declines in the American currency.

Most American policy makers argued that, as a cure is found for domestic inflation, the dollar overhang will take care of itself. Other specialists, such as Robert Triffin, warned of the dangers in permitting the dollar to continue as the linchpin of the world monetary system: a domestic economy managed to please foreign holders of dollars; an international economy plagued by instability as the demand for dollars rises and falls. No other national currency could assume the role that the dollar plays in the international economy.

In the long term, the European Currency Unit (ECU) used in the newly established European Monetary System might serve as an alternative to the American dollar. An international solution would award a larger role to SDRs (internationally created money) and establish a substitution account to which foreign governments could transfer unwanted dollars for SDRs. After persistent resistance from the United States, the question was discussed at the annual meeting of the International Monetary Fund in September 1979. Negotiations broke down in April 1980, and the substitution account once again became a minor theme in discussions of international monetary reform.

For the first time, an American administration seemed to admit, however cautiously, that the United States no longer desired the burden of sustaining the international monetary system on its own. Devising an alternative, however, would require time and a willingness by the other principal economies to share in the responsibility for managing the international monetary system.

Trade Policy

Although the Carter administration completed the Geneva trade negotiations and saw the resulting agreement through Congress, the test of the new codes lies in the future. Both internationally and domestically, the nibbling away at free trade is likely to continue. In an economic downturn, the new under-standings on nontariff barriers would have to contend with demands for subsidies and other forms of assistance that could distort trade patterns. Even with favorable economic circumstances, states would play an increas-ing role in international economic relations. It is a role difficult to regulate or monitor.

On the domestic front, the new agreement might be insufficient to stifle demands for "fair trade" in industries that would be threatened by competi-tion from not only Japan and Europe, but also the newly industrializing countries of the Third World. The Carter administration directed its atten-tion outward, toward maintaining the openness of the world trading system. But liberalization had already increased the competitive pressure on such industries as textiles and steel, and others would join the list in the future.

The need to adjust to changing world economic conditions was vital, but also painful and politically explosive, as the travail of the steel industry had shown in 1977. Yet, the internal dimension of trade policy—assistance for adjustment and the creation of an industrial policy—continued to be neglected.

International Economic Coordination

With the advent of floating exchange rates, many policy makers hoped for increased autonomy in setting domestic economic policy. By the end of the Carter administration, ironically, emphasis was being placed on the coordi-nation of national economic policies to stabilize the international monetary system, to deal with trade disruptions, and to avoid self-defeating energy policies.

However necessary coordination might be, the domestic obstacles re-mained awesome—whether the power of the farm lobby in Japan or the unwillingness of the Congress to enact an energy program. Management of the economy itself seems less and less adequate, even without political impediments. Whatever the progress toward harmonizing national choices on economic policy, ability to attain common goals remained doubtful.

THE REAGAN ADMINISTRATION: ISSUES FOR THE 1980s

If the Carter administration had witnessed a slow chipping away at liberal preconceptions that had guided American foreign economic policy, the Reagan administration, which succeeded it in January 1981, gave every sign of reinstituting laissez-faire solutions in a form more resistant to compro-mise. Not since the 1920s had the United States seen an administration so intensely committed to reducing the role of government, particularly in eco-nomic policy, or one so convinced of the virtues of unhindered capitalism.

The administration took office during a major trade crisis over the levels of Japanese automobile imports. The dispute followed a familiar pat-tern. The automobile industry mobilized its congressional representatives to threaten legislative protection if some relief was not granted from Japanese competition. The Reagan administration was divided between those who favored the politically prudent course of pressuring the Japanese for export restraints (the Departments of Transportation, Commerce, and Labor) and those who opposed such restraints as a violation of the administration's economic philosophy and a spur to inflation (Office of Management and Budget, Council of Economic Advisers, and Treasury Department). The counsels of political prudence finally triumphed, and the Japanese government and automobile manufacturers reluctantly announced curbs on their exports of automobiles to the United States market. Apart from the cost to the American consumer, this resolution contributed to an early souring of relations with Japan, complicated by conflicts over Japanese military spending.

Although automobiles seemed to fit a familiar model from other administrations—verbal commitment to free trade combined with political concessions to protectionist demands—other trade issues, involving less significant sectors, were resolved in accord with the administration's laissez-faire preferences. In June, 1981, despite congressional opposition, President Reagan ended four years of quotas on shoe imports. Other more politically significant industries (notably textiles and steel) promised future crises of conscience for an administration concerned not only with economic doctrine, but also with constructing a new Republican majority.

High American interest rates awarded the new administration a strong dollar in early 1981. The ideological divisions within the Republican camp on questions of international monetary policy were muted as a result. The dominant, monetarist strand, represented by Beryl Sprinkel, Treasury Undersecretary for Monetary Affairs, has been more intent on a stance of nonintervention in the exchange markets than the early Carter administration. The president, on the other hand, has expressed some support for a return to the gold standard, an idea for controlling inflation that has won proponents in supply-side circles. A third group, the "old right" and Wall Street financial interests, was probably more satisfied with the Volcker policy of managing the dollar more closely in 1979 and 1980. With the dollar at a ten-year high against other major currencies, however, the divergent preferences within the administration were not subjected to an immediate test.

Whatever the satisfaction within the United States regarding the strength of the dollar, American economic policy brought complaints from European trading partners attempting to recover from recession. The Reagan administration, intent upon its own combination of supply-side and monetarist economic policies, seems even more unlikely than its predecessors to bend before the complaints and entreaties about high-interest rates that were heard at the Ottawa summit in July. Coordination among the industrial countries that might reduce interest rate levels and spur recovery was even made less likely after the 1981 elections in France brought to power a Socialist team with its own, very different choices of economic strategy.

The nationalism and laissez-faire attitudes of the Reagan administration signaled a shift in energy policy toward a strictly supply-side approach, emphasizing traditional energy sources. The question was no longer whether American energy policy would take international consequences into account, but whether there would *be* a national energy policy at all, apart from "unleashing" the energy industry. Here, as in international monetary policy, the new administration has been granted a respite by the oil glut that had appeared in early 1981. If and when that oversupply disappeared, the noninterventionist bias of the Republicans would be tested.

The Reagan administration has embraced, with more fervor than ever before, the "old-time religion" of American foreign economic policy. It seems unlikely that it will take a new look at questions raised by the turbulent course of the international economy during the 1970s. Both the international and the domestic dimensions of participation and equity in foreign economic policy have been set aside. During the 1970s, the developing countries had appeared and reappeared like unwanted guests at a rather meager feast. By accumulating debt, by exporting manufactures, and by ratcheting up oil prices, the poorer countries have become increasingly influential participants in the world economy. Yet, they have not been granted equality with the rich nations in determining the outline of international economic institutions or policies. The Reagan administration seemed content to place the Third World in the context of East-West confrontation, while devaluing the importance of North-South economic negotiations.

Within the United States, the growing domestic effects of foreign economic policy raise questions of equity that were easier to ignore when the international and domestic sides of policy were distinct. International conflict surrounds the question of who will bear the burden of adjustment; within American society, the question arises as well. When steel mills shut down or energy prices go up, certain groups and regions are more vulnerable than others.[11] If inequity in supporting the costs of foreign economic policy are not dealt with, a revulsion against existing international economic arrangements may arise, already apparent in widespread hostility toward Japanese imports throughout the depressed industrial belt of the Midwest. Nevertheless, the budgetary choices of the new administration and its hostility toward industrial and trade adjustment policies suggest that this aspect of foreign economic policy will remain neglected as well.

Only a pressing need to deal with strains imposed on the international financial system by Third World debt pushed the Reagan administration toward greater activism in foreign economic policy. Even in that instance, however, domestic criticism of any "bail-out" of the banks made a longer-term policy difficult. The fundamental ideological commitment of the Reagan administration to laissez-faire and automatic market mechanisms had not been undermined. Nevertheless, the experience of earlier adminis-

---

[11]The regional and social effects of the new trade agreements, for example, were criticized in reports by the Congressional Budget Office and the Senate subcommittee on International Trade.

trations suggested that international economic well-being might require more than ad hoc crisis management, undertaken reluctantly, and that domestic support for American foreign policy might require some turning toward government activism to preserve support for openness in the context of economic stagnation. In the absence of more severe external shocks, the laissez-faire nostrums of the Reagan administration might survive. But the sensitivity of the American economy to the outside world—whether reflected in a fluctuating dollar, unpredictable energy prices, or imports of textiles and steel—is unlikely to recede, and those traditional solutions may yet be called into question.

FOR FURTHER READING

General

Destler, I. M. *Making Foreign Economic Policy* (Washington, D.C.: The Brookings Institution, 1980).

Krasner, Stephen D. *Defending the National Interest: Raw Materials Investments and U.S. Foreign Policy* (Princeton, N.J.: Princeton University Press, 1978).

Monetary Policy

A useful summary of international monetary and economic developments can be found in the *Annual Reports* of the International Monetary Fund, published each autumn.

Cohen, Benjamin J. "Europe's Money, America's Problem," *Foreign Policy,* 35 (Summer 1979), 31–47.

de Vries, Tom. "The Inconstant Dollar," *Foreign Policy,* 32 (Fall 1978), 161–183.

Morse, Jeremy. "The Dollar as a Reserve Currency," *International Affairs,* 55 (July 1979), 359–366, (a European view).

Solomon, Robert. *The International Monetary System, 1945–1976, An Insider's View* (New York, N.Y.: Harper & Row, 1977).

Triffin, Robert. "The International Role and Fate of the Dollar," *Foreign Affairs,* 57 (Winter 1978/79), 269–286.

Volcker, Paul. "The Political Economy of the Dollar," *The Banker,* 129 (January 1979), 41–51.

Trade

Abegglen, James C. and Hout, Thomas M. "Facing up to the Trade Gap with Japan," *Foreign Affairs,* 57 (Fall 1978), 146–168.

Balassa, Bela et al. *World Trade: Constraints and Opportunities in the 80s* (Paris, France: Atlantic Institute for International Affairs, 1979).

———. *The Rise in Protectionism* (IMF Pamphlet No. 24) (Washington, D.C.: International Monetary Fund, 1978).

Strange, Susan. "The Management of Surplus Capacity: How Does Theory Stand Up to Protectionism 1970s Style?" *International Organization*, 33 (Summer 1979), 303–334.

The Future of the International Economy

OECD Interfutures Project. *Facing the Future: Mastering the Probable and Manging the Unpredictable* (Paris, France: OECD, 1979).

Heilbroner, Robert. *Beyond Boom and Crash* (New York, N.Y.: W. W. Norton, 1978).

index

85 86 9 8 7 6 5 4 3